Quick Cash for Teens

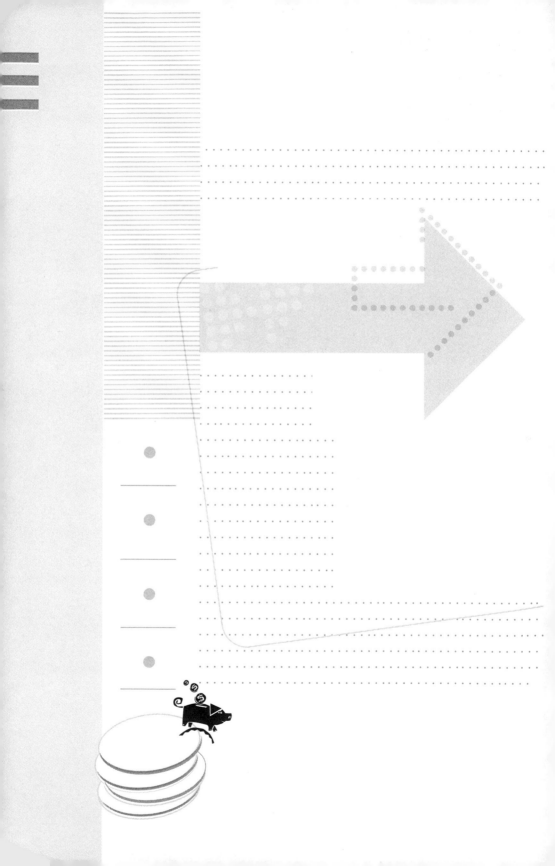

BE YOUR OWN BOSS AND MAKE BIG BUCKS

Quick Ca$h for Teens

Peter G. Bielagus

STERLING

New York / London
www.sterlingpublishing.com

*This book is dedicated to my niece, Mei Ling
Ann Bielagus. You bring me much joy.*

STERLING and the distinctive Sterling logo are registered trademarks
of Sterling Publishing Co., Inc.

Library of Congress Cataloging-in-Publication Data

Bielagus, Peter G.
Quick cash for teens : be your own boss and make big bucks /
Peter G. Bielagus.
  p. cm.
  Includes index.
  ISBN 978-1-4027-6038-9
 1. Entrepreneurship—Juvenile literature. 2. Small business—Juvenile
literature. 3. Part-time self-employment—Juvenile literature. I. Title.
 HD62.5.B52 2009
  658.110835—dc22

                                                     2008042793

10 9 8 7 6 5 4 3 2 1

Published by Sterling Publishing Co., Inc.
387 Park Avenue South, New York, NY 10016
© 2009 by Peter G. Bielagus
Distributed in Canada by Sterling Publishing
ᶜ/₀ Canadian Manda Group, 165 Dufferin Street
Toronto, Ontario, Canada M6K 3H6
Distributed in the United Kingdom by GMC Distribution Services
Castle Place, 166 High Street, Lewes, East Sussex, England BN7 1XU
Distributed in Australia by Capricorn Link (Australia) Pty. Ltd.
P.O. Box 704, Windsor, NSW 2756, Australia

Manufactured in the United States of America
All rights reserved

Book design and layout by Guenet Abraham

Sterling ISBN 978-1-4027-6038-9

For information about custom editions, special sales, premium and
corporate purchases, please contact Sterling Special Sales
Department at 800-805-5489 or specialsales@sterlingpublishing.com.

CONTENTS

Introduction

Can You Really Become
an Entrepreneur?

Cha-ching!

You know the sound. The universal signal that easy money has just been made. The question is, have *you* heard it lately? Are you disappointed with the lack of money in your pocket? Have you thought about getting a job but never gone through with it, because you were told you were too young or because the pay was pathetic and you were asked to work the worst hours (like the Saturday morning shift)? Or can you just not find a job you'd enjoy?

If any or all of these problems are up your alley, you've come to the right place. I'm here to tell you firsthand that regardless of your age, you DO NOT have to start out by earning minimum wage; you can start right now earning double, triple, even *ten* times the minimum wage! You DO NOT have to work the worst hours; you can choose your own hours! You DO NOT have to continually reach into your pocket and feel that it's empty. You can have all the money you need and work the hours you want to work—all while doing something you love. How? You can start your own business.

"Hmmm," you say, "Me? Start my own biz? I don't know. Can I even do that?"

The answer is YES! I started my first business when I was in sixth grade. It was a landscaping company. I started with just one push lawn mower that I rented from my parents. I started mowing one lawn for $100 a week; it took me about six hours to mow the whole lawn. Each time, I spent about $20 in expenses, so for six hours of work I got paid 80 bucks. That's $13 an hour, more than double the minimum wage. Then I added another lawn for $65 a week, then another one for $45, and another for $35, and one more for $50. Soon this sixth grader was making $300 a week. As my business grew more efficient, I figured out how to do all the lawns in a day and a half and was soon making $25 an hour as a sixth-grade landscaper.

It didn't stop there either. Over the years, I began offering more landscaping services, like leaf raking, planting, and yard cleanup. I soon had a crew of four people working for me. I would charge my customer $25 an hour for each person in my crew who was working (including me). I would pay the workers in my crew $10 an hour (still almost double the minimum wage). So if four of us were working a job, I would charge my customer $100 an hour ($25 per person) and pay out to my crew $30 ($10 an hour for each person working for me). That means I was making $70 an hour before I even reached high school!

When I turned sixteen and got my driver's license, my business continued to grow. My service area expanded because now I could drive to my customers. By the time I was a senior in high school, I was making more part-time than many people were earning full-time!

Keep in mind that I am just *one* example of a young entrepreneur. My friend Stephen also started a landscaping company while he was in middle school, and by the time he was a senior he had sold his landscaping company for more than $400,000!

How about Omer A., a Web-site developer who made over $40,000 designing Web sites before he was eighteen! Even younger was twelve-year-old Shennendoah Hollsten, who, with her nine-year-old brother, founded a nonprofit corporation, NeuroKids, to teach children about how the human brain works. Shennendoah and her brother have already raised more than $11,000 for charity! Or you can check out *www.grandslamgaragesales.com*, where 17-year-old Ben Weissenstein has *thirty* employees and annual revenues of more than $30,000 a year.

You too can do what Stephen, Omer, Ben, Shennendoah, thousands of young entrepreneurs across the country, and I have done. This book will show you step-by-step how to start any business, even if you have no money and no experience. It will also provide more than 100 mini-business plans you can start on as soon as you finish reading this book (you can even start some right in the middle of the book). In addition to these mini-business plans, you'll find a complete business plan at the end of the book, so you can learn exactly how to write one. I've also included some of the most common worksheets that entrepreneurs need to use to plan and organize their business. You'll even find a glossary filled with all the key terms in this book. (By the way, whenever you see a word in **_bold italics_**, you can find the definition in the glossary.) Also keep an eye out for boxes with the following icons:

Dollars & Sense
These boxes sum up some of the most important concepts in the chapter, so be sure to read these carefully.

Extra Credit
These provide a little extra information on the topic at hand. Sometimes it's just cool trivia; other times, they answer a question or clear up a misconception.

Tales from the Front Lines
Here is where you'll read about dozens of successful entrepreneurs who were once—just like you—sitting there reading a book and wondering, "When do I get started? Where do I go? And what the heck am I supposed to do?"

You can get started right now.

You can get started right here.

And as to what the heck you are supposed to do,

you can start by turning the page!

HOW TO START A BUSINESS

Okay, here is the bad news: The overwhelming majority of new businesses fail in the first two years of start-up. The reasons vary, but it's mostly because people don't learn the fundamentals of how to start a business. They think that because they are good at washing cars or teaching piano, that's all they need to be successful. In reality, there's a lot more stuff. But don't worry. I've included that "stuff" right here in Part One. Read on, and you won't be one of the statistics.

CHAPTER 1

Your Entrée to Entrepreneurship

An *entrepreneur* is someone who starts and operates his or her own business. Okay, so what exactly is a business? Business is a word whose meaning we think we know, but when we have to explain it to someone else, we get stuck.

A *business* is nothing more than a group or an individual who charges money to solve a problem. Some businesses, like Walmart, are enormous, with millions of people working for them. One reason Walmart is so huge is because it solves a problem that nearly everyone has: We all want to buy stuff at the lowest price possible, whether it's clothes, toilet paper, or baseball bats; we want to spend as little as possible on these items. Walmart acts as a solution to this problem because it can provide these items (and thousands more) at very cheap prices.

Look at Coca-Cola, another huge business. Everyone has the problem of thirst. We get thirsty, so Coca-Cola charges for the solution to this problem. The company doesn't give away its tasty beverages; it charges money for them.

However, businesses can also be very small, made up of just one person. Maybe your parents hire someone to paint your house or mow your lawn. The problem is that the lawn needs to be mowed every week. A person offers the solution—to mow the lawn—and charges to do it. In the world of business, *solutions* to problems come in the form of *products* and *services*.

The size of a business isn't important. What is important is that no matter how big or small the business is, it solves a problem and people are willing to pay for the solution. Entrepreneurs call these problems *opportunities*.

There are many problems that we all have, but aren't willing to pay to remedy them. Every morning when you wake up, your hair is a mess. That's a problem. (And for some of you, it's a *real* problem.) And every day you solve that problem by running a comb through your hair. That's the solution. But you probably aren't willing to *pay* someone to comb your hair. So while there are several problems we need to deal with every day, there are only so many we will actually pay money for someone to solve. In addition, there are times when we are willing to pay and other times when we are not, for solutions to the same problem. Sometimes you will pay to buy a Coke. Other times, you will just save money and drink tap water.

DOLLARS & SENSE

To an entrepreneur, the difference between a *problem* and an *opportunity* is simply that an opportunity is a problem that someone will pay to have solved.

So to sum up, all businesses work like this:

1. The business owners spot a problem (opportunity).
2. They spend money, or create **expenses**, while trying to find a solution to the problem. They call these solutions products and services.
3. They sell these solutions (products and services) to consumers. The money they collect from selling these products and services to customers is called **revenue**.
4. The business takes all the money (revenue) it made from selling its solution, and from that amount it subtracts all the money it spent trying to find that solution (its expenses). Whatever is left over is called **profit**.
5. Business owners then use their profits to either:
   - Spend for themselves
   - Save for a rainy day
   - Donate to charity
   - Invest in the business
   - Invest in *other* businesses

Entrepreneurs sum up this whole process with a simple math equation. I promise there will be very little math in this book, but this is the most basic equation for entrepreneurs:

$$REVENUE - EXPENSES = PROFIT$$

To survive, businesses need to make money. What is important to the person who starts that business is not the money the company makes, but the money the business owner gets to *keep* in his or her pocket: the *profit*. I like to think of profit as simply your reward for solving problems.

Is Entrepreneurship for You?

So that's what entrepreneurship is. The question now is, is it for you? People typically become entrepreneurs for one of three reasons:

1. THEY WANT TO MAKE MONEY. There are lots of problems out there in the world that people are willing to pay to have someone else solve. Sometimes, if entrepreneurs can find those problems and find a way to solve them, they can make a lot of money.

2. THEY WANT MORE FREEDOM. Picture Kim's dad, who has to drive an hour to work every day. Then he has to drive another hour just to get home. Two hours of every day he spends in his car, just driving to and from work. (Worst of all, his radio is broken.) Kim's dad sells medical equipment to doctors. After years of doing this, he got sick of making that one-hour drive every morning and night. So he quit his job and started his own business selling medical equipment out of his home. Now he actually makes *less* money than he did when he was working for his old company. But money wasn't the main reason he started his own business. He wanted more freedom.

3. THEY WANT TO DO SOMETHING THEY LOVE. Todd worked at the hamburger shack near the beach all summer. While he made good money flipping burgers and making fries, his real passion is painting. Every day after work, Todd set up his easel and painted the sunset on the beach. Todd didn't want to give up the steady money he made at the hamburger shack, but his passion for painting was too powerful. So Todd quit his job and started giving painting lessons and selling his paintings.

These are the three most common reasons people start their own business. Sometimes they do it for just one of these reasons; other times, they do it because of all three. For people under the age of fourteen, there is actually a fourth reason to start a business: *because that's your only way to make money.*

Unfortunately, people under the age of fourteen can't actually work for someone else. There are exceptions to this, but by and large it's prohibited. There are federal laws to protect young people from working too many hours for employers. The funny thing is that you can work as much as you want if you work for yourself, running your own business! So when people under the age of fourteen want money, they have *no choice* but to start their own business.

You might be thinking, "Okay, money, freedom, and doing something I love. That all sounds good to me. I'll start my own business!" But hold on. While everyone loves more money, more freedom, and working on things they are passionate about, starting your own business involves a lot more.

What I Mean by "Starting a Business Involves a Lot More"

Business owners share several traits that seem to ensure their businesses will be successful. Whether they are personal chefs or they wash cars, you'll find entrepreneurs share these characteristics:

- *They meet one of the three criteria above.* They want more money, or more freedom, or they have a desire to do something they love.
- *They have found a problem that people are willing to pay someone else to solve.* Remember, there are many problems in the world, but not all of them are ones that people are willing to pay someone else to solve.
- *They are organized.* Entrepreneurs need to be careful and keep track of many things. For instance, they need to know who has already paid them and who still needs to pay. They also need to keep a list of people who don't want their service yet, but have told them, "Call me in a month."
- *They are disciplined.* Many times, entrepreneurs have to do things that aren't fun. They may have to spend an hour licking envelopes to send out brochures describing their business. Or maybe they spend an entire day knocking on doors, looking for customers. Let's face it: these things are boring. But they are necessary, and business owners need the discipline to do them.

- *They are creative.* Business owners, as you know, are problem solvers. They started their business by solving one problem and charging a fee to do it. But many other problems will come up that entrepreneurs need to solve. What if, after two years in business, you suddenly don't have any more customers? What if someone moves in next door and starts competing with your lawn mowing business? What if someone starts making necklaces that are better and cheaper than yours? To conquer the unexpected, you need to be creative: find new ways to offer your products and services and new products and services to offer.

DOLLARS & SENSE

If you're the boss, no one is bossing you around! You need to crack your own whip to make sure you get done what you need to in a certain amount of time. No one is looking over your shoulder. That's your job, being the boss.

Do you meet these criteria? Even if you don't meet all of them, it's okay. Personally, I am not very organized. (That's definitely a problem I am willing to pay to have solved.) Luckily, another entrepreneur friend of mine is a professional organizer. She helps business owners like me make sure their bills are paid, files are in order, and basically that everything runs smoothly. Businesses of all sizes hire other businesses to help them stay creative, organized, and disciplined. So it's okay if you can't do it all—you just need to know who can help you do the things that you can't do!

Now you know what an entrepreneur is and roughly how a business operates. You know why people become entrepreneurs and what characteristics they typically share. So before we end this chapter, you need to decide: Is it for you? If you can answer yes, then turn the page; we will try to find the ideal business for you to start.

CHAPTER 2

What Type of Business Should You Start?

There are thousands of businesses out there. There are even more businesses that haven't been created yet! With so many ideas, how do you pick? Well, the good news is that a lot of the deciding has already been done for you. Let's face it: many businesses are too expensive for a young entrepreneur to start. You may love cars, but you probably aren't going to start a car manufacturing company. Unless you have a few *billion* dollars stuffed under your mattress, that just won't work! Over the years of being an entrepreneur and working with entrepreneurs, I've developed an easy way to help you determine the business that's right for you. When you get what seems to be a great idea, you can run that idea through what I call the ***Five S Formula***. The Five *S*s stand for:

- Simple
- Safe
- Skills
- Satisfying
- Self-seller

Let's look at each part of the formula more closely.

Simple. The business you start should be simple. That means it can be started without a lot of money, without a lot of time, and without a lot of hassle. Like the person in the example above, you may be fascinated by cars. But think of all the time, money, and hassle it would be to start manufacturing them, so that isn't a simple business.

Safe. The business needs to be safe for you and your customers. Avoid businesses that are dangerous. Businesses that are "high risk" need to pay a lot more for insurance. Maybe you have a trampoline in your backyard, and you and your friends love jumping on it. People love it so much you think you could charge people to use it. Great idea, right? But what if someone attempts the Amazon Triple Backward Double Reverse Kansas City Praying Mantis Flip and gets hurt? Renting your trampoline is simple, but it doesn't meet the *safe* requirement.

Skills. Try to use one of your skills or talents. Maybe you are really good at math. Get a pencil, a calculator, and some paper, and you're in the math tutoring business! It is that simple. Can anyone get hurt by being a math tutor? Nope. It's safe. Best of all, you're already good at it!

Satisfying. You might make a lot of money typing term papers for your friends, but if you hate typing, the business won't be any fun. You'll just be working for the money and, as I said, money is only one of the reasons why people start a business. So think about what you love to do. Look at your hobbies for great ideas that you could consider turning into a business. Don't think you can't be paid to do what you love. Remember Web designer Omer A. from the introduction? He got started by playing an online game called Ultima Online. In the game, he won virtual gold. He then sold that virtual gold on eBay for real money. So, yes, he got paid to play!

Self-Seller. *Self-seller* simply means your product or service sells itself. If you have a self-seller, every job you will have as the business owner will be easier. Your marketing, your sales, your customer service are all simple if you have a product or a service that everyone wants and everyone talks about. There are many ways to achieve a self-seller, but typically, your product is somehow the best. As marketing guru Seth Godin says, "Go out and be remarkable."

TALES FROM THE FRONT LINES

A friend of mine owns a cardboard recycling company. He has been very successful simply because he has a *self-seller*. Normally, a company has to pay to have its garbage removed. The more garbage it has, the more it has to pay. My friend's business actually *pays* other companies to take their cardboard. He takes their scrap cardboard, recycles it, and then sells it for less than what new cardboard costs. The companies he buys the scrap from make money not only from selling their old cardboard but also because their garbage load is smaller. His sales pitch is simply, "Why *not* do business with me?" If you want your entrepreneurial efforts to go smoothly, try to find a business that is a *self-seller*.

Testing the Five *S* Formula

The ideal business to start is one that meets all five criteria in the Five *S* Formula. Let's look at some examples.

> *Timmy loves jumping his mountain bike on homemade jumps that he makes out of scrap plywood. He's become so good at jumping that other kids have asked him to give lessons. So many kids have asked that Timmy thinks he could charge for the lessons.*

Is this a good business for Timmy?

Well, it is *simple*. Timmy already has a bike and his friends all have bikes too. He builds all the jumps himself out of plywood. It also takes advantage of his *skills*. Timmy is really good on a mountain bike. And, of course, Timmy loves it, so it is a *satisfying* business. It is a bit of a *self-seller*. Timmy is so good that kids have *asked* for lessons—he never had to advertise. But it does fail big-time on one of the *S*s; it is not a *safe* business. Kids who aren't as skilled as Timmy could get hurt.

How about this business?

> *Several of Kelly's friends have asked if they could buy Kelly's pottery. She has brought several projects home from school, and family friends noticed them displayed around the house. So many people have asked if they could buy items that Kelly thinks she could sell pottery. She looks into what it would take to start a pottery business. She could sell an item for an average profit of $15. A potter's wheel, a kiln, and all the supplies cost $3,500 total.*

Is this a good business for Kelly?

Well, it is certainly *safe*. Making pottery isn't really dangerous. It's obvious Kelly is good at it, so that meets the *skills* test. Because Kelly's friends have requested the pottery before it was ever for sale, it seems like Kelly has a *self-seller* on her hands. It also appears as if Kelly enjoys pottery, so she'll certainly find the business *satisfying*. But is it *simple*? She has to come up with $3,500 just to get started. Maybe this isn't the best business for her.

What do you think of Kaitlin's idea?

Kaitlin has been playing the flute for five years. She loves it. She has become so good at it that people are now asking her if she will play a song at their weddings.

How about this business?

Kaitlin loves the flute so it is *satisfying*. She is certainly *skilled* at it. It's *simple* because all she needs to start the business is a flute, which she already has. In the history of flute playing, no one has ever been killed in a tragic flute accident. So it is a *safe* business. The requests for her service tell us it's a *self-seller*. Kaitlin's business meets all the criteria of the Five *S* Formula.

The Art of Tweaking

But wait a minute! What if Timmy and Kelly *really* want to start their businesses? What if a business doesn't meet all five criteria but you *really* want to pursue it? What then?

That brings us to the art of **tweaking**. Tweaking your business idea simply means to make slight changes so it meets the criteria of the Five *S* Formula. Let's start with Timmy.

Timmy tells his dad his idea for the bike-jumping business. His dad is a little concerned that it might be dangerous and suggests that Timmy write down some alternatives that still allow him to make money through his love of bike jumping. So Timmy comes up with a tweak to his business:

Timmy contacts all the local bike stores and tells them that he is really good at jumping mountain bikes. He tells the store he can help them get customers by offering to do a display during the store's promotion. Customers come to watch Timmy jump his bike in the parking lot of the store. Timmy charges a flat fee for an all-day promotion in which he does several jumps and then answers questions about bikes and bike jumping. Because the store has insurance, Timmy's business is now a lot safer.

Kelly totals up the cost of all the materials to start her pottery business, and she realizes she doesn't have the $3,500 necessary to buy all the stuff. Her parents are willing to give her a loan of $1,000, but she is still $2,500 short. Frustrated, Kelly starts to think of ways to tweak her business. Here's what she comes up with:

Kelly finds a local pottery store that already has a kiln and a potter's wheel in the back shop. She approaches the owner and shows him some of her pottery. He's impressed, so Kelly offers him a deal. If she can use his potter's wheel and the kiln for five hours a week, she will make one pot for the owner per week for free. She basically pays for the potter's wheel and kiln by giving the owner free pottery.

Maybe your business idea doesn't fit perfectly into the Five *S* Formula. But with a few simple tweaks, you can still have the business you want and the comfort of knowing it's *simple, safe,* uses your *skills,* and it's a *satisfying self-seller.* The Five *S* Formula Checklist on the opposite page can help you see if your idea is a good fit. For other safety issues to consider, and to get a parents' point of view, see Chapter 21, *Keeping Them Safe.* This will help you to plan for and work out any potential problems early in your thinking about your business.

The Five *S* Formula can help you determine what type of business you are looking for. But how do you actually find opportunities that are worth turning into a business? Turn to the next chapter and find out.

The Five *S* Formula Checklist

My business idea is:

_____

_____

_____

_____

_____

_____

_____

_____

THE FIVE *S* FORMULA

1. Is this a simple business? _____ yes _____ no

2. Is this a safe business? _____ yes _____ no

3. Does this business make use of my skills? _____ yes _____ no

4. Do I find this business satisfying? _____ yes _____ no

5. Is this business a self-seller? _____ yes _____ no

If you answered *no* to any of the above, write some ideas for tweaks here:

_____

_____

_____

_____

_____

_____

_____

_____

CHAPTER 3

Turning What Sucks into Bucks

The Groaning Goldmine

You now know you are looking for businesses that fit the Five *S* Formula. Although the Five *S* Formula goes a long way in limiting your business search, there are still thousands of businesses you can start. How do you select the best one out of all the businesses out there? And how do you make sure that yours can compete?

Believe it or not, getting all the information you will ever need about which business to start and how to make it successful couldn't be easier. Remember that we said that all businesses solve a problem? And that when someone is willing to pay to solve a problem, an entrepreneur calls that problem an opportunity? Well, most people don't see the world that way, they just see the problems. Luckily for you, they love to complain about them!

What Is a Groaning Goldmine?

Let me introduce you to the Groaning Goldmine™. If problems are really opportunities in disguise, then behind every groan is a goldmine! Whenever someone is upset, angry, scared, confused, tired, bored, or frustrated, there is an opportunity nearby. Keep your ears open for key words that tell you an opportunity is lurking. The following phrases are almost always surefire paths to Groaning Goldmines:

"It sucks when . . ."

"I hate it when . . ."

"You know what pisses me off?"

"I'm scared of . . ."

"I wish this included a . . ."

"I'm confused about . . ."

"I'm so frustrated with . . ."

"It's a pain in the butt that I have to . . ."

"I wish that . . ."

"I get bored when I . . ."

"It would be nice if . . ."

"It worries me that . . ."

"This place really should . . ."

"It's too expensive to . . ."

"It's so difficult to . . ."

"It takes too long to . . ."

"It's too far to drive to . . ."

The Groaning Goldmine in Action

The Groaning Goldmine prompted me to write my first book. I was sitting in my college dorm room, reading a book on investing in the stock market. As people popped in and out of my room and saw the many investment books strewn about my floor, a few of them said, "I should really start investing." When I heard this, I would hand them the latest investment book I had just finished reading and suggest they take a look at it. A few weeks later, however, they would give it back to me and groan, "I didn't finish it. I found it boring."

After this happened three times, I decided there was a need for a fun investment guide written by a young person for young people.

TALES FROM THE FRONT LINES

Recent college grad Nicole Newman knew that most college students hate creating a résumé. What's more, most of them do it the wrong way. Her solution was Resume Nation LLC! After one too many eighty-hour workweeks at her job, Nicole wanted a better future for herself. She knew the best way to do that was to do something that her academic peers hated. She knew that if people hate doing something, they will often pay you to do it for them!

I'm not saying that every time you hear someone complain, you have to go start a business. (If that were true, I would've started a business every *day* I was dating my ex-girlfriend.) You'll have to decide whether or not the complaint is worth your time and effort to pursue. At least, now you know how to identify opportunities. You'll find that there are countless opportunities out there, once your ears are tuned into the right signals.

Not only can you use the Groaning Goldmine to find a brand new business, you can use it to improve an existing business. When I started my first business, the landscaping company, I used the Five *S* Formula. I found the business *satisfying* because I wanted to spend my summers working outdoors. It was *safe*; as long as I was careful with the equipment, I knew I wouldn't get hurt. The business was *simple*. When I started, I didn't have much equipment, but my parents did. I worked out a deal where I would "rent" the equipment from them: I promised to keep it in good condition and agreed to take care of their yard every week. Landscaping did make use of my *skills*. My father loved to landscape, so my brother and I spent half our childhood in the freaking garden! I learned about landscaping at an early age.

Although I knew a landscaping company was for me, I didn't really have a *self-seller* on my hands. There were already several landscaping companies in town, companies that had a lot more experience than I did. I didn't know how to compete.

But my *customers* told me how I could compete. One woman simply called me up and complained, "Peter, my usual landscaper can only mow the lawn on Mondays. I hate it that they won't let me pick the day. I wanted the lawn mowed on Friday so it would look nice for my son's birthday party on Saturday. Can you mow it Friday?"

There was a goldmine in this groan. This woman let me in on a landscaping secret: it is very important to people to pick the day their grass gets cut. What's more, they want the ability to switch that day. Most of the larger landscaping companies were so busy that they couldn't move their schedule around to accommodate such requests. But I could. I started printing up fliers that said: *"You pick the day we mow your lawn! Want to switch to another day? No problem, just call us!"*

DOLLARS & SENSE
Groaning Goldmines can help you identify how to make your business a *self-seller.*

All businesses solve problems. Your customers know more about these problems than you ever will, so if you are unsure, ask them.

Think about this: If you want to start a babysitting business, it may appear that babysitting is simple; there isn't really a difference from one babysitting service to another. But then one night you are having dinner with your parents and some of their friends and you hear their friends complain: "We had tickets to the concert, but we had to give them away because it's impossible getting a sitter at the last minute."

Hmmm . . . *impossible* to get a sitter at the last minute? Sounds like a pretty tough problem this family has if they use the word *impossible.* But their groan is your goldmine! That very night you can hop on your computer and print up some fliers that read: *"Think It's Impossible to Get a Babysitter Last Minute? Think Again! Call Last-Minute Sitters. Guaranteed sitters; just give us three hours' notice and we guarantee a sitter."*

Maybe a babysitting service that specializes in last-minute bookings is too difficult for you to offer. You decide. The key is to keep listening, because the world is constantly telling you how to improve your business. Everyone is giving you a map to the next Groaning Goldmine.

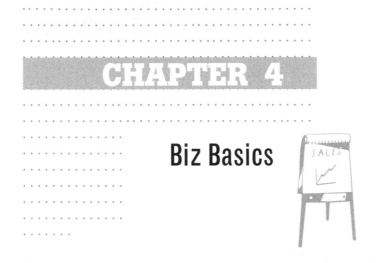

CHAPTER 4

Biz Basics

You're now at the bridge to cross over from a business idea into an up-and-running business. Your eyes and ears are open, looking and listening for Groaning Goldmines that fit into the Five *S* Formula. This period of searching is the perfect time to go over some business basics. It's funny how many seasoned businesspeople forget these fundamentals. If you continually remember them throughout your journey into entrepreneurship, your business will be a success. Let's start with a term you have probably heard before: **economics**.

Societies form because people need help solving their problems. (I know, I know, I'll get to the definition of *economics* in a minute.) Since the beginning of civilization, people have realized they could be safer, eat better, and accomplish more by living together than they could alone. From the days of hunter-gatherers, people realized that they could gather more and hunt more effectively in groups. These small groups of people grew more complex and eventually became societies. **Societies** are nothing more than groups of people who have banded together to help solve the problems of the group.

In order to make this problem-solving process as efficient as possible, societies have developed **economic systems**. The word *economy* has its roots in the Greek word *oikonomos*, which translates roughly to "household manager." So an economic system is the way we have chosen to manage our "house," or society. It's the procedure for solving society's problems. Economics then is simply the study of how we manage our society. Economists look at tons of data, from the total electrical output to the number of homes being built to the number of homeless people currently living in New York City. Economists process all these data, searching for ideas about how a society can improve and also predicting what the economy might look like in the future.

Different countries have chosen different ways to manage their "homes." You've heard terms such as *socialism* and *capitalism*. These are just different ways that societies can manage themselves.

In school, you may have learned that under socialism, the government or community owns everything (the businesses, the banks, maybe even people's homes) and under capitalism, the individuals own their own businesses, banks, and homes. But I don't like to categorize economies by looking at ownership. The way I separate economies is by asking the key question: *Who gets to solve the problems?*

Remember that the whole purpose of forming a society is to solve the problems of the people within that society. No one can solve all the problems by him- or herself. We all need help. We have needs for things like companionship, protection, food, shelter, water, and *Monday Night Football*. Who will help meet these and other needs and solve the problems of the society?

If you want more wealth, you simply need to start solving problems. If you live in a monarchy, you'd first have to figure out how to become king or queen. (Good luck!) In a socialist economy, you'd have to figure out how to get a government position. In a capitalist economy, however, the problems are open to anyone.

The Law of Supply and Demand

The overwhelming majority of people who are reading this book live in a capitalist society. So let's go over a few basic concepts in the world of capitalist economics. Some of these concepts are so well-respected that people have come to call them laws. The first is the *law of supply and demand*. Let me break this down:

> **Demand measures how aggressively people want to buy something.** What often determines *demand* is price. Think about this: You see a designer pair of jeans in the mall for $200. How many pairs are you going to buy? Two? One? Probably none. Because the price is so high, your demand (and the demand of all your friends) is very low. What if those jeans suddenly go on sale for $20 a pair? The demand is going to go way up. You and your friends will probably buy as many pairs as you can.

While price often controls demand, it isn't always the case. Perhaps a new Dave Mathews Band CD sells for $14 at the mall. At that price, you'd buy it, but you might not go out of your way to do so. Suppose, however, that next Thursday Dave Matthews *himself* is going to be at the mall, signing CDs, only these signed CDs are $50. Even though the price is way up, you can be sure that all the little ants will go marching down to see him.

Supply measures how aggressively a business wants to sell something. Like demand, what often determines *supply* is price. Imagine you are about to start marketing your lawn-mowing service. You think you can charge $5 an hour for that service. You decide to distribute flyers only to the houses within a quarter-mile of your house. At $5 an hour, you're not all that motivated to supply customers that are farther away. More than a quarter-mile away is too far to travel for just five bucks an hour. Later that evening, however, you show your marketing plan to your dad and he says, "Ya know, when we used to hire that boy up the street to cut our lawn, he charged $25 an hour. I think you can do the same." What happens next? Probably your mildly aggressive marketing plan is going to get a lot more aggressive. If you know you could make $25 an hour, you'll probably market to every house within 20 miles of your home.

DOLLARS & SENSE

If a business knows it can charge more, it will try its hardest to supply more.

The real key to supply and demand is how they work together. Customers want to buy at the lowest prices possible. Businesses want to sell at the highest prices possible. Somewhere in the middle is a happy medium, and that happy medium is often called the *market price*. Smart businesses are constantly experimenting with their prices. They know where they want to be on the scale between demand and supply. Look at stores like Walmart: they want the highest possible demand. How do they create that? Simple. They make sure they have the lowest prices.

On the other end of the scale might be Ferrari Automobiles. A Ferrari can cost more than $250,000! Obviously, the demand for a car at that price is very low, but because its price is so high, Ferrari doesn't need to sell a lot of them. The company wants to sell at the highest price possible, even if that means demand will go down. (Personally, I am waiting for the day when Walmart starts selling Ferraris.)

Getting Rich with a Niche

Walmart and Ferrari Automobiles are examples of two companies that know their competitive advantage. Your *competitive advantage* is sometimes referred to as your *niche*. A niche explains how you are different or better than all the companies like yours. It's important for you to find your niche; otherwise, competition is going to be tough. A good niche helps make your business a *self-seller*.

DOLLARS & SENSE

Your niche can be that you are the:

Fastest	Most convenient
Cheapest	Most luxurious
Newest	Biggest
Oldest	Smallest
Nearest (in the neighborhood)	Loudest
Best	Quietest

In a capitalist society, businesses are competing against each other for everyone's money. Competition keeps businesses on their toes. Businesses are always trying to be better, faster, cheaper, or different. In a society where the government solves all the problems, often things aren't of as high a quality, simply because there is little motivation to be better: Government-run businesses know that you have to buy from them, regardless of their prices, regardless of their quality. Lack of competition can throw off the law of supply and demand, because when customers have nowhere else to shop, they will buy what is in front of them. When customers have a choice, businesses are forced to improve every day.

Problems for Which You Can't Charge

Of course, some businesses have to be run by the government. The fire department is one example. Think about how much money people would pay a fire department if their house were burning! We can't have fire departments picking and choosing which houses they will save and which ones they will let burn, so we as a society have agreed that the government will run the fire departments.

Because fire departments can't charge people to save their homes, they need their funding from somewhere else, namely **taxes**. Taxes are fees we pay to local, state, and national governments to solve the societal problems that businesses either cannot or should not solve. Think about it. It would be dangerous if *everyone* tried to raise his or her own army. It would be silly if everyone had to build his or her own road. Protection and transportation are two things every society needs and are two things that are best left to government. As a society, we all agree on that, and we've all agreed to chip in and pay taxes.

How Taxes Work

In our society, there are several types of taxes. Sometimes the tax is charged by the local government, sometimes it is charged by the state government, and sometimes, the federal government. When you drive your car through a tollbooth, you actually pay a tax called a **per-use tax**. You only pay for it when you use it. If you don't drive on that particular road, you don't ever have to pay the tax. While there are many types of taxes, as business owners we are primarily focused on two of them: **sales tax** and **income tax**. *Sales taxes* are fees charged when something is sold. Sales taxes are charged by state and local governments. Not every state has a sales tax, but most of them do.

To find out if your state has a sales tax, take notice next time you buy something. If the price says $5, but the cashier charges you $5.35, you have a sales tax. The seller adds on the sales tax at the time of sale. Throughout the year, the business sends all its sales tax money to the government. (I'll explain how this works in a minute.)

The other type of tax that business owners worry about is the *income tax*. Income taxes are fees charged as a percentage of income or business profits. If the income tax is 10%, and your business made a profit of $1,000 last year, then you will send the government $100, or 10% of $1,000.

Talking about taxes is pretty boring to most people, but it is important to know how they work and why we have to pay them. This is especially true for business owners. If you are an employee, most of the tax work is handled by your employer. But as a business owner, you are in charge of everything, including taxes.

Hold on, don't fall asleep on me here! You know that taxes are fees paid to the government to solve the problems individual businesses cannot or should not solve. But how does the government keep track of who owes what and how much? Simple. They ask every entrepreneur who has earned at least $400 in profits to file a ***tax return***. A tax return is nothing more than a written summary of how much an individual or business has earned and how much it owes in taxes. Tax returns are filed once per year; in the United States, they are due every year on April 15. People refer to the period of late January to April 15 as ***tax time***. (Here's a non-entrepreneurial tip: If you ever want to ask your parents for something, NEVER do it between April 1 and April 15! They are too stressed out from tax time!) When people file their taxes on April 15, 2010, the taxes are being paid for the year of 2009. When people files on April 15, 2011, that tax return covers the year of 2010, and so on. Remember that people file both state and federal tax returns at the same time, and city tax, if there is one.

With whom do people file their taxes? Who receives all these tax returns and reviews them to make sure they are accurate? All federal tax returns in the United States are sent to the ***Internal Revenue Service*** or IRS. State tax returns are sent to your state's Department of Revenue.

Although tax *returns* are due once per year, salaried people actually pay taxes all year long. If you have ever had a job working for someone else, you know that your paycheck is always smaller than you thought it would be. If you were supposed to get $8 an hour working at a movie theater and you worked for 10 hours, you probably expected to get an $80 paycheck. As soon as you opened it, you saw it was for only $62! What happened? Your employer took out income taxes from the total and sent the taxes to the federal and state governments. This process is known as ***withholding***. As you work throughout the year, your employer keeps hacking away at your paycheck and sending those payments to the government. (Ouch!) Once the year has passed, you start preparing tax return forms for IRS and for the state (and city, if applicable).

If you are working for someone else, you calculate how much tax you owe the federal government and then subtract the amount of tax your employer has already sent to the IRS throughout the year. Sometimes an employer hasn't sent in enough money over the year, so you have to send in an additional check with the tax return. Other times, an employer has sent in too much money. In that case, you can request and receive a ***tax refund***. The state tax functions in the same way as the federal, but you send the money to the State Department of Revenue. (By the way, when your parents get a refund, *that's* when you should ask them for something!)

DOLLARS & SENSE

Many people believe that a tax refund is found money, but in reality, it's not. It's *your* money. It means that you overpaid the government, and now it has to pay you back.

When You're Self-Employed

So that's what happens to people who are employed by someone else, but what if you are the employer? In that case, it's all up to you. The big idea here is to remember that taxes need to be paid on your business's profits and, if your state has a sales tax, on business sales. You need to make sure you are setting aside the proper amount for income taxes, and you need to collect the proper amount for sales tax.

Because taxes are due on money *as you earn it*, you, as the business owner, have to pay what are known as ***estimated taxes***. Estimated taxes are taxes paid by business owners throughout the year. The big difference between estimated taxes and withholding (which an employer deducts if you work for him or her) is that it's up to you to make sure those estimated taxes are paid. When a customer pays you, you need to be sure to put some of that money aside to pay your estimated income taxes. Estimated taxes, both federal and state, are due four times a year in the United States, on April 15, June 15, September 15, and January 15. (January 15 is for the last quarter of the previous year.)

Sales Tax

How do you make sure you are setting aside the proper amount for taxes? Sales tax is easy. Multiply the cost of the item you're selling by the rate of sales tax in your area to get the amount of sales tax on the item. Then just add the sales tax to your sales price. For example, if you sell used college textbooks online and your state's sales tax rate is 5%, add 5% of the sales price to every sale, and charge that amount. For a $20-dollar book, you would add $1 (or 5%) and charge the customer $21. When the customer pays you, you take the sales money ($20), and put that money into one bank account and put the sales tax ($1) into another account. (We'll talk more about how to set up accounts in Chapter 10.)

In states with a sales tax, you often have to apply for a sales **tax ID number**. This number allows the government to easily monitor businesses collecting sales tax. Your state's Department of Revenue can help you with this form. How do *you* find the Department of Revenue? Simply go to your state's Web site—it should be on there. They make themselves easy to find, because they want your tax money!

Estimated Income Taxes

Estimated income taxes are a bit more complicated than sales tax, because they are charged as a percentage of your business *profits*. So although your revenue this month is $1,000, your profit may only be $250, after you have subtracted all your expenses. There are several precise calculations you can use to figure out the exact amount of money you need to set aside for estimated income taxes, but I use a simple formula that never gets me into trouble. Sometimes I overpay the government a little bit, sometimes I owe them a little bit more at tax time, but I never worry with this method. Remember the Five S Formula: We want our businesses to be *simple*. Even if you picked a simple business to start, it can turn into a big accounting hassle if you're not careful. I prefer simple calculations. You can also use this calculation as a brand new business owner who doesn't have all the financial data yet to calculate estimated taxes.

You know the basic equation to calculate your profit:

$$\text{REVENUE} - \text{EXPENSES} = \text{PROFIT}$$

To figure your federal and state estimated income taxes, just use the following simple equation once you have figured out your profit:

$$\text{PROFIT} \times 30\% = \text{ESTIMATED TAX}$$

At first 30% might seem a little bit high to pay in taxes. But in many states you have both state and federal income taxes. Using the 30% estimate, you may send in a bit more money than you need to. But don't worry; you will get any tax money you overpaid back when you file your annual tax return early in the next year. Remember that some of this money will go to the state, while most of it will go to the federal government.

File your estimated tax every quarter year (April 15, July 15, September 15, and January 15). Always make photocopies of all the payments or other correspondence you send to the state or federal government, and file them in an easy-to-locate place. Set up a special file for your business's papers; this could be a drawer in a file cabinet or a separate file box with hanging folders, which you can get for a few dollars at an office supply store. The federal government requests that you keep business records for at least 7 years, so it's a good idea to start in an organized way.

If you are confused, scared, or flat-out bored with the subject of taxes (and most people are), then don't feel bad about getting some help. Surprisingly, the IRS has a very friendly Web site at *www.irs.gov*. You can get tax forms there also. You may also want to ask your parent's tax preparer for some guidance on how to do all your tax tasks properly.

Thanks for sticking with me through this tax lesson. I'll be the first to admit that reading about taxes is the *best* cure for insomnia. So I'll mix it up here with a fun chapter. Next, we'll talk about naming your business and getting a title for yourself. Curious? Just read on.

CHAPTER 5

The Name Game and the Title Bout

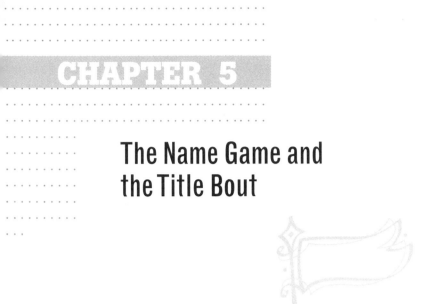

Every business has a name. Even if the business is using your name, like John's Kitchen Repair, that's still a name. While picking a name for your business seems simple, major corporations spend millions of dollars coming up with the perfect name for their company or their new product lines. A name is important, because the wrong name can be dangerous or misleading.

In this chapter, we'll look at names—names you give your business, and names you'll give yourself (and any partners or employees you may have), as well as names for the various duties you'll perform.

Solving Your Identity Crisis

Okay, hold on, you say. How can a name be dangerous? Chevrolet used to have a car called the Chevy Nova. Not such a bad name, right? The problem came about when Chevy tried to sell the car in Spanish-speaking countries. If you fell asleep in Spanish class, you missed that *No va* means "It doesn't go." There's probably a worse name for a car, but I can't think of it.

Movie stars go so far as to change their own names! Martial arts action star Jean Claude Van Damme's real name is *Jean-Claude Camille François Van Varenberg*. Originally, he thought his Van Varenberg name wasn't tough enough for the action star image he was going for. So he changed it *first* to Frank Cujo. Now *that* is a tough-sounding name! The only trouble was around the same time he switched to Frank Cujo, the film *Cujo* was hitting the theaters. *Cujo* was about a dog that contracted rabies and went psycho. Needless to say, as Frank Cujo, Van Damme didn't get very far, because when people heard the word *cujo* they thought *rabies*. So he switched again (and for the final time) to Van Damme, and his career took off from there. (Okay, fine. I admit that as you read this Van Damme is long overdue for a hit, but you get the idea.)

It's important to get the right name for your business. In fact, it's actually important that you come up with *five* names for your business because sometimes your first choices are taken. People can spend years trying to come up with a good name for their business, but if you follow these four keys, you can shave the time down considerably:

1. HAVE THE NAME DESCRIBE EXACTLY WHAT THE BUSINESS DOES. In high school, my friends had a business called Discount Dirty Work. They handled all those "dirty" jobs no one wanted to do, such as cleaning gutters and hauling away trash and landscaping debris. Because they were high school students, living rent-free with their parents, their services were often much cheaper than most landscaping companies, hence the "discount."

2. HAVE THE NAME BE FUNNY. While you don't want to come off as unprofessional, a funny name is easy to remember. There is a discount car-rental company called Rent A Wreck. There is another handyman company called Rent a Husband for all those jobs that wives wish their husbands would do but never will. Funny names also have built-in advertising because people say, "Oh I saw this clever ad for a business, and it was called _____." I did that after seeing an ice cream truck with the name The Ice Cream Man from Hell.

3. BE SURE THE NAME CONVERTS EASILY INTO AN INTERNET DOMAIN NAME. My first book was called *Getting Loaded*, and I thought that was a great title. But, when I went to register *www.gettingloaded.com*, it was already taken by a trucking company! (Luckily, about a year later, I grabbed it when it became available.) So as you are thinking of names, double-check them on the Internet. A great site to help you register a domain name is *www.godaddy.com*.

4. AVOID NAMING THE BUSINESS AFTER YOURSELF. Steve Mariotti, the founder of the National Foundation for Teaching Entrepreneurship, warns against the temptation to use your last name as the business name. In his book, *The Young Entrepreneur's Guide to Starting and Running a Busi-*

ness, he warns, "If the business fails, your name is attached to it." If, on the other hand, it succeeds, and you sell it for a lot of money, "what if [the new owner] engages in dishonest business practices? Your name is still on the door."

Following these four tips can instantly shrink your name-searching time.

DOLLARS & SENSE
It's important for you to register your business's name with the state you live in. That way there won't be 15 different "John's Kitchen Repair" businesses. Once a name is taken, that's it. To register your business's name, first contact your state's Corporations Division, which you can find by searching online on your state's Web site. They often have to do a search to be sure someone hasn't already registered your chosen name. (Sometimes you can register the same name if the products and services are different, but I still recommend that you have the most unique name you can find.) While many states allow you to register a name by mail, I think it is worth a trip to the Corporations Division office (in large states there is probably more than one) to register the name in person. Also, keep in mind that some states handle this on the county level. However it works in your state, call first, and ask them if there is a fee to register a name and how much it is.

Getting Your License (No, Not Your Driver's License)

Once you have decided on a name and have registered it with the proper government agency, you want to investigate whether or not your business needs a license. Many businesses are not allowed to operate unless they obtain a certificate from the state. Perhaps your business is picking up kids from elementary school. Do you need a chauffeur's license to do that? Maybe you want to prepare meals at home and deliver them to busy parents. Does this type of business fall under the watch of the Board of Health?

Often the prospect of getting a license turns many entrepreneurs away at the start. At times, it should. Choosing a business that requires licensure might violate the *safe* rule of the Five *S* Formula. However, if you are certain that, despite the need to get a license, your business idea will work, you might want to inquire about license exemptions. If you call the appropriate authorities and ask a general question like, "Do I need a chauffeur's license to drive kids to and from school?" the person on the other end of the phone might answer a standard yes. But there may be some license exemptions. For instance, if there are no more than two kids in the car at any one time, you might not need a chauffeur's license. Maybe if you spend less than twenty hours a week as a chauffeur you don't need a license. Be sure to ask about exemptions. Perhaps if you make slight tweaks to your business, you can slide under the requirements to get a chauffeur's license.

Got the name? Got it registered? Got a license (if necessary)? Then you're just about ready to start earning some money. But first, you need to create your business's organizational structure.

Who's in Charge Here?

Your business's **organizational structure** answers the question "Who does what and when?" Many entrepreneurs laugh at me when I ask these questions. "Peter," they say, "I am the only worker! I do everything." Although this may be true for you too, it is still important to have an organizational structure—even if you are flying solo.

TALES FROM THE FRONT LINES

I run a one-man business. I am the president, the accountant, the janitor, and everything in between. At times, my business has suffered because the janitor didn't do his job. My office was such a mess that I lost a speaking contract. I had to call the client back and ask for another one, which was a huge inconvenience because the person who signs contracts only signs them once a month. Because of this, I got paid a month late. Because of that, I was charged a late fee on my credit card (not to mention that I looked unprofessional in front of my client). I knew that I was the janitor, but I never put into writing when the janitor was supposed to do his job. So my policy was, "Whenever the trash cans are overflowing, the janitor will get to work."

I also never scheduled time for the accountant (still me) to do his job. And the receipts just kept piling up. Money was coming in, so I was fine—that is, until I checked my bank account and found only $45 in there! A little fact-checking revealed that several clients owed me several *thousand* dollars. I got lucky this time. If I had written a check before I noticed my cash-flow problem, it would have *bounced*, because there wasn't enough money in the account.

Michael Gerber calls this lack of organizational structure "The E Myth." (He tells all about it in his book by the same title.) Imagine that I work at a sandwich shop making sandwiches. Every day I hear Groaning Goldmines from the customers: the sandwiches should include this; the owners shouldn't charge for that. After hearing enough of these complaints I think, "I could go into business for myself making sandwiches. Look at all this great knowledge I have from customers!"

So I open my own sandwich shop, and it's a disaster! But I had such great inside information from my customers! So what happened? Simple. I know how to make a great sandwich, but I had no idea how to mop a floor. Or negotiate with my suppliers. Or keep good financial records. *I was only good at making a great sandwich.* The E Myth then, that so many entrepreneurs fall for, is that someone who opens a sandwich shop will be successful if he or she can make a good sandwich. The reality is that in order to *sell* that sandwich for a profit, a lot more things need to be done.

This is why an organizational structure is so important. When we start our businesses, we often think only about the main task that we are going to be doing: playing with little kids, making jewelry, mowing lawns, painting houses. All of these businesses include smaller tasks that need to be done in order for them to be successful. If you are your entire business, you need to identify each of these jobs and set aside time to do them.

The C Suite

Think about your business idea and which jobs will be necessary. Here are some common jobs at every company (they can all be performed by one person):

- *Chief Executive Officer, or CEO.* The **CEO** is the big cheese, the person who has the power to make big decisions for a company.
- *Chief Operations Officer, or COO.* The **COO** is in charge of making the business more efficient. If your business is mowing lawns, do you ever think about the order in which you mow those lawns? Or do you simply make sure you mow the lawns near the coffee shop in the morning, the lawns near the hamburger shack in the afternoon, and the lawns near the pizza shop in the evening? When you put on your COO hat, you'll probably scrap the "Munch and Mow" schedule that you've been using and switch to something guided by your profits and not by your stomach.
- *Chief Financial Officer, or CFO.* The **CFO** is responsible for making the company more profitable and making sure all the financial statements are accurate. Personally, I find that this is the most boring of these jobs but probably the most necessary. Remember, if your business doesn't make a profit, it is not a business!
- *Chief Marketing Officer, or CMO.* The **CMO** is responsible for bringing in new customers and keeping the old customers coming back for more. (By the way, never refer to your past customers as "old.")

The people with the above titles are often referred to as the *C Suite*. They pretty much run the company. There can be several people, several hundred people, or even several thousand people working below them. These folks can have all sorts of different titles like **controller**, which is someone who works under the CFO, or like *vice president of marketing*, who obviously would work under the CMO. Depending on the size of the company, there can be dozens of layers between the high school intern and the CEO.

EXTRA CREDIT

Companies keep track of who reports to whom using an *organizational chart.* This is literally a tree diagram that is handed out to all employees in the company. If you are the only member of your company, you don't need an organizational chart, but you should schedule times that you will do each of the jobs in the C Suite.

The C Suite in Action

Imagine that Katie's business is playing a violin at weddings. Normally, Katie works Saturdays and Sundays from 10 a.m. to 2 p.m. (to play at a morning wedding) and then 4 p.m. to 8 p.m. (for an evening wedding). Katie charges $50 per wedding and gets paid on the day of the wedding.

Below is a description of how Katie might organize her time when she is not actually playing the violin.

Chief Marketing Officer Tasks. Katie puts on her CMO hat twice a year at the spring and fall wedding conventions that come to her city. For two weekends a year, she rents a booth at conventions and spends long hours on her feet selling her musical services. Katie also takes every third Wednesday afternoon of every month to drive to all the hotels in her area to meet with the hotel's events planner. She drops off a flyer or sometimes she brings a small gift. Whatever she does, she makes sure she visits them at least once a month.

Chief Financial Officer Tasks. Every Monday night from 7 to 9 p.m., Katie plays the role of CFO. She takes all the money she made last weekend from weddings, adds it up, and subtracts from that all her expenses for gas, dry cleaning her dress, and violin lessons. Every week she records all her revenues and expenses in a journal. The first Monday of every month, she creates financial statements (which I'll discuss in Chapter 8).

Chief Executive Officer Tasks and Chief Operations Officer Tasks. Every other Thursday night, Katie plays the roles of COO and CEO. She looks at her journal of revenues and expenses and tries to think of ways to cut back costs and increase profits. She looks at her clients and determines which ones are the greatest sources of referrals. She tries to figure out why certain hotels she markets to have never recommended her. She always writes up a quick action plan with two or three simple things she will do in the next week to improve her business.

Katie's office is in her bedroom in her parents' house. One Friday night per month, she plays the role of ***executive assistant***. This is a person who assists those in the C Suite with everyday tasks such as opening mail, sending mail, and responding to e-mails. This "busy work" is often easy to ignore, and it does build up if it's not taken care of. While the jobs in the C Suite might be a little more fun and rewarding, Katie knows that one Friday a month she has to put on the executive assistant cap and get the office work done.

The nice thing about the organizational structure of your business is that once you set it up, you're done. Spend an hour or two setting it up and then move on. Speaking of moving on, we need to move on so we can talk about getting customers.

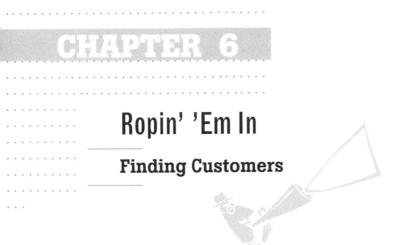

CHAPTER 6

Ropin' 'Em In

Finding Customers

Customers are the people who give you money for your products and services. They are essential to the survival of your business. Remember, all businesses depend on money to survive, and customers are the folks with the money! Whether you're looking for your first customer or for your 101st, this chapter will help. There are only three types of customers out there:

1. NEW CUSTOMERS. These customers are total strangers. They know very little—perhaps nothing—about you or your business. By far, these are the toughest customers to get, simply because you have no connection to them.

2. CURRENT CUSTOMERS. These are the people you are already doing business with. Current customers are very valuable to your business because those who have already bought your product or service are very likely to buy from you again. Some businesses take such good care of their current customers that they no longer need to find new ones. Often businesses grow not by getting new customers, but by offering their current customers new products and services. Current customers can also be a good source of referral customers.

3. REFERRAL CUSTOMERS. These customers have heard about you through one of your current customers. Referral customers are easier to get than new ones, because even though referral customers have never worked with you, they know someone who has. That someone, your current customer, has given you a rave review. It's important to continually ask your current customers for referrals. It's also important that your business be a *self-seller*, so people will refer you even when you don't ask them to, simply because your product or service is so amazing.

Whether they are going after new customers, referral customers, or trying to get more business out of their current customers, smart business owners develop a **marketing plan**. The marketing plan is simply an outline of how they will find more customers. Because new customers are the toughest, let's start with them.

You Gotta Start Somewhere

At some point, your business needs a new customer—your first one! How do you find that person? The first step is to figure out who that person is. A lot of money is wasted by small and big businesses alike in trying to capture new customers who may never buy a thing. Imagine you are trying to start a pool-cleaning business; you advertise in your local newspaper. Many people read the newspaper, but only a small percentage of them actually have a pool. The price of the newspaper ad is based on the total newspaper readership, not just the readership of pool owners. You paid a lot of money to advertise to many people who will never buy your service.

The key is to describe your ideal customers. Who are they? How old are they? Are they male or female? Where do they hang out? How much money do they make? What problems do they have? What do they like to do? Answering questions like this can help you identify your **target market**. Your target market is the group of people who are your ideal customers. Sure, you may get customers who are outside your target market, but the people who are most likely to buy from you are those in your target market.

The more you know about your target market, the better your marketing will be. Here's an example: Pretend you determine that the target market for your landscaping business is families with yards and small children. You could write up a flier that says: *"Pete's Landscaping Service. Call me today!"* That's not a bad advertisement, but if you knew a little bit more about your target market, you could improve your advertisement. Suppose you learned that the most important thing to the people in your target market wasn't getting their lawn mowed, but was having more time to spend with their kids. You could change your ad by saying something like this: *"Want more time with your kids? Let me do the yard work, and you can spend the day with your family! Call Pete's Landscaping Service today!"*

See the difference? One ad announces your service, plain and simple. But the second ad reminds customers of the problem that is on their minds—that they don't get enough time to spend with their kids. Because you reminded them of a good reason to use your services, you're likely to get more business.

DOLLARS & SENSE

In all of your advertising, try to remind your customers of the problems they have—and that you are the one with the solutions!

Once you have a written description of your target market, a great way to learn more about it is simply to ask! Maybe you're about to start a car-washing business, and you think everyone in your neighborhood is in your target market. Next time your neighbor up the street is washing his own car, ask to talk to him for a few minutes. Ask him why he washes his own car. Ask him how long it takes him to do it alone. Ask him if he ever paid someone else to do it.

Answers from people in your target market can help you easily create your marketing plan. Maybe after talking to four or five of your neighbors, you learned that the reason they all seem to wash their own cars is because several years ago they all hired a boy to do it, and he never did a good job. Your neighbors don't like to go to the automatic car wash either. They feel that machine doesn't do a good job, and of course it doesn't clean the inside of the car.

Having this information, you can be sure to address people's concerns in your marketing plan. You can offer a "satisfaction guarantee" so that people never have to worry about a sloppy job. You can offer to clean the inside of the cars as well. If you simply went around telling people that you wash cars, they might turn you down out of fear that you would do a lousy job, just like the boy before you.

Ways to Get Customers

Once you know the people in your target market and you have addressed some of their concerns, you can start implementing your marketing plan to actually get some customers! There are only a few ways to reach new customers, which we'll describe below.

1. ADVERTISING. This is the most expensive option, but it will reach the largest number of people. Many new small businesses should NOT advertise, simply because the costs are too high and the business is too focused to justify an advertisement to a large group of people. If you plan on being a chef for hire in your neighborhood, there is no reason to put an ad on the radio, as you will pay to reach thousands of people, many of whom live nowhere nearby. If, however, your business has mass appeal, then you may want to consider advertising. Your best bet is often to do targeted advertising. If you run a babysitting service, advertising in your apartment complex's newsletter is a great use of your advertising dollars. Advertising can come in many forms, from ads on TV and radio and in newspapers, to posters on the library bulletin board, to hiring a plane to drag a banner of your business across the sky! (It's probably best to wait on that last one though.) Just be sure you are reaching the people you want to reach.

2. SAMPLING. Sampling involves giving away your product or service for free. In the car-washing example, you learned that many of your neighbors were hesitant to hire someone to wash their car, because the boy who did it a few years ago didn't do a good job. It's going to be tough to convince these people you can do a good job by just giving them a flier. You'll have to prove it by washing their cars once for free. Samples can be expensive, but they are also very effective in getting business. One way to cut back on the costs of sampling is to state something like, "You only pay if you are satisfied." This way, customers can try your service with very little risk. They don't have to pay until they know you've done a good job they are happy with. (Sampling, by the way, also helps you test new products and services. If sixteen people puke after trying your Pumpkin Surprise Cookies, you know you need to make some adjustments!)

3. ASKING FOR REFERRALS. Even if you are trying to get new customers, you can still use the referral technique. Though your business is brand new and no one has used your products or services, there are many people out there who know you personally and know that if you say you will do something, you will. Announce to these people that you are starting a new business and that you are looking for customers. Do they know anyone? Would they be willing to hand out some of your business cards? Would they give you some names you could call? Often businesses pay for referrals, either by offering cash or a free product or service to anyone who refers them business. While paying for referrals is a cost, it's a cost you *don't* have to pay until you get more business!

4. SALES CALLS. These can be made in person, over the phone, or even via e-mail. A *sales call* happens when you approach someone in your target market and actually try to get the person to buy. Unlike advertising or sampling, where you simply wait for the customer to respond, the purpose of the sales call is to leave with a yes or no answer—preferably a yes! Although sales calls can be made "cold" (meaning that the call is your very first interaction with the customer), they are best used when combined with another form of marketing. If you dropped off a flier to everyone in your neighborhood, some good sales calls would be to contact everyone who received a flier who has not called you back yet. Because sales calls are personal, they can be very effective. However, they do take up a lot of time, so you must also focus your sales calls.

5. SURVEYING. Surveying is advertising in disguise. Rather than trying to sell something, you simply ask the people in your target market to fill out a survey. If you are going to start a chef-for-hire business in your apartment building, maybe you can give a survey to everyone in your building. On it are several questions, such as: How often do you order out? Would you ever hire a personal chef to come to your apartment to cook dinner for you and your family? If so, would you pay $30 for this service? $40? $50? What nights of the week are you most likely to hire a personal chef? And of course: Are you interested in a free sample of my services? Often entrepreneurs offer a reward, such as a free sample, to someone filling out the surveys. While many in your target market will simply recycle your survey, those who do answer it are usually pretty serious customers. In that case, arrange for a sales call!

6. PUBLIC RELATIONS. Public relations (PR) is another form of advertising in disguise. Often PR campaigns are cheaper than advertising campaigns. Public relations campaigns simply use the media to establish a *relationship* with the **public**. They differ from advertising in that the campaign is not trying to sell anything directly. PR gets customers interested in your business because you are doing something good, funny, or amazing. Imagine you have a cookie-baking business. One idea for an amazing PR campaign would be to try to break the world record for baking the biggest cookie. You could put on a huge event and have samples of your cookies at the event. People would come just to see the giant cookie you were trying to bake. Or you could have a funny PR campaign, in which you could bake cookies and decorate them with jokes. Your local newspaper might like a story like that. Or you could use a PR campaign to do something good, like bake 100 cookies and give them to an orphanage in your city. People will talk about what you do as long as it is newsworthy. In Chapter 12, I'll talk about another common PR strategy, "the Grand Opening." Even though PR is not a traditional advertisement, the results are the same!

7. FORM A PARTNERSHIP. Who already has a bunch of customers? Another business owner just like you does. Many business owners seek to form relationships of *synergy*. Synergy happens when the whole is greater than the sum of the parts. In other words, 1 + 1 = 3. Maybe your friend sells handmade necklaces for her business. You, on the other hand, sell handmade bracelets. It's a good bet that at least some of her customers might want bracelets and some of your customers might want necklaces. You can form a partnership and together create more business! Partnerships can work in many different ways. A simple way might be that you both agree to tell your current customers about each other's businesses. Perhaps you get a percentage of the profits that you create for one another. Maybe you both put your products on a flier and split the cost of printing the flyers.

8. OUTSOURCING. So far we've been *targeting* individuals as potential customers. However, *businesses* also represent a potential customer base, in that they can *outsource* jobs to you. Outsourcing is the practice of one business hiring another business to do part of its work. Businesses do it all the time, either because they can't handle all the business they have or because they are trying to cut costs. If I have a car-detailing business (cleaning and refurbishing cars), I might offer to completely detail cars, but outsource the vacuuming to another company. My clients never know that I outsource the vacuuming—they deal directly with me. If they complain about the vacuuming, they complain directly to me, and I deal with the vacuuming company. Outsourcing is becoming more and more popular as businesses try to cut costs. As you develop your marketing plan, consider approaching other businesses about outsourcing opportunities.

Getting Started on Your Marketing Plan

So now you know the eight ways to get customers. Let's put them together with a plan. There are four keys to a successful marketing plan:

1. *Keep costs down.* This is always a good idea, no matter what aspect of business you're dealing with.
2. *Use graduated spending.* Graduated spending basically means as you earn more, you can spend more on advertising. This may seem obvious (your lemonade stand is not going to pay for a 30-second ad during the Super Bowl), but many entrepreneurs spend a lot of money on advertising with the hope of getting a lot of business quickly. What often happens is they run out of money before they get any customers!
3. *Test and track.* Suppose you hand out fliers in your neighborhood.

Then you advertise in your local newspaper. Then you e-mail all your friends and tell them you are starting your business. Then you get eight new customers. Good news? Not exactly—unless you know *how* those customers heard about you. Was it the fliers? The ad in the paper? The e-mails? Smart marketers *test* their marketing plan, which means they try different variations of their e-mails, advertisements, sales calls, and other marketing materials. They also *track* their marketing, which means they work to uncover exactly how the customer found them. The simplest way to track your marketing efforts is to ask every customer, "How did you hear about me?" You can put tracking incentives in your ads, which give people a discount. (You've seen ads that say, "Mention this ad and receive 10% off.")

4. *Use a multimedia approach. Multimedia advertising* simply means you are targeting your customers in several areas at once.

DOLLARS & SENSE

There is an unwritten rule in the world of marketers: *You need to hit your customers SEVEN times before they will buy something.* Indeed, some customers will buy from you the very first time you contact them, but plan on approaching them seven times before you get their business. That way any surprises will be pleasant ones!

You already know the first part of your marketing plan: determining your target market. This costs nothing except the price of a piece of paper. It's best to describe the person you are looking for in a sentence. That way, when you are asking for referrals from family and friends, you can quickly and easily explain who you are looking for.

The next step is to determine your advertising budget. If you are just starting your business, it can be tough to determine how much you should spend. Existing businesses usually know how much they are willing to spend on advertising, and they make it a constant section in their company's budget. As a brand new business, you don't have that luxury. A great way to sidestep this problem is to first use only free advertising. Then graduate to the cheaper forms of advertising. Then finally (and only if necessary), consider more expensive forms of advertising. Want some help with this? Try the Marketing Plan Worksheet on the next page.

Marketing Plan Worksheet

STEP ONE: IDENTIFY YOUR MARKET

Who is your target customer?

_____
_____
_____

List possible customers:

_____   _____
_____   _____
_____   _____
_____   _____

STEP TWO: FREE ADVERTISING

What kind of free advertising can you do?

_____
_____

What are some businesses that you could market to for out-sourcing opportunities?

_____
_____

Write some quick ideas for a PR campaign here:

_____
_____

List three other young entrepreneurs like yourself who might want to form a partnership with your company:

1. _____
2. _____
3. _____

STEP THREE: CHEAP ADVERTISING

What kind of cheap advertising can you do?

_____
_____

STEP FOUR: EXPENSIVE ADVERTISING

Where can you pay to advertise?

_____

STEP FIVE: PUTTING TOGETHER A SURVEY

What do you need to know from your customers?

_____

Which customers will you send surveys to?

_____
_____

From Plan to Action

Let's take a look at how an actual plan might work. Imagine that Sally wants to start a Web-design business. Here is a mini-sample marketing plan she created.

Step One: Target Market

Her niche. Sally determines that her company is going to be called Affordable Web Solutions. She is going to target ultra-small businesses and individuals who believe that having a Web site designed and uploaded is too expensive. Her niche is that she is the cheapest Web designer around.

Step Two: Free Stuff First

Sales calling. Sally's parents have a calling plan that allows free calls after 7 p.m. Sally gets permission from her parents to use the phone on Tuesday and Thursday nights from 7 to 9 p.m. for the next three weeks. Sally makes a list of all her friends, her family, and all the small businesses she can think of. She spends two hours every Tuesday and Thursday evening in calling people and informing them she is starting a new Web-design company. She also asks people if they already have a Web site, and if so, she asks what they like and dislike about it. If they don't have one, she asks them why not.

Referrals. At the end of every call, Sally offers $10 to anyone who refers a customer to her.

E-mail. On all her calls, Sally also asks people for their e-mail address. After she calls on Tuesdays and Thursdays, she e-mails everyone on Wednesdays and Fridays, thanking each one for talking to her on the phone and reminding the person that she pays a $10 referral fee for every customer referred.

Partnerships. Sally calls all the computer-repair shops in the phone book. She offers each one a partnership. She agrees to tell her clients (who all have computers) about the repair stores if the stores agree to tell their clients about her Web service. Of the eight places she calls, six tell her no because they already have an in-house Web design business. Two, however, agree to her partnership idea.

More referrals. After three weeks of making calls, Sally has gotten four Web-design clients. She works extra hard on these four Web sites and makes sure her customers love her. When the Web site is finished, she asks every customer for two things: First, she asks for referrals to others who might be interested in her services. She reminds her customers that they too can get $10 for every customer they send her. Second, she asks each customer for a *testimonial*. A testimonial is the single best piece of advertising you can have. It is a positive statement from one of your satisfied customers.

More E-mails. Sally takes the four testimonials she received and puts them into an e-mail that she sends once again to all her friends, her family, and potential businesses. From this second round of e-mails, Sally gets six more customers.

Public relations. Sally knows that she has many potential customers who just need to be convinced that a Web site can help them out. Sally decides to write an article for her local newspaper titled "Why Every Small Business Needs a Web Site." In the article, Sally addresses some of the concerns she has heard from chatting with friends and family over the phone: it's too expensive, I'm afraid of technology, and so on. While Sally doesn't come right out and advertise, she does sell in the article. She writes many sentences like, "While many people think a Web site will cost several thousand dollars, there are many great services that offer affordable Web design. For example, my company, Affordable Web Solutions, charges just $50 for a basic site." At the end, Sally includes her *byline*, which is a one- or two-sentence description about herself and her business. (See the sample press release in the Resources section of this book.) Sally e-mails the article to four local newspapers, and one of them decides to publish it!

Outsourcing. One day Sally gets a thought: Six computer repair businesses turned down her idea of a partnership because they already had in-house Web design services. She decides to call them again and ask them to outsource to her any business that those services can't handle. Upon suggesting this, she gets two projects.

Step Three: Cheap Stuff Next

Flyers. Sally has gotten a great response from her free marketing efforts, but she would like to step it up and grab some more customers, especially now since she has some revenue coming in. Sally prints up 200 flyers, one for every apartment in her complex. The cost is 10 cents per flyer for a total of $20. She asks the property manager if she can slip them under the doors. The manager tells her no, but says that if she knocks on the door and someone answers, she is free to give a flyer to the person.

Door knocking. Sally spends the next two Saturdays knocking on doors. Of the 200 doors she hits, only about 125 people answer; only 70 of those actually take a flyer.

Posting. Since Sally has several flyers left over, she posts them at all the locations she can walk to in her neighborhood. She makes sure she checks with the person in charge before posting anything. She puts up three flyers at the library, one on her apartment building's bulletin board, five on her school bulletin boards, one at the post office, and another five on the boards of local businesses.

Step Four: Most Expensive Stuff Last

Surveys. Although Sally has been surveying her family, friends, and customers all along by asking them questions, she really wants to do a formal survey of all the small businesses in her town. Her market research tells her that people would rather fill out a paper survey than an electronic one, so Sally spends $1,000 printing up 150 three-page surveys, renting a mailing list from a local mailing-list company, and mailing them out. She offers a 50% discount on her services to any business that completes the survey. Of the 150 sent out, Sally only receives 50 responses, but the information she gets from them is invaluable. For one thing, she realizes that she can raise her prices. Sally also discovers that many businesses want help creating a "temporary" Web page that promotes a single event, product, or sale. She has never offered this before, but now she knows to make it one of her main points in all her marketing materials.

Paid advertising. While Sally is a little nervous about spending $600 to place an ad in a magazine for entrepreneurs, she wants to expand quickly. This magazine has more than one million readers, and she needs only 12 customers from the ad to make it pay for itself, so she is going to go for it.

Sally's marketing plan is a very simple marketing plan that you can copy, no matter what your business is. Are you ready to go and get customers yet? Well, before you go out, be sure to read the next chapter, because it will help to you handle the money side of your business.

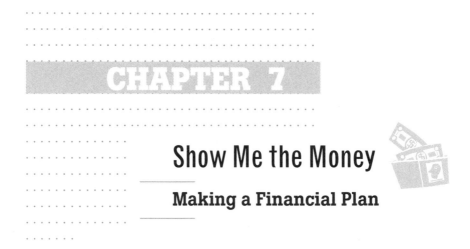

CHAPTER 7

Show Me the Money

Making a Financial Plan

Just as every business has a plan for how to go out and get customers, it also has a plan for what to do with its money. This includes the money the business starts with as well as the money it earns. So let's talk about forming your business's *financial plan*.

A financial plan is just a road map of how and when your business collects and distributes money. Starting a business costs money. (Remember the old saying, "It takes money to make money!") Of course, running a business also requires that money keep coming in. And every time you make your product, it costs you money. All businesses have three basic costs that entrepreneurs need to deal with. They are:

1. Start-up costs
2. Operating costs
3. Cost of goods sold (often called COGS)

> **Start-up costs.** *Start-up costs* are those one-time expenses that you need to make in order to start the business. If you are starting a sewing business, somewhere, somehow, you need to buy a sewing machine. That sewing machine is one of your start-up costs. These are often the most intimidating costs, because your business doesn't have any revenue yet to pay for them.
>
> **Operating Costs.** *Operating costs* are the ongoing expenses that the business must continue to pay to stay open. These expenses could be the cost of utilities, insurance, licenses, salaries, rent, advertising, Web-site fees, and the like. Mind you, operating costs

are costs related to the business, not to the product itself. Operating costs are divided once again into *fixed costs* and *variable costs*. As you can probably guess, fixed costs don't change, but variable costs do. If you rent a power washer for your power-washing business for $10 a month, well, that's a fixed cost. If you work every day, the rent for that power washer is $10 a month. If you don't work at all in a month, that rent is still $10. Fixed costs are certainly easier to plan than variable costs. An example of a variable cost might be the costs of tune-ups for the power washer. This cost varies, because the frequency of tune-ups depends on how much business you get. The more often the power washer is used, the more often it needs to be tuned up.

Cost of goods sold. Just as operating costs are costs related to the business, the *cost of goods sold (COGS)* includes all the costs related to the product itself. If you bake cookies, the costs of flour, sugar, eggs, and milk are part of the COGS. The more you sell, the higher your COGS will be. But you *don't* have to pay COGS if you aren't doing any business.

A++

EXTRA CREDIT
Sometimes it can be difficult to distinguish between COGS (cost of goods sold) and variable costs. It's often better if you can turn a variable cost into a COGS. For instance, if a power-washer tune-up costs $20 and you know you need to perform a tune-up with every twenty washes, then that variable cost can now be assigned to the COGS. Your COGS just went up by $1 to account for tune-ups. Converting variable costs to COGS makes it easier to predict your total costs.

Digging for Dollars

Because start-up costs can be the toughest to come up with, let's start with them. When a business is being started, it often has to determine its *financing strategy*. The word *finance* simply means "to pay for." So when someone asks, "how are you going to finance your business?" They are really asking, "How are you going to pay for this?"

In the theoretical business world, there are basically two types of financing: ***debt financing*** and ***equity financing***. In the real business world, there are several other financing options, which I'll discuss in a minute. First, let's look at debt financing and equity financing.

Debt is money that you *owe*. ***Equity*** is money that you *own*. So if you finance (pay for) your business with debt that means you borrowed money to start your business. If you financed with equity, that means that you sold some of your business to someone else and used that money to start your business. Whoever you sold to is now a part owner of the business.

Rather than using the words *debt* and *equity*, I find it easier to remember the words *loaners* and *owners*. If I want to raise money to start my business, I need to find either owners or loaners. Let's first look at raising some cash with loaners.

You know that when you rent something, you pay a rental fee to get it. Go to the store and rent a DVD, and you are charged a rental fee. Money is no different. When you rent or borrow money, you are charged a rental fee. That rental fee is called ***interest***. Interest is rarely charged as a flat fee. Instead, it is often charged as a percentage of the money you borrowed. So if you borrowed $1,000 with a 10% annual interest rate, the rental fee comes out to be $100 a year. The person borrowing the money is often referred to as the ***borrower;*** the person loaning the money is often referred to as the ***creditor***. (This isn't brain surgery!)

Loans come in all shapes and sizes, but all of them have four basic parts: The ***interest rate***, as you know, is the percentage of the loan charged as the fee for borrowing that money. The ***principal*** is the original amount you borrowed. In the above example, 10% is the interest rate and $1,000 is the principal. Every loan also has a ***repayment period***, the amount of time you have in which to pay back the loan. Perhaps the above loan has a five-year repayment period. Finally, all loans have ***repayment terms***. While the repayment period outlines when the money will be paid back, the repayment terms outline how the money will be paid back. Are you supposed to pay once a month? Twice a year? All of it at the end?

To ensure that you get the best deal, remember to consider all four parts of the loan. Most young entrepreneurs, however, borrow from the Bank of Mom and Dad, and I can assure you that those loans are always a good deal.

When borrowing money to pay for the start-up costs of your business, there are a few pros and cons to consider.

Borrowing Money: Pros
- You still own the whole business.
- As long as you make your loan payments on time, no one else has a say in how the business is run.

Borrowing Money: Cons
- You have to make those loan payments, even if the business is not making a dime!
- Creditors can legally take some of the stuff the business owns in order to repay the debt if you can't repay it another way. If you use a loan to buy a T-shirt silk-screening machine and you fail to make the loan payments, you could end up losing the silk-screening machine to your creditors.
- Since you are a brand new business, many creditors won't loan you any money at all, because they don't know you. Your business doesn't have any sort of track record, and they may view you as too high a risk.

Finding a loaner is one way to scrape together some cash. But what do you do if your requests for loans are met with moans? Well, you can sell part of your business to an owner. I like to think of this as "selling the future." Right now, your business is essentially worthless. I mean no offense, but think about it: Sure, you have a great idea, but your business doesn't own anything, and it isn't making any money. What could you possibly have to offer someone who is willing to give you cash? The only thing you can sell is the future value of your business, by offering a partial ownership in the business.

If I were to be an owner-investor in your business, I might give you $2,000 in exchange for a 25% ownership in the business. That means I am entitled to 25% of all the profits that come in. If, five years down the road, you sell your business for $25,000, I would get $6,250 because

$$\$25,000 \times 25\% = \$6,250$$

Becoming a part owner may also mean that I have a say in what the business does and how it spends its money, 25% of which is *my* money. Getting cash from people who become part owners has its own list of pros and cons.

Getting Cash from Part Owners: Pros
- There are no scheduled payments.
- It is usually easier to get than a loan.

Getting Cash from Part Owners: Cons
- You give up a piece of the company.

- You may even give up control of the company.

Now you've seen the two basic ways of raising cash for your business. The question is: Which one is for you?

The Real Deal

Many companies use a combination of owners and loaners. Often they start with owners; once they get established, they can begin borrowing money. But for a small start-up business like yours, there are other types of financing. While the theoretical business world recognizes mainly owners and loaners, the real-world entrepreneur has several places to go for money, described below.

- *Trade your time.* You may not have a lot of money to buy equipment, but what you do have a lot of is time. You can trade your time for the equipment you need. This is how I financed my landscaping business. When I started, I didn't have any money to buy lawn mowers and rakes, so I made a deal with my dad that I could borrow his stuff if I took care of his yard for free. Your parents may not have the equipment you need hanging in their garage, but maybe someone you know does. Many entrepreneurs work part-time for free in a business like the one they hope to have one day. You might want to sell handblown glass items, but you hardly have the money to buy a furnace and all the tools to get started. So you find a store owner and offer to work five hours a week for free if you can use his equipment for ten hours a week to make your own stuff.
- *Have a yard sale.* There aren't piles of cash sitting around your house, but if your parents are anything like mine, there are piles of "stuff" floating around your house, and that stuff can be turned into cash. Don't overlook this cool shot at getting some money. I've had yard sales that have made over $1,000! Best of all, any money you make off a yard sale is tax-free, because you are selling everything at a loss. (Your dad bought that pasta maker for $75, never made any pasta, and now you've sold it for $15.)
- *Sell stuff online.* Don't have a yard? The Internet, of course, is the yard sale of the future. Sites such as eBay and craigslist are great ways to unload some of your stuff. And unlike yard

sales (which must be done all at once), with Internet sales, you can sell stuff anytime you need more money!

- *Rent equipment.* Rather than renting money to buy equipment, it's often far easier to just rent the equipment. Visit local rental shops that rent the equipment that you need and ask what their policies are. Ask if you can put down a small deposit and pay the remaining balance when you return the item.
- *Credit cards.* Nice idea but . . . no. First of all, you need to be eighteen years old to have one. And while many entrepreneurs charge their start-up costs to a credit card, this is a *very* high-interest loan. Unless your business can make buckets of cash quickly, it's unlikely you can make credit-card financing work.
- *Save.* This is the old-fashioned way to finance a business. While you're searching for the ideal business to start, set aside a little bit of money for the day you finally stumble upon that great idea!
- *Customers.* You don't have any money, but your customers do! Ask them to pay half of the cost of the job up front. You can use that money to rent or buy the equipment you need. Many entrepreneurs give their first customers a deep discount, simply to get the cash flowing.
- *Donations.* Most businesses can't convince people to donate cash to them. But many people will donate their stuff, if for no other reason than just to get rid of some of the junk in their house! Remember, one person's trash is another person's treasure. Maybe your family's friends are moving from a large home to a small condo because both their kids are now in college. They're probably happy to get rid of a lot of their stuff, everything from desks to gardening tools.
- *Howdy, partners!* Partnership financing is like owner financing, only the partner is not just throwing in her money, she is also going to help run the business. Maybe you and your friend want to make and sell handmade wooden crafts. Your friend has saved $500 to buy the woodworking tools, but she lives in an apartment building and has no room to set up a shop. You've only saved $50, but your parents will allow you to use one side of the garage to set up your business. You supply the shop, your friend supplies the money, and you are now partners in business. While partnerships are a wonderful opportunity for synergy, they can damage a friendship if the

partnership goes sour. Partnerships can also be ruined if the *friendship* goes sour. Create a written partnership agreement to clearly spell out everyone's duties. It's also a smart idea to chat about what happens if the business goes bankrupt or if one person wants to leave the partnership. Ideally, this will address any problems in advance.

- *Step right up!* If you look hard enough, I bet you can find a contest for young entrepreneurs. As promotion for this book, I gave away $1,000 to the entrepreneur who had the best essay describing his or her business or business idea. *Ideablob.com* gives away $10,000 *a month* to entrepreneurs who receive the most votes on its Web site. The good news is: many of the contests have rules that are the same. Most of them ask for an essay or business plan (which you will soon have!), and many give the award to the person with the most online votes. So hop onto the Internet and search around. There are a lot of contests out there, and more pop up every day.
- *The bank of Mom and Dad.* You've probably knocked on the doors of the Bank of Mom and Dad before, but this time you have a great story to tell them. You're not looking for money to go to the movies or order a pizza: you want to start your own business. Your parents can be owners in your company or they can loan you the money and charge an interest rate. If you get a loan from your parents, treat it as seriously as you would a loan from a bank. Check out the Sample Loan Agreement Form in the Resources section of the book, which you can use as a guide.

The good news is that most of the businesses in this book can be started with little or no money. While you now know about owner and loaner financing, you probably won't have to do either to get your business started. And as your business grows, you'll be prepared with some knowledge of financing.

Operating Costs

Operating costs are the ongoing costs that your business incurs just to stay open. I hope you will have some money coming in to cover your operating costs. Remember that I said that operating costs are divided into fixed costs and variable costs? It's important to know and constantly check what your business's fixed and variable costs are, even before you start the business. Take a moment and write down everything you think would be a fixed cost for your business and everything that may be a variable cost for your business on the Monthly Operating Costs Worksheet on page 58. One tip I give entrepreneurs is: Whenever you can, seek to change a variable cost into a fixed cost or a cost of goods sold. In my office, I pay my heating bill all year long, even though I only heat the office about seven months a year. I got tired of heating oil being a variable cost—very high in the winter and almost nothing in the summer, so I signed up for a payment plan with my oil company in which they spread the heating bill payments out throughout the year. The payment is the same every month, be it December or July.

As you write down your list of variable costs, ask yourself if there are ways you can convert them into fixed costs.

Cost of Goods Sold (COGS)

To determine your cost of goods sold (COGS), you really need to determine your cost of a *good* sold. In order to determine that, you need to define one unit of what you are selling. If you sell cookies, one unit might be one cookie. It might be one batch of 12 cookies if you only sell in batches. If your business cleans pools, one unit might be one hour of pool cleaning, or it might be the cost to clean one pool. Do whatever makes the math easiest (and makes sense for how you plan to sell) in order to answer this question: *How much does it cost me to sell one unit?*

Here's a great tip for calculating costs: Use imprecise math. I know what you are thinking: *Imprecise math? Aren't I supposed to be accurate in my calculations?* What I mean is, overestimate the cost of a good sold and that way any surprises will be pleasant ones. Again, imagine your business is cleaning pools. Now, most pools are the same size, but some people have very large pools, and others have very small pools. It's better to calculate your cost of a good sold based on the larger pool than it is the smaller one. That way you'll never come up short!

Here's an example of calculating cost of a good sold for a woodworking business that sells hand-carved wooden dolls.

Wooden Doll Business

Define the unit: The unit is defined as one doll.
Below are the calculations of costs to make one unit:

- **Wood.** $20 for one block. One block of wood can make 10 dolls, so $20/10 = $2 in wood costs per doll.

Monthly Operating Costs Worksheet

VARIABLE COSTS:

_____
_____
_____
_____
_____
_____
_____
_____
_____
_____
_____
_____
_____
_____
_____
_____

FIXED COSTS:

_____
_____
_____
_____
_____
_____
_____
_____
_____
_____
_____
_____
_____
_____

TOTAL MONTHLY COSTS:

Variable: _____

Fixed: _____

VARIABLE COSTS THAT COULD BECOME FIXED COSTS:

_____   _____
_____   _____
_____   _____
_____   _____
_____   _____

- *Paints.* $40. All dolls are four colors. One quart of paint is $10 so four colors cost $40. Four quarts can paint 50 dolls. To get the cost per doll, $40/50 = $0.80 paint costs per doll.
- *Brushes.* $8. Each doll requires four different brushes, one for each color of paint. Each brush is $2; all four total $8. A brush lasts for 30 dolls. $8/30 = $0.26 brush costs per doll.

When we put all the costs together, we see that the cost of a good sold (COGS) is $3.06 for one unit:

$$\$2 + \$0.80 + \$0.26 = \$3.06$$

From the dollmaking example, we see that the simple process for determining the COGS is:

1. Define one unit.
2. Determine the total cost of materials (overestimate with imprecise math).
3. Determine how many total units those materials can make (underestimate with imprecise math).
4. Divide the total cost into the total number of units that can be made.

To make it easy for you to figure out your COGS, try using the Cost of Goods Sold Worksheet included on page 60.

Now you know what your start-up costs, operating costs, and COGS are. It's time to make all these numbers work together. The reason these numbers are so important (as you may have guessed by now) is that these numbers will help your determine your prices. Remember the basic business equation:

$$PROFIT = REVENUE - EXPENSES$$

Well, suppose you never bothered to figure out your COGS for your wooden doll business; you just started selling them at $3 each. Without knowing your COGS, you would be losing a *minimum* of 6 cents per item sold (and that doesn't even count your start-up or operating costs!). There is an old saying in business that, surprisingly, many people ignore and that is, "Sell it for more than it costs!" Seems obvious, but many businesses that seem to be established don't know their costs. So let's find yours.

Total It Up

Now that you know your three main expenses, let's put them all together to see just how many units you need to sell to actually make a profit.

1. DETERMINE YOUR START-UP COSTS. How much money do you need to start your business? Can you replace any of the start-up costs with donations, rentals, or items you already own? Make a list and total it up.

2. DETERMINE THE PAYMENT STRUCTURE OF YOUR START-UP COSTS. Whether you borrowed money or sold a piece of the company to an owner, this is easy. If you borrowed money, your start-up costs instantly convert to

Cost of Goods Sold Worksheet

STEP 1. Define the unit: _____

STEP 2. Make a list of all materials and their costs:

MATERIAL:	COST OF MATERIAL:
_____	_____
_____	_____
_____	_____
_____	_____
_____	_____
_____	_____
_____	_____
_____	_____

STEP 3. Total the cost of materials: _____

STEP 4. List the number of units created with above materials:

_____

STEP 5. Divide the answer in Step 3 by the answer in Step 4:

Total cost of materials: _____ / Number of units: _____ = Cost of

Goods Sold (COGS) for one unit: _____

---

fixed operating costs. Let's say you get a $1,000 loan from your parents at 12% interest. The terms of the loan say that you are supposed to pay $110 a month to them for one year. That $110 a month is now a fixed operating cost. The terms are already set for you. It's easy. Or perhaps you put in $500 of your own dough. That $500 is paid back not through operating costs, but through the growth in value of the business and through the profits of the business. The good news is that because it is your own money, you can determine when to take that $500 out of the business. You don't add to operating costs. Although businesses that raise a lot of money will have a detailed plan of how and when investors will be paid back, it's okay to start your business without a clear idea of when that will be. It's important to just get started. The money will come!

3. DETERMINE YOUR OPERATING COSTS. What does it cost for your business to "keep the lights on"? Remember, try to convert as many variable costs to fixed costs as possible.

4. DETERMINE YOUR COST OF GOODS SOLD. Use the four-step process on pages 59–60 and the Cost of Goods Sold Worksheet on page 60.

5. DO A LITTLE RESEARCH TO DETERMINE THE MARKET PRICE FOR YOUR GOODS OR SERVICES. The market price, as you know, is that middle of the road that both buyers and sellers think is reasonable. A great way for a new business to find this is to just take an average of the prices of its competitors. You might call three pool-cleaning companies and find out that one charges $50 for a cleaning, one charges $45, and the third, $65. So the average price to clean a pool in your area is $53. This is not an exact science. You might include extra work in your pool-cleaning fee compared to these other companies, or you might do less. (Or your wooden dolls might use four colors of paint, and everyone else's might use just two.) However, the market rate is very helpful in your calculations, and it at least provides the ballpark of where your prices will eventually be.

6. SUBTRACT THE MARKET PRICE FROM YOUR COGS AND YOU HAVE WHAT IS CALLED GROSS PROFIT. In the business world, *gross* doesn't mean disgusting. ***Gross profit*** means your profits before subtracting operating costs. Suppose you check out a few flea markets and determine that wooden dolls like yours sell for about $6 each. Your COGS for one doll is $3.06. So your gross profit per doll would be $2.94: $6.00 − $3.06 = $2.94.

7. DIVIDE GROSS PROFIT PER UNIT INTO YOUR OPERATING COSTS TO DETERMINE YOUR BREAK-EVEN NUMBER. The ***break-even number*** is the number of units you need to sell to cover all your operating costs. It is the *minimum* your business must sell before it can make a profit. Imagine your total monthly operating cost for your doll-carving business is $100. This includes a $35 fee to have a table at the flea market, $5 in gas to get to and from the flea market, $25 to advertise in the flea market magazine, $15 to parents for use of work space, and $20 into a fund you use to replace and sharpen your wood-carving tools. Divide $2.94 (gross profit per unit) into $100 (monthly operating costs) and you get 34 (your break-even point). So you have to sell 34 dolls a month just to stay in business.

8. GUESSTIMATE HOW MANY UNITS YOU THINK YOU CAN SELL EACH MONTH. Remember, when you sell your thirty-fifth doll, and with every doll you sell after that, your business will start to make a profit! So how many units do you think you can sell? This is a difficult one to answer. You might try asking the other people at the flea market how many dolls they sell on an average weekend. If they won't tell you, just watch them for an hour or two. How many dolls move? Ask the owner of the flea market how much money the average person takes in each weekend. Ask pool owners how often they get their pools cleaned. Do all the research that you can, but at the end of it all, this number is a guesstimate. When your business is up and running, you can make changes in your calculations as you will have hard data. For the doll business, multiply the units sold number by $2.94 to come up with your *profit before taxes* for the month.

9. MULTIPLY YOUR PROFIT BEFORE TAXES BY 30% (OUR ESTIMATE FOR TAXES), SUBTRACT THE TAX AMOUNT FROM YOUR PROFIT, AND YOU WILL HAVE YOUR NET PROFIT. *Net profit* is what people refer to as "the bottom line." It literally is the last line on the income statement (which we will talk about in the next chapter). Whatever is on that bottom line is the amount of profit your business makes. It is what you can take home if you want to. For calculating the profit of your particular business, use the Total Costs Worksheet on the next page.

So you're staring at your bottom line, and it doesn't look as good as you hoped. Remember that when businesses first start, they often don't make a profit. Some don't make a profit for years, but they at least need to be close to breaking even. They can only lose money for so long. If you still feel that profits are an unlikely possibility, don't worry. There are three pieces of good news:

- *Maybe your prices are too low.* Yes, you checked the market price, but investigate further. No one but you uses four different colors to paint her dolls. How much more is that worth? Your pool-cleaning service comes with a guarantee. Isn't that worth at least 10% more?
- *Maybe your guesstimate of units you can sell is too low.* We said this is a guesstimate. Do some more research on how many units you can sell. Do your competitors market as hard as you will? For the most accurate measure of all, keep very good track during your first few days of business, and use these numbers as a guide.
- *Maybe your costs are too high.* You are buying your wood from a local hardware store. Maybe that big home renovation superstore by the highway has lower prices. You also planned on having your tools sharpened once a month. Even though it is a bit more work for you to use dull tools, for the first few months in business could you have them sharpened every 45 days?

Total Costs Worksheet

1. DETERMINE YOUR START-UP COSTS:

List all costs required to start your business: Remember, you can pay back many start-up costs at your leisure, such as money you have saved up for your business. However, you must pay off your start-up costs on a predetermined schedule (for example, loan payments back to Mom and Dad), and you must put those start-up costs back into operating costs. Use the Operating Costs Worksheet (page 58) to help.

_____

_____

_____

_____

Total start-up costs: _____

2. LIST THE TOTAL OPERATING COSTS FROM THE OPERATING COST WORKSHEET (BE SURE TO INCLUDE SCHEDULED LOAN PAYMENTS):

_____

3. DETERMINE THE COST OF GOODS SOLD FOR ONE UNIT (FROM COGS WORKSHEET): _____

4. MARKET PRICE OF YOUR SERVICES: _____

5. MARKET PRICE _____ **– COST OF GOODS SOLD** _____
= GROSS PROFIT PER UNIT _____

6. OPERATING COSTS DIVIDED BY GROSS PROFIT PER UNIT = BREAK-EVEN NUMBER:

_____ / _____ = break-even number _____

7. ESTIMATE NUMBER OF UNITS SOLD: _____

8. CALCULATE PROFIT BEFORE TAXES: _____

Estimated number of units sold _____ – break-even number _____
$\times$ gross profit per unit _____ = profit before taxes _____

9. MULTIPLY YOUR PROFIT BEFORE TAXES BY 30% (AVERAGE AMOUNT OF TAXES) TO GET ESTIMATED TAXES:

Profit $\times$ .30 = Estimated taxes

10. SUBTRACT YOUR ESTIMATED TAXES FROM YOUR PROFIT BEFORE TAXES TO GET YOUR ESTIMATED NET PROFIT:

Profit before taxes _____ – Estimated taxes = Net profit _____

In the end, there are only three ways to increase profits:

1. Raise prices
2. Cut costs
3. Sell more

Knowing the basic numbers of your business can save you from a lot of headaches. You may choose not to go into that business at all, which may help you avoid the biggest headache—starting a business where the numbers can't work. Sometimes people have a great idea for a business, but they simply cannot get the numbers to work. And that's okay. Not every business idea can be turned into a business. Now that you know the basic numbers in a business, let's put them into use.

CHAPTER 8

Meet the Trio

The Income Statement,
the Cash-Flow Statement,
and the Balance Sheet

Believe it or not, all companies from the largest multinational, multi-billion dollar corporations to the one-person pool-cleaning business can be financially reduced to just three documents:

- The Income Statement
- The Cash-Flow Statement
- The Balance Sheet

Sure, bigger corporations have more complex versions of these documents, but every business uses the same three. Yours should too! Let's look at each of these items individually and see what they are used for.

The Income Statement helps you project if your business is profitable. The key word here is *project*—in other words, you might be taking into account payments you haven't received yet. For example, you have a client who hired you to design his Web site, but he isn't obligated to pay you until you complete the project one month from now. The income statement tracks all these revenues and expenses. Remember the basic equation: Profit equals revenue minus expenses. If there are too many expenses and not enough revenue, you'll know from your income statement that your business is not profitable. Income statements are usually prepared monthly (which is easy once you do it for one or two months) and most businesses calculate a yearly income statement. If your income statement isn't showing a profit, month after month, then you have a problem.

The Cash-Flow Statement sounds a bit like the income statement. But there is one big difference. Remember how I said the key word in the definition of income statement is *project*? Well, the income statement records money you project to be coming in and going out, but the cash-flow statement records these same amounts *when they actually occur*. As a professional speaker, I don't ask clients to pay my speaking fee until the day of the speech. Yet I sign contracts with some of them a year in advance. My income statement might show a nice steady profit (Wahoo—look at all those speeches!), but my cash-flow statement might show I am in trouble. My Internet, cell phone, and heating bills are due every month, even though my clients don't have to pay me for a year! Like the income statement, the cash-flow statement is prepared monthly (but once you do a few, they're easy!).

DOLLARS & SENSE

One easy way to increase your cash flow is to simply request the longest time possible to pay your bills and to demand your customers pay as soon as possible—or even ask them to pay some money in advance.

The Balance Sheet determines a company's *net worth*. Net worth is the value of the business to the owner (also called the *owner's equity*), once all the debts are paid. Imagine your business is playing guitar at birthday parties. Suppose you bought the $600 guitar with $300 of your own money and a $300 loan from your parents. To determine the net worth of your business, you would subtract the current amount left on the loan from your parents from the fair-market value of the guitar. If you owe your parents another $220, and the guitar, after a year of wear and tear, is now worth $450, the net worth of your business is $230, because $450 – $220 = $230.

The things your business owns are called *assets*. The monies your business owes are called *liabilities*. So the equation for net worth is:

$$NET\ WORTH = ASSETS - LIABILITIES$$

Or to put it even more simply:

NET WORTH = WHAT YOU OWN – WHAT YOU OWE

So why is it called a **balance sheet?** What exactly balances? Believe it or not, no matter what you have for assets and liabilities on a balance sheet, *assets always equal liabilities.*

How can this be? Simple. Remember, you always owe the net worth of the business to the owners. This is true even though you're the owner! When you subtract liabilities from assets, the difference is what you owe the owners.

Let's take a look at a very simple (actually, oversimplified) balance sheet for your guitar-playing business. As you can see, it *always* balances.

SIMPLIFIED BALANCE SHEET FOR GUITAR PLAYING

ASSETS	LIABILITIES
Guitar: $450	Loan from parents: $220
	Owed to the owner: $230
Total Assets: $450	**Total Liabilities: $450**

Still confused? Think about it this way. If you sold the business right now, you would get $450 for the guitar and you would "owe" money to your parents *and* to yourself. If you sell the business in a year, the balance sheet would still balance, even though the guitar has gone down in value and the amount of the loan has also gone down. Here's what it would look like a year from now:

SIMPLIFIED BALANCE SHEET FOR GUITAR PLAYING A YEAR LATER

ASSETS	LIABILITIES
Guitar: $300	Loan from parents: $120
	Owed to the owner: $280
Total Assets: $300	**Total Liabilities: $300**

Again, this balance sheet is very oversimplified, but the message is always the same. The balance sheet *must always balance!*

So the income statement helps you forecast your business's financial future. The cash-flow statement tells you what is going on right now, and the balance sheet tells you the value of your business. Easy, right? Well . . .

How to Really Determine the Value of a Business

Okay, the basics are all there, but what we have so far is drastically over-simplified. For instance, suppose I ask you, "What would you sell your guitar business for?" The balance sheet would tell you it's worth $450, the total value of the business's only asset. If I bought it, I would give you $450; you'd use $220 of that to pay back your parents and keep $230 for yourself.

Imagine, however, you had five birthday gigs this month at $50 apiece. That's $250 worth of revenue you would lose if you sold the business to me. If you had another five next month, you would have lost $500 of future revenues by selling it to me.

When you look at the profits, or *earnings*, of a company, the value of that company changes. Sometimes business owners add the price of all the assets on top of that. When you sell based on your earnings, you are selling your customers, your relationships, your reputation—lots of things besides the assets. If your guitar business had annual profits of $1,000 and sold for three times earnings plus assets, you would receive $3,450 for your business ($3,000 from three years of earnings at $1,000 a year plus $450 for the assets of the business). Again, you'd pay back your parents' loan of $220 and your profit would now be $3,230. See how nice it is to include earnings in addition to net worth?

DOLLARS & SENSE
Most small businesses will sell for 3 to 5 times earnings.

Of course, what a business sells for is always negotiable. Some businesses have sold for less than two times their earnings while others have sold for twenty times their earnings or more. Sometimes people buy businesses just to get their assets (their earnings could be terrible).

Sometimes a business has almost no assets, but its earnings are great. It all depends on the buyer or seller. The point is that it is crucial for you to keep good records. If you can't prove how much your business makes and what its net worth is, no one will ever buy it! Good records are also important if you ever want your business to take out a loan. Bankers will want to see how much the business owns and what its cash flow is before they loan it any money.

The Bottom Lines (All Three of Them)

One big idea to remember when it comes to these documents is how they work together, especially the income statement and the balance sheet. You could sum up the financial strategy of every single business in the world today by saying these three statements:

1. *Lots of cash in, little cash out.* My goal on the income statement is to maximize income and minimize expenses.
2. *Delay and demand.* My goal on the cash-flow statement is to delay my bills as late possible (but still pay on time!) and to demand payments (nicely) as quickly as possible.
3. *Own more, owe less.* I use the cash from my business to either (a) buy stuff that will bring in even more cash or (b) pay off the people I owe.

In a nutshell, this is what every business does. As simple as this may seem, many businesses fail because they ignore one or all of these items. You might want to write these down on a piece of paper and post them somewhere you can see them. They are the golden financial rules in business!

So now that you know the three main business forms, how do you go about preparing them?

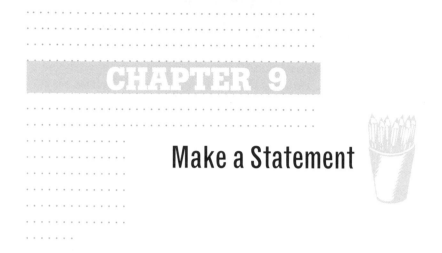

CHAPTER 9

Make a Statement

Okay, I know you want to skip this chapter. Unless you love math, preparing the financial statements of your business isn't going to be all that fun. But before you jump ahead, remember these two things: After you have prepared these statements once, it's very easy to update them. Second—and more important—your business won't survive if you don't keep track of your finances. I've seen businesses limp along doing very little marketing. I've seen businesses that fail the Five *S* Formula still do well. But I haven't seen a business that doesn't know its costs stay alive for long. Boring as it may be, this stuff is essential.

DOLLARS & SENSE
Without good financial records, you will be out of business. Period!

There are several great computer programs out there to help you keep track of your financial statements. If you are the computer type, I recommend that you find one and use it. It can save you a lot of time. Those of you who insist that math was invented solely to bring unhappiness to your life can buy your way out of preparing financial statements, but it is expensive. You can hire a ***bookkeeper*** for a few hours a month, and he or she will prepare all of these statements for you. Mind you, the costs for this will probably start at around $200 a month, which most new businesses cannot afford. But it is something to tuck away in the back of your head when you ask yourself, *Why am I working so hard?* Add this to your long list of goals: to hire a bookkeeper!

Whether you choose the computer route or plan to eventually hire someone to do it, it is essential that you prepare your own balance sheet, cash-flow statement, and income statement at least once. For start-up entrepreneurs, many of the lines on these documents will be estimations that can be tweaked when you have real data from sales.

Alright, enough delay. Let's get to it! Since we have a bunch of data already from the example of the wooden doll business from Chapter 7, we'll pretend that we are preparing financial statements for that business. (Keep in mind that some numbers are different, to enhance the examples. For instance, we never talked about a loan from your parents in Chapter 7, as we do here.) We'll start with the income statement.

The Income Statement

The income statement has two parts. The top lists all of your revenues; the bottom lists all of your expenses. Pretend that you started the wooden doll business with $500 of your own cash and a $500 zero-interest loan from your parents that is paid back at $20 a month. With that start-up money, you bought a $300 carving tool set. The rest of the money you put into a bank *savings account* that pays interest. The June Income Statement for the wooden doll business on page 72 is what your monthly income statement might look like.

Let's take a closer look at the June Income Statement for the wooden doll business. See anything interesting? Well, first, under Cost of Goods Sold, did you notice that I didn't charge anything for labor? Most entrepreneurs don't charge for labor. They simply take the business's profits as their salary. If you spent 5 hours making dolls and selling them at the flea market, you would have made an after-tax profit of $8.26 per hour ($41.30/5). Not bad. Remember, you've already paid taxes on that money, so it is yours to keep. Your friend who works for the movie theater might brag to you that he makes $10 an hour, but ask to see his paycheck and you'll notice his hourly wage is more like $7.

Of course, even if you are the only one working in the business, labor is a cost. I've worked with several entrepreneurs who claimed, "Peter, last month my business had a profit of $500!" After a little more investigation, I found out they weren't figuring in any labor costs. "How many hours did you work to get a $500 profit," I asked. They then revealed that they had worked 40 hours a week for four weeks. That

June Income Statement,
Wooden Doll Business

REVENUES:	
Sales:	$ 300.00
Interest from bank account:	$ 2.00
Total revenues:	$302.00
COST OF GOODS SOLD (COGS):	
Materials:	$ 153.00
Labor (5 hours at $0 per hour):	$ 0.00
Total COGS:	$153.00
GROSS PROFIT	
Total revenues – Total COGS:	$ 149.00
OPERATING COSTS:	
FIXED COSTS:	
Loan repayment:	$ 20.00
Flea market fees:	$ 35.00
Tool replacement fund:	$ 5.00
VARIABLE COSTS:	
Gas:	$ 5.00
Advertising:	$ 25.00
TOTAL OPERATING COSTS:	$ 90.00
PROFIT BEFORE TAXES:	
Gross profit – Total operating costs:	$ 59.00
TAXES:	
Profit before taxes × 30%:	$ 17.70
NET PROFIT:	
Profit before taxes – Taxes:	$ 41.30

comes out to an hourly wage of only $3.13. Heck, Mickey D's can beat that! So, while in the beginning you are willing to list labor as a zero cost on your income statement, eventually you need figure it in. Even when it remains a zero cost, be sure your profits are enough to justify your time!

Use our Income Statement as a guide to create an income statement for your business.

Show Your Depreciation

Look at the line in the Wooden Doll Business Income Statement called "tool replacement fund." That's an expense, but where did that money go? You didn't give it to anyone, because you haven't bought the tools yet. That money stayed in the business. So if the money didn't leave the business, why is it an expense?

Most income statements factor in something called *depreciation*— just a fancy way of saying that as stuff ages, it loses value; losing value is just like losing money. Maybe your $300 woodworking tool kit needs to be replaced every five years. That means five years from now you need to come up with $300 to replace it. Rather than subtracting that amount when it is actually due, the income statement allows us to deduct smaller chunks of it over time. That's why you're figuring in $5 a month as an expense:

$$\$300/5 \text{ YEARS} = \$60/\text{YEAR}$$

$$\$60/12 \text{ MONTHS PER YEAR} = \$5 \text{ A MONTH}$$

Depreciation, we'll see, is one of the big differences between the income statement and the cash-flow statement.

A++

EXTRA CREDIT
Remember that profits equal revenue minus expenses? The higher the profits, the more taxes we pay. Taking depreciation allows you to take on a *noncash expense* that, as you can guess, is an expense that doesn't require you to fork over actual cash. In a way, it "secretly" lowers profits, thereby lowering taxes. More money for you, less for the Tax Man! Wahoo!

Study your income statements to determine how you can improve your business. Look again at labor. Perhaps you spend three hours making the dolls and then two hours sitting at the table selling them. After a few weeks of doing this, you notice that other craft makers are making their crafts *right at the table*. The next week, you spend two hours making dolls at home and two hours making them at your table. You actually sell more dolls this way, because people are naturally interested when they see you making what they are about to buy. You sell a little *more* and work less.

You'll see your income jump when that loan from your parents goes away. Because it is at 0% interest, there is no rush to pay the loan back. You'll like having the cash, just in case sales slow down. And what about advertising? After you've done the flea market for several weeks, do people still need to see an advertisement? Can you sign a multi-week deal with the owner of the flea market to reduce the flea market fee by $5? Can you carpool to and from the flea market? (Not only is carpooling good for your wallet, it's good for the environment!) Little tweaks to your income statement like this can quickly and easily increase profits.

Smart entrepreneurs also use the income statement to test the market. It can help answer questions like the following ones:

- How did sales do when you didn't advertise that week?
- If you switched to three colors of paint for the dolls instead of four, what did that do to the income statement?
- How many months must you be in business before you can upgrade to that automatic woodworking machine?

Flowing with the Cash-Flow Statement

Okay, we have one financial statement out of the way, and you're still alive. Let's take a look at the cash-flow statement. Most start-ups are simple enough businesses that the cash-flow statement will look a lot like the income statement. In a small start-up, cash flows very quickly because: (a) you can't afford to give your customers the luxury of taking a long time to pay you, and (b) your suppliers are still getting to know you and your business. Until they do, they want to be paid immediately.

For the example here, let us assume all cash comes in and goes out in the same month, as it does on the income statement. However, let's pretend (for purposes of the cash-flow statement) that in June, half of your customers asked you if they could pay next month.

June Cash-Flow Statement, Wooden Doll Business

TRANSACTION	CASH IN	CASH OUT
Sales:	$150	
Interest:	$ 2	
Materials:		$153.00
Loan repayment:		$ 20.00
Flea market fees:		$ 35.00
Gas:		$ 5.00
Advertising:		$ 25.00
Subtotals:	$152	$238.00

Total cash flow June: **($ 86.00)***

*Parentheses around a number indicate a loss, or negative number.

Do you see the big difference in the June and July (page 76) cash flow statements, even though your sales and expenses (except for taxes) were exactly same from month to month? In case you didn't already guess, the parentheses around a number in an accounting table indicate a *loss*. Maybe at the end of June you say, "Ya know, I sold $300 worth of product this month, I deserve to treat myself to a movie." Not so fast. Your cash-flow statement would tell you that you actually can't afford it! Even though you sold $300 worth of stuff, you were only paid for half of it ($150) in June!

The other thing to notice about the cash-flow statement is that all the numbers are moving. Either stuff is coming in, or it's going out. Nothing just sits there. Since June did not have any profits, there was no money set aside for taxes. In the accounting world, on a cash-flow statement people refer to money coming in as ***credits*** and money going out as ***debits***. Also, notice that the expense of "tool replacement fund" is gone. Remember, depreciation is a noncash expense. The tool depreciation money doesn't actually move, so it doesn't show up on the cash-flow statement.

Use these examples to create your own cash-flow statement for your business.

July Cash-Flow Statement, Wooden Doll Business

TRANSACTION	CASH IN	CASH OUT
Sales:	$ 450*	
Interest:	$ 2	
Materials:		$153.00
Loan repayment:		$ 20.00
Flea market fees:		$ 35.00
Gas:		$ 5.00
Advertising:		$ 25.00
Taxes:		$ 64.20
Subtotals:	$ 452	$302.20
Total cash flow July:	**$ 149.80**	

Even though you earned $300 in July, there is also the additional $150 from the half of the June earnings that was received in July, which is reflected in this figure.

The Grand Finale: The Balance Sheet

Two down, one to go! Let's take a look at the evolution of your wooden doll business balance sheet, starting with Day 1 and going up to a year of being in business. You can see the balance sheet on page 77. Remember that you originally borrowed $500 from your parents at 0% interest? To keep it simple, let's pretend your parents agreed to give you a break the first year of the loan and require only one payment of $20. Let's further assume you're paying them out of the cash you put into the business. You're taking depreciation on your woodcarving tools. You also threw in $500 of your own money.

On a balance sheet, stuff you own, or assets, are usually placed on the left column (or left page) and money you owe, your liabilities, are placed in the right column (or right page). Of course, at the end, both columns must balance!

Beginning Balance Sheet, Wooden Doll Business

ASSETS		LIABILITIES	
Cash:	$ 1000	Loan:	$ 500
		Owed to the owner:	$ 500
Total Assets	$ 1,000	Total Liabilities:	$ 1,000

Balance Sheet after Purchase of Tools, Wooden Doll Business

ASSETS		LIABILITIES	
Cash:	$ 700	Loan:	$ 500
Woodcarving tools:	$ 300	Owed to the owner:	$ 500*
Total Assets:	$ 1,000	Total Liabilities:	$ 1,000

*$200 in cash + $300 tool set.

Balance Sheet after One Loan Payment and One Year of Depreciation, Wooden Doll Business

ASSETS		LIABILITIES	
Cash:	$ 680	Loan:	$ 480
Woodcarving tools:	$ 300	Owed to the owner:	$ 440*
Subtotal Assets:	$ 980		
Minus depreciation:	($ 60)		
Total Assets:	$ 920	Total Liabilities:	$ 920

*$200 in cash + $300 woodcarving tools – $60 in depreciation.

DOLLARS & SENSE

Whenever something happens on one side of the
balance sheet, something must happen on the other.

When looking at a balance sheet from an up-and-running business, you
may see one final subject line saying: ***accounts payable*** and ***accounts
receivable***. Accounts receivable are assets. This is money that is owed
to you but has not yet been paid, such as the second half of your Web-
site development fee, if you are in the midst of designing one for someone. (Once it is paid, the money becomes cash.) Accounts payable are
liabilities. They are bills that you need to pay but haven't yet, such as
your cell phone bill. Even though you don't yet have the cash from
accounts receivable and you haven't disbursed the cash from accounts
payable, they still show up on the balance sheet.

Use the Balance Sheet examples to create your own balance sheet for
your business.

Tah dah! You're done with all three financial documents. That wasn't
so hard, was it? There's one final thing you need to do before we leave
the realm of math. You need to set up an ***accounting system***. Don't
worry—just turn to the next chapter. It's not that hard.

CHAPTER 10

Account for Your Accounting

An accounting system is simply a system to handle the money that goes in and out of your business. Although the income statement, cash-flow statement, and balance sheet help you keep track of this money, an accounting system will help you know what to do when someone physically hands you cash (which we hope will be quite often).

The first step is to decide where to physically put the money that is given to you. I recommend that every entrepreneur have five bank accounts (yes, five). To make it simple, keep these all at the same bank. That way it will be easy to move money around (which is something you'll be doing quite often). Here's what the five bank accounts are for:

1. Business checking
2. Business savings
3. Taxes checking
4. Personal checking
5. Personal savings

The bank accounts will serve as containers for your money. You could pile all the money into one account and keep track of what goes where, but I prefer to put it exactly where it belongs as soon as I get it. What's more, some banks even have automatic withdrawal features that allow you to have a set amount withdrawn from a bank account on a certain date and moved to another bank account. Because it's automatic, you don't have to worry. (Remember our timeless goal of keeping our businesses simple!)

A++

EXTRA CREDIT

Ever wonder what happens to your money when you deposit it into the bank? Well, here's the funny thing: Most of your money doesn't stay in the bank! The bank loans out your money to other people. The bank pays you interest for your money, not because it likes you, but because it takes your money and loans it out to someone else at a higher interest rate than it is paying you. The bank might pay you a 4% interest rate and then loan your money out to someone else at 10%. That 6% difference is the bank's profit. Not such a bad gig, huh?

Types of Bank Accounts

*A **checking account*** is a bank account that allows you to write checks against the account. A ***check*** is a legal contract to exchange money. Like all other contracts, checks are signed by all of the involved parties. If I write you a check, then I, the check writer (often referred to as the ***maker***), sign the front side of the check and state that you or your business is to be paid a certain amount of money from my account. You (often referred to as the ***payee***) then take the check (the legal contract that says you are to be paid) and convert it to cash at your bank. In order to convert a check into cash, the person to whom it is made out must ***endorse*** the back side of the check. *Endorsing* means signing the check (signing your part of the contract) to indicate that you are now accepting the money. On page 81 there is an example of a typical check.

Checking accounts make it easy to move money around. I could write you a check for $1,000, and you could carry it to your bank without fear of losing the actual cash it represents. If someone stole the check from you, it would be worthless to the thief, because the contract (the check) is only valuable to you, the payee.

Here is the key to understanding our sample check:

1. Checks need to include the check writer's name and address so people know who wrote the check.
2. Checks are always numbered so that you can keep track of them.

FIGURE 1.

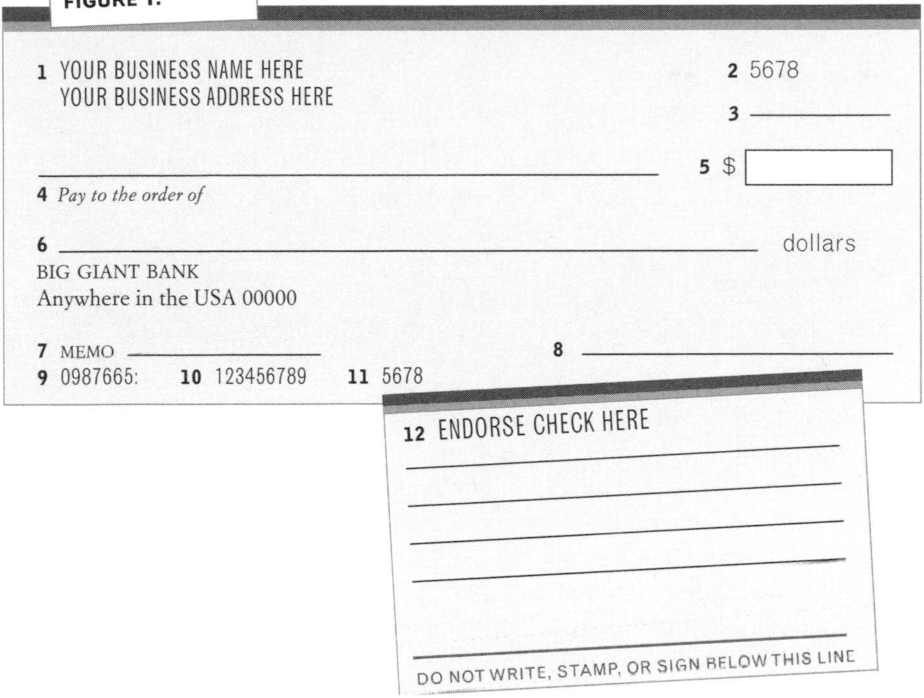

1 YOUR BUSINESS NAME HERE
YOUR BUSINESS ADDRESS HERE

2 5678

3 ——————

5 $ ▢

4 *Pay to the order of*

6 ——————————————————————————— dollars

BIG GIANT BANK
Anywhere in the USA 00000

7 MEMO ————————   **8** ——————————————

9 0987665:   **10** 123456789   **11** 5678

12 ENDORSE CHECK HERE
————————————————
————————————————
————————————————
————————————————
————————————————
DO NOT WRITE, STAMP, OR SIGN BELOW THIS LINE

3. Be sure to write in the date, month, and year on which you are filling out the check.

4. The name of the party (the payee) to whom you are making a payment is written here.

5. The amount you are writing the check for is written in numerals at 5.

6. To eliminate errors, banks ask that you write out in words the same amount you put in numerals at 5.

7. The memo line allows you write a note to yourself to help you remember the check's purpose. You may, for instance, write "Internet hosting fees, December" on this line.

8. Remember, a check is a contract, so it must be signed by you at 8.

9. The first set of numbers at the bottom of each check is what is known as a *routing number*. Each bank has its own unique routing number to easily help banks sort the checks they receive.

10. The second set of numbers is your checking account number. Rather than naming your account something like Peter's Account, banks "name" your bank account with a number.

11. The check's individual number also appears at the bottom.

12. The back of the check is where the payee (the person to whom the check was written) signs the check to cash it, legally agreeing to accept the money.

DOLLARS & SENSE

These days nobody wants cash. It's too dangerous to carry around. If you lose it, that's it. Customers are going to pay you with checks, and you're going to pay your bills with checks. In order to do that, you need a checking account.

Suppose, however, that the person that stole a check from you had a fake ID, showing he was you. What then? Well, banks have protection against check fraud by having a **check-clearing policy**, or **funds-availability policy**. This is a written policy by the bank (and it can vary from bank to bank) stating that the bank does not allow checks to be immediately converted to cash. Often the check-clearing period is three business days. If you are waiting for a check to clear, you are waiting for the check writer's bank to literally transfer money to your bank. (Ever wonder what's in those armored trucks you see driving around? Some of the money they carry is yours!)

Suppose that while you are waiting for a check to clear in your own account, you write a check for a new lawn mower for your landscaping business. Suppose also that the seller tries to cash it, and his bank clears checks faster than yours does. If his bank asks for the funds and your funds aren't ready yet at your bank, the check will bounce. Bouncing a check simply means that someone attempted to cash a check against an account that did not have enough funds in it. So before you write a check, make sure that you not only deposited enough money into your account to cover it, but also that the money has actually cleared.

The interval that it takes for check-clearing also helps protect against fraud. Suppose a thief tried to use a fake ID to get a check cashed. The bank, even if it believed the ID, would still force him to wait three days for the check to clear. That's more than enough time for you to call the person who wrote you the check and ask that he or she **cancel**, or terminate, it.

Most checking accounts these days come with a **debit card**. A debit card is a like a dynamic checkbook. It allows you to deposit money in an **ATM** (Automated Teller Machine) and withdraw cash from that same machine. The ATM is just like a live bank teller. If you have just deposited a check at an ATM, you will still need to wait for the check-clearing period to expire before you can get the cash from that check. If there is cash sitting in your account though (and I hope there is), you can get that money instantly, 24 hours a day, seven days a week, from an ATM.

In addition to letting you do electronic banking, debit cards also allow you to pay your bills. When you swipe your debit card at a cash register, the register reads your account number off the magnetic strip on the back of your card. Each debit card requires a personal identification number, or PIN, which is agreed to between you and the bank. It is a password to your account. When you swipe your card and enter your PIN at a store or bank, it is like electronically signing for the payment. At a store, it means that you authorize that a certain amount of money be transferred from your account to the store's account as payment for what you are buying.

Debit cards are a double-edged sword. Money that is easy to get is money that is easy to spend. However, if you are responsible enough to run your own business, then I say you're responsible enough to handle a debit card. The other danger with debit cards is that many banks charge ATM fees when you use an ATM outside of the bank's network. If my checking account is at Bank A, and I use an ATM owned by Bank B (not in the same banking network), it is very likely that *both* Bank A and Bank B will charge me a fee. Because these fees are normally between $1 and $3, people never get too worried about them. But they should. If you pay a $2 fee to take out $20, you just paid 10% to get your cash! That's a pretty high interest rate to get your own money.

The beauty of debit cards is they make transactions easy and you can pay over the phone or online, which you can't do with checks. When you go to your bank, ask if you can get a debit card with your account.

Keep in mind that debit cards are quite different from ***credit cards***. When you use a debit card, you are accessing your own money. Even though credit cards look the same as debit cards, when you use a credit card, you are borrowing a bank's or other company's money, which means that with every swipe, you take out a mini-loan. The trouble with credit cards really boils down to high interest rates. It's so easy to swipe and forget that interest is being charged to you—sometimes as much as 29%. At some time far down the road, credit cards may have a place in your business. For young start-up entrepreneurs, I say hold off from using credit cards as long as you can.

Savings accounts differ from checking accounts in two major ways: they pay a higher interest rate and you can't write checks against them. Their main purpose is (of course) for saving. Savings accounts often come with an ATM card. If one is offered, I suggest that you decline it.

You'll already have an ATM card for your checking account. The money that is in savings, whether it is business or personal, should stay in savings. Don't make it too easy to get to the money in your savings account.

Picking the Right Bank

It can be a bit difficult to compare banks. This one has a lot of free ATMs but charges you 10 cents every time you write a check. That one charges a $5 a month maintenance fee, but you can write an unlimited number of checks. Another one has very few ATMs, but will help you set up online bill-paying for free. Apples-to-apples comparisons in the banking world aren't easy. The trick to choosing is threefold:

1. As a brand-new business, you want to keep those fixed costs down, so avoid any banks that charge a fee, no matter what. (For example, steer clear of monthly maintenance fees.)

2. Determine what service you need the most. Does your business need to write a lot of checks? Access the ATM a lot? Pay all its bills online? Making your selection based on the one or two services that you need most can quickly narrow down your bank search.

3. Perhaps most important of all is your relationship with the banker. This is especially true for a new business owner. Your banker can help out with many of your business needs. She can approve a loan, serve as a financial reference for you, and even shorten the check-clearing period! Many banks, because of their size, don't want to deal with a small business. How do you tell? Simply call the banks you are considering and ask to meet with a representative who handles small business accounts. If people are unwilling to meet with you because they think you are a "kid," that's a pretty good signal that that's not the bank you want to deal with. As a small business, you won't have as much money on deposit as the bigger businesses, so you will rely heavily on your relationship with your banker.

A great alternative to using a traditional bank is to work with a credit union. Briefly, credit unions are nonprofit banks. They are associations that will make small loans to customers at lower percentage rates than bigger banks would. Because it's not all about the money for credit unions, they are often willing to listen to the unique needs of each of their customers (although in the credit union world, they don't call them *customers*; they call them *members*). If you don't already have an account somewhere, definitely look into working with a credit union.

The Flow of Your Business's Money

Once you have found a bank, you have to set up a system so your money flows easily to where it should be. Let's return to those five bank accounts that I suggested you set up earlier in the chapter. Think of money as water, and think of these bank accounts as buckets. Every month, you need to readjust the water levels in all of the buckets. Some of the buckets have tiny holes in them, so the water that flows out needs to be replaced. Other buckets keep getting fuller and fuller until one day you will need to empty them almost completely. As more water (cash) comes in, the process keeps repeating itself.

I like to rearrange my accounts monthly. Suppose that in the month of October, $1,000 of revenue and $90 of sales tax came in. That $90 of sales tax money goes straight into the tax checking account. The $1,000 goes immediately into my business checking account. While that $1,000 is still in that account, I pay all my bills for that month—except taxes, as those are due quarterly. For this example, let's pretend my bills totaled $600. That leaves me with a profit of $400. I multiply that number by 30% to figure my income tax bill for that month. I calculate that $400 × 30% = $120, so $120 goes into the tax checking account, where it sits until estimated taxes are due.

That leaves me with an after-tax profit of $280 ($400 − $120 = $280). Of that money, I take 10% and put that into my business savings account. While every business owner will have a different opinion of how much money to set aside, saving 10% of after-tax profits is a good benchmark. If you can afford to save more, do it, but don't save any less. It's tempting to skip business savings, but when you hit that slow period, you'll thank me for suggesting this.

So $28, or 10% of $280, has been put into my business savings account. That leaves me with $252. This is the business's profit, and it is mine to keep, which means I first need to transfer it over to my personal checking account.

There is one big exception to this rule: *During the first few months of your business, most of the profit should stay in your business savings account, until you build up a reserve of three to five months' worth of operating expenses.* You need to do this for two reasons. One, because you are a new business owner, many vendors are going to ask you to pay for stuff in advance, since they don't know you yet. You'll need cash to pay for supplies up front, and it might be a month before your customers pay you. Also, you're going to make mistakes, or people might not pay you on time or at all, and you need to be prepared for the worst.

So for the first three to five months of your business, leave nearly all of the money in your business savings and checking accounts.

However, once you have a nice little cushion saved up in there, you can and should start taking your profits. After all, you earned them! When we last left our example, I had $252 once all taxes, expenses, and even business savings had been taken care of. This $252 should be transferred into my personal checking account. Ten percent of that money should go into my personal savings account to pay for big expenses in my personal life. The remaining $226.80 is mine to spend! (Wahoo!) The flow of my money would look as shown in Figure 2.

This system ensures that money is being allocated and saved as it flows from the customer's hand into your pocket. Budgeting becomes very easy, because once the money hits your pocket, you've already paid all your bills and taxes and have set aside some for savings. Enjoy!

DOLLARS & SENSE
It's crucial for you to build up a cash reserve to carry you through the slow times and through the times when you make business mistakes.

Hitting the Books

You now know where to physically put the money that comes into your hands. Once you set up the five-account system, feel free to tweak it to your own needs. I've seen businesses that have two tax accounts: one for income taxes and one for sales taxes. I've seen people who have three personal savings accounts: one for general savings, one for charity donations, and one for the "item of the year," which could be a bicycle or a flat-screen TV. However you set up the system is up to you, as long as it is simple to use and ensures that bills, taxes, and savings are taken care of along the way.

Once you have the accounts set up to physically warehouse the money you make, you will need to create a ***bookkeeping system***. Businesses nickname their financial statements "the books," so "keeping the books" simply means you are preparing and tending to the financial statements of your business. Keeping good books allows you to easily

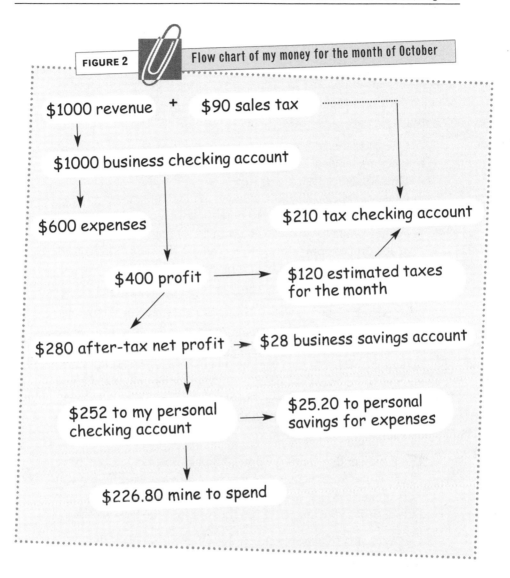

FIGURE 2 — Flow chart of my money for the month of October

$1000 revenue + $90 sales tax

$1000 business checking account

$600 expenses

$210 tax checking account

$400 profit → $120 estimated taxes for the month

$280 after-tax net profit ⇀ $28 business savings account

$252 to my personal checking account → $25.20 to personal savings for expenses

$226.80 mine to spend

prepare a balance sheet, income statement, and cash-flow statement. If your books are a mess, your business will be a mess.

Just like financial statements, bookkeeping can be done using a computer program; however, you can also hire someone to do it. My advice is the same as last time. If you are talented with computers, test out a program or two and keep your books that way. Probably the most popular system is QuickBooks. If you want to hire someone to do your bookkeeping, that is your choice; but remember that it will be expensive (probably in the neighborhood of around $200 a month).

Boxing Lessons: Filing the Easy Way

Whichever way you choose to keep your records, it helps to do it once or twice the old-fashioned way so you understand how it works. To set up a simple all-paper bookkeeping system, you will need:

- One box labeled *Income*
- One box labeled *Expenses*
- One box labeled *Accounts Receivable*
- One box labeled *Accounts Payable*
- A **business ledger**, which is a notebook with preprinted columns to help you keep your books. These can be bought at any office supply store, or you can use the sample ledger on my Web site, *www.quickcashforteens.com*.

The Income Box holds copies of checks that you have already received and cashed as well as copies of paid **invoices**. An invoice is just a fancy term for a bill. Every time you sell a product or service, you need to send or give your customer an invoice, clearly outlining how much the customer needs to pay you and reminding him or her what the invoice is for and when you need to be paid. Use the sample invoice in this book to create your own. Remember: If something is in the Income Box, that means you have already received the money for it.

The Expense Box holds receipts and paid invoices you get from other people for expenses that you have already paid. When you write a check to pay an invoice, make a photocopy of the check and staple it to the invoice. Then throw it into the Expense Box.

The Accounts Receivable Box holds all of the invoices that your customers have not yet paid. These include invoices for customers who still have some time left to pay you (perhaps because you give them 30 days to pay their bills) as well as those for customers who are late paying you. Remember: This is money that you are owed, but you do not have it yet, so it does not show up on the cash-flow statement. When an invoice is paid, write *Paid* on the invoice. Make a photocopy of that invoice. Send one copy of the paid invoice back to your customer, letting him know you received his payment. Also, make a photocopy of the customer's check, and staple it to the original copy of the paid invoice. Throw the paid invoice with the check copy stapled to it into your Income Box.

The Accounts Payable Box holds all of your own unpaid invoices. This is money that you have to pay out, but which hasn't left your account yet. This money does not show up on the cash-flow statement either. When you pay a bill, make a photocopy of the check you wrote. When that check is cashed, the business that cashed it will send you a paid invoice or receipt. Take that paid invoice or receipt, attach the photocopy of your payment check, and throw it into the Expense Box. Easy!

I like to call this system "keeping the boxes." Believe or not, simply putting receipts in the right boxes is half the battle. Even if you never had actually bothered to do any bookkeeping, if your invoices and receipts were in the correct boxes, it wouldn't be all that hard to get your books in order. You would know what money you have, what money you sent out, what money you were owed, and what money you needed to send out.

Pulling It Together: The Business Ledger

Although the four-box system is an easy way to get organized, you can't carry those four boxes around to look at every time you want to know your cash balance. The business ledger puts all the information you have in the boxes on one easy-to-use page. Business ledgers can differ slightly; I prefer to make mine as simple as possible. I use these column heads:

DATE   SOURCE   CASH IN   CASH OUT   CASH BALANCE

Once a week, look at your Income Box and Expense Box and transfer the information they hold onto the business ledger. For instance, suppose that in the week of April 10 a customer bought 20 wooden dolls for his toy shop. You also bought $40 worth of paints at the store and printed $10 worth of flyers. Also, suppose you had $1,000 in cash in your business checking account. Your ledger would look like the Ledger for the Week of April 10 to April 17, shown on page 90.

Net cash balances should match what's in your business checking account. If they don't, either you or the bank has made a mistake. Comparing your net cash balance to what's in your bank account is called *balancing the books.*

I like to keep it simple. While many bigger businesses have **sub-ledgers**, which are specific business ledgers that support the main ledger, I like to keep it all one on page. Notice that this ledger also does

Ledger for the Week of April 10 to April 17

DATE	SOURCE	CASH IN	CASH OUT	CASH BALANCE
4/10	Existing cash:			$1,000.00
4/11	Sale to toy store:	$120.00		$1,120.00
4/12	Paints:		$40.00	$1,080.00
4/13	Flyers:		$10.00	$1,070.00
4/17	**Net Cash Balance:**			**$1,070.00**

not count the money in the Accounts Payable and Accounts Receivable boxes; that isn't "real" money until it arrives in or leaves your hands.

When you are about to pay a $600 bill and you're wondering, *Can I afford this?* simply look at your business ledger. Notice how this business ledger quickly transfers into the cash-flow statement. Notice also how, once you add in the accounts payable and accounts receivable, you can easily create your income statement.

As your business grows, your ledger can become more advanced in order to help you budget better. For instance, you may decide to start putting accounts payable (AP) and accounts receivable (AR) onto the ledger. Some larger businesses have accounts receivables in the millions of dollars, some of which have been outstanding for years! So don't forget about those people who need to pay you.

The ledger just keeps running and running, week after week, month after month, year after year. It helps you easily generate your business's financial statements: the income statement, the cash-flow statement, and the balance sheet.

Don't get too wrapped up in trying to find the perfect accounting system. Just get started with a simple system like the four-boxes method described above. As your business becomes more complex, you can use a computer program or maybe even hire someone else to do the accounting. The point is to get something going.

Speaking of getting going, it's time we put all this information together. It's time for you to write your business plan. To find out what that is, just read Chapter 11.

What's the Plan, Man?

Writing Your Business Plan

So you're out there, keeping your ears alert. You are listening carefully to people's problems because you know that there may be a goldmine behind every one of their groans. After a few weeks of listening, you uncovered some opportunities that might make good businesses for you to start. To further narrow down your list, you ran all the business ideas through the Five *S* Formula, and one emerged as the clear winner. You've even come up with a name, thought about the different jobs involved, and given the finances some serious thought. Now what?

Once you have the idea for the business you want to start, it's a good idea to write what is known as a ***business plan***. A business plan is nothing more than a road map of how you will start and grow your business. Some business plans are very long and complex, totaling more than 100 pages. Some are simple one-page documents. Some of them are even written on paper napkins! Entrepreneurs employ business plans for their own personal use—to give them direction and keep them focused. Business plans can also be used to raise money or to help your business get a loan. Regardless of the length or the purpose, all business plans are broken down into three parts:

- *The organizational plan*
- *The marketing plan*
- *The financial plan*

All of these plans should be easy for you to write, because you now know how to market your business, prepare financial statements, and organize the tasks of a business. Let's look at each of these plans in more detail.

The Organizational Plan tells who does what job within your company. Most likely you are doing all the jobs, but it's still important to decide when you will do these tasks. When will you do the marketing for the company? When will you prepare the financial statements? The organizational plan answers all of these questions. Whereas the organizational chart shows who reports to whom, the organizational plan actually spells out the specific tasks that each person will be doing, and it also justifies why those people were chosen for those tasks.

The Marketing Plan basically describes what the business will do in order to get customers. Your marketing plan can be as simple as one line: "I will knock on every door in my neighborhood and hand-deliver a flier about my car-washing service." While this will work, I suggest a little more meat in your marketing plan. Remember, in Chapter 6, we learned that you had to hit your customers seven times? Your marketing plan should incorporate a multimedia approach to be sure that happens.

The Financial Plan consists of your cash-flow statement, your income statement, and your balance sheet. When you write a business plan, you are just starting out, so many of these numbers will be estimates.

Don't be intimidated by writing a business plan. The fact that you have read this far in the book means you have thought out most of the business plan in your head anyway. If you are still scared, then I present to you the Quick and Dirty Business Plan Worksheet. If you simply follow along and answer the questions in this worksheet, the business plan will flow out naturally. Also, there is a Sample Business Plan at the end of the book for you to consult (see pages 231 to 238).

There are a lot of questions in the plans, but as you'll see from reading the Sample Business Plan in the Resources section of this book, you can answer most of these in one or two sentences. Besides, these are the questions that parents, bankers, partners, and customers are going to be asking you, so it helps to think about them all now.

Congratulations! You know everything you need to know to start your business. Turn to the next chapter for some tips before you open for business.

Quick and Dirty
Business Plan Worksheet

Name of your business: _____

Location of your business: _____

Your contact phone number: _____

Your e-mail address: _____

Web site: _____

Describe your business in two or three sentences. This is often called the Executive Summary:

_____

_____

_____

PART ONE: THE ORGANIZATIONAL PLAN

IDENTIFY YOUR BUSINESS

1. What product(s) or service(s) will you sell? (Describe in detail.)
2. How is your business different from/better than your competitors' businesses?
3. What is your market niche? (Are you the biggest, the cheapest, the newest, the oldest, etc.?)

IDENTIFY MANAGEMENT*

1. Who will be running the business?
2. What experience do the managers have?
3. Why are they qualified to manage the business?
4. When will they do their assigned tasks?

OUTLINE OPERATIONS

1. What equipment will you need to start the business?
2. Do you already own any of this equipment?
3. Will you need employees to start the business? If so, who do you need and how will you hire and pay them?
4. Do you need any insurance or a license to start this business?
5. Who do you know that can help you or advise you on this business (lawyers, accountants, consultants)?
6. What businesses will supply your business with office supplies, Internet service, etc.?

Remember: Even if "management" is one person—you—you still need to answer these questions.

PART TWO: THE MARKETING PLAN

IDENTIFY YOUR MARKET

1. Who are your customers? (Age, income, geographic location, etc., are all helpful.)
2. What is the condition of the business you are in? For instance, are you starting your snow shoveling business in July? Are there already over a dozen landscaping companies in your town alone?
3. How will you reach your customers (e.g., radio, flyers, word of mouth)?
4. How much will you charge for the product or service?
5. Will you offer any money-back guarantees? If so, what exactly is the guarantee?
6. Who else sells a product or service like yours?
7. What do they charge for the product?
8. What will you do to gain customers that your competitors do not do?

IDENTIFY YOUR RISKS

1. What can go wrong?
2. What can you do to prevent it?
3. How have you prepared for disasters?
4. Where is your business weak?
5. What can you do to make it stronger?

SCHEDULE

1. Grab a calendar and write down what you will do each week for the first 30, 60, and 90 days.
2. Using that same calendar, write your yearly goals for the business for this year.

PART THREE: THE FINANCIAL PLAN

FINANCIAL ANALYSIS

1. How much will it cost to start the business? (You should itemize each expense.)
2. How much will it cost each month to run the business? What are the operating expenses (both fixed and variable costs)?
3. Define one unit.
4. What is the cost per unit?
5. How much profit will you make when you sell one product or perform one service? Remember: PROFIT = REVENUE – EXPENSES
6. What will you spend your start-up money on?
7. Where can you cut costs as the business grows?

FINANCIAL STATEMENTS

1. Prepare an income statement.
2. Prepare a cash-flow statement.
3. Prepare a balance sheet.

CHAPTER 12

Setting Up Shop

Okay, no more learning about starting your business. No more writing about setting up your business. It's time to get started!

Step into My Office

Let's start with something simple: your location. Where will your business be set up? Remember that many entrepreneurs want a cushy, air-conditioned corner office in a building they own, but for start-ups, we are trying to keep our fixed costs down. So think about all those "free" available office spaces like your bedroom, your dorm room, and your parent's garage.

DOLLARS & SENSE
Even if you hope your business will one day have its own storefront, the number-one goal when it comes to picking your location is to keep those fixed costs down!

Your office also needs to have enough room for your bookkeeping system, if you are using the four-box system. It's a good idea to have a computer with a high-speed Internet connection, a printer, a file cabinet, and some storage space for office supplies, marketing materials, and maybe even your actual products.

Though it is expensive and adds to the fixed cost, I think it's very important that you have your own phone line. Sometimes adding a second line to your parent's house phone isn't all that expensive. When someone calls, you alone should answer, or else the caller should be directed to leave a message on a professional-sounding answering machine. If your mom answers your business phone, it comes off as unprofessional.

If a landline is too much money, consider using your cell phone as your business phone. You can use it as both a business phone and a personal phone by always answering, "Hi this is_____." That will sound professional to a customer but won't sound too stiff for your friends. When recording your phone message, make it professional but neutral—something like, "You've reached the mobile phone of _____. I'm sorry I could not take your call. Please leave a message and I would be happy to call you back." Though this doesn't mention your business name, customers will be happy to have your personal cell phone as the number at which they can reach you. (Too many people are sick of business recordings that say, "All operators are currently assisting other customers. You're call is very important to us, so please continue to hold.") Giving out your cell phone number is one way you can stand out from the big guys.

Here's My Card

Although every business uses a different array of marketing materials—from brochures, to samples, to DVDs—nearly every business has stationery and business cards. Stationery includes the sheets of paper, envelopes, and labels that display your address and *logo*. A logo is a small, simple symbol or picture that helps people recognize your business. Everyone knows Nike's logo, the "swoosh." When you think swoosh, you think sports and athletes—and so you think Nike. Southwest Airlines' logo is a heart with wings on it. Fly Southwest and youinstantly know it's the fun airline where flight attendants make jokes during the safety announcements. Your logo can't be too complex, because it needs to fit onto your business card and your stationery. If you are The Happy Cookie Company, maybe your logo is a cookie with a yellow smiley face on it. If you are Gentlemen's Lawn Care, maybe your logo is a cartoon picture of a man in a suit and tie mowing a lawn. Think of something simple that visually explains your business.

It's okay to start your business without a logo, but keep it in the back of your mind that you will need one eventually. (I actually still don't have one.) It's also okay to make your own stationery and business cards when you're just starting out. As long as your stationery has your name, address, e-mail, Web site (if you have one), phone number, and logo, you are all set.

Never leave the house without your business cards. While it's a bit cumbersome to carry around product samples or even just brochures, 25 business cards will easily fit into your pocket. Business cards are mini-marketing materials that have your name, address, Web site, e-mail, phone number, and logo on them. Although nearly everyone in business has a business card, many business cards fail to serve their primary purpose, which is to market! I get handed so many business cards that read something like this:

CLIFTON CONSULTING
Gerard Clifton, *President*
123 Happy Street
Anywhere, MA, USA
617-555-1234

The problem with this card is that I have no idea what Clifton Consulting does. Do they consult farmers? Circus clowns? Automobile companies? Small businesses? Maybe the back side of Gerard Clifton's card could read:

Consulting services to help small farmers become organic
farmers. Save money and save the environment with the help
of Clifton Consulting.

Aha! Now we know exactly what it is they do. If I found this business card in my desk drawer six months later, I would still know what it is they do, because it's written right on the card!

DOLLARS & SENSE
Your business card should clearly state exactly what it is you do.

Your Web Site

We'll talk more about Web sites in Chapter 13, but for now know that these days every business needs a Web site. They are absolutely essential for businesses that sell products. They do add a bit to your fixed costs but, in this day and age, a Web site is a necessary expense. Customers you weren't even marketing to will find you. Maybe they're from Australia. Or Sri Lanka. You'll never know, unless you have a Web site.

Business Hours

Many start-ups seem to be open 24/7. The theory behind these hours is that if someone wants to give you his money, you take it! While this is a tempting way to do business, chances are that after a few months of this you will burn out. You can't work seven days a week forever.

What's more, like many young entrepreneurs, you may still be in school. More than a few parents have pulled the plug on businesses because grades started dropping off. An easy way around this problem is to set *business hours* and *office hours*. We already went over office hours. These are times when your business is closed to customers, but you are performing one of the tasks done in the C suite (accounting, marketing, etc.). Business hours are the hours when you actually are open to customers. This is the time you are taking phone orders, baking cookies, walking dogs, and waxing cars.

It's tempting to be open all the time. For the first few months of your business, maybe you should do just that. It will allow you to build up a cash reserve quickly and get some current customers that you can use for testimonials and referral sources. But after six months of craziness, you should scale back to normal business hours, and you should stick to them. You don't want your customers to think they can call you anytime. You need to have a life. There's no point in making a ton of money if you never have time to enjoy it.

TALES FROM THE FRONT LINES
Your hours, of course, need to be in line with your other commitments such as school, sports, piano lessons, and household chores. Remember how I told you I used to

"rent" lawn-mowing equipment from my dad by mowing his yard for free? Well, my business got to be so big that I started neglecting my dad's lawn in order to be at the beck and call of my customers. My father soon put an end to that. He told me if I wanted to keep renting his equipment, his yard would have to get done first. Your hours are up to you; just make sure they accommodate the other promises you have already made.

Help! I Need Some Help!

Suppose you can't do this all on your own; you need some help. How do you go about hiring employees? The best piece of advice about hiring employees is to try not to hire employees. An employee is a fixed cost, and as a new business, you know that you want to keep those fixed costs down. It's better to hire *independent contractors*. These are like employees, but you hire them to work on a job—not to work for your company. You might hire an independent contractor to rake the leaves off one of the lawns in your neighborhood. You can pay independent contractors by the job or by the hour. And when the job is done, you don't have to pay them again until you need them for another job. So it's best to make a list of some of the tasks you might need help with and a list of people who can help.

Remember Katie's violin business? Maybe her friend Megan also plays the violin. Katie might hire Megan as an independent contractor for when Katie can't make a gig or when she books two weddings at the same time on the same day. (Remember, I hire a woman who helps me stay organized.) Which of your friends can help with the extra work in your business?

Of course, there are drawbacks to hiring your friends. They might not work as hard as you do. They might show up late, but still want to be paid the full amount. Troubles in your business relationship can spill over into your personal relationship. My advice is to inform them up front of exactly what it is you expect, even if you are only hiring them for a few hours. It's also a good idea to tell them that your policy is to hire people on an initial "test" basis. This way your friends don't think they have scored a summer job simply because they worked for you for one day. When they help you out, let them know the first few days are part of a testing process to see if you'll want them to work for you long-term (and vice versa). Not only will this be good for your friendship, it will be good for your business.

Save Big Bucks with Bulk Buying

A *retail* business is a business that sells directly to customers. Most likely, this is the business you are going to start. Whether you sell products or services, chances are you are selling them directly to your customers.

A *wholesale* business sells products to retail businesses. A beef wholesaler might sell a 300-pound slab of beef to a butcher, who is the retailer. The butcher then chops up that 300-pound slab into 12-ounce steaks and sells those to the customer. Wholesalers usually get their products directly from manufacturers. The farmer doesn't want to sell one beef cow at a time, so he sells 1,000 at a time to a wholesaler at a drastically discounted price. The wholesaler then warehouses the meat and sells it in small chunks to the retailer. The retailer divides that up into even smaller chunks to sell to the customer.

In recent years, the line between retailer and wholesaler has blurred. Stores like Walmart are a new blend of retailer/wholesalers. Walmart buys at wholesale prices and stores the products in its warehouse. But its warehouse *is* the store, which is open to customers. Walmart eliminates the middleman, as the expression goes. Normally, the manufacturer makes a product for one price and sells it to the wholesaler at a slightly higher price. Then the wholesaler sells it to retailers for a slightly higher price. Then the retailer sells it to the customer for a slightly higher price. The more people in the chain, the higher the price goes. Stores like Walmart have cut down the number of links in the chain, which is why its prices are so low.

With new technology like the Internet, some businesses are everything at once. You might make your own nail polish, so you're the manufacturer. You might sell your nail polish to customers online, so you are a retailer. But you might also sell large orders directly to beauty salons, so you are also a wholesaler.

Depending on your business, you might not need to deal with a wholesaler. In fact, many businesses start out paying retail prices simply because they don't have the cash to buy large portions of the product, or *inventory*, that wholesalers require. As you are starting a brand-new small business, dealing with a traditional wholesaler can be tough. When wholesalers sell something to a new business, they often want payment up front. That's a payment that most new businesses can't afford. However, if you do need to buy a large quantity of something, here are some tips for dealing with wholesalers:

- *Use a retailer/wholesaler.* When you shop at a store like Costco, Walmart, or Sam's Club, you're getting wholesale prices without all the hassle of setting up an account with a wholesaler.
- *Ask for free samples.* While some wholesalers are reluctant to work with a new business, others are dying for new customers. Sometimes they will send some free samples. Free samples can be a unique way of financing!
- *Try to meet a representative from the wholesaler in person.* An in-person visit can be your chance to show that you are a serious businessperson. Bring your business cards, marketing materials, and, if you have it, a sample of your product.
- *Ask for a size discount.* In dealing with a wholesaler, you often don't need a better price; you need a to be able to buy a smaller quantity at the wholesaler's price. If you explain to the wholesaler that your business is new and that you want to start slowly, maybe their people will allow you to order an amount smaller than their typical minimum order without raising the cost.
- *Get a reference.* If you're getting nowhere, then do good business with a retailer and use the retailer as a reference. Be sure to be known as someone who always pays the bills on time. Once you get a reputation, a wholesaler will be easier to work with.

Making a Grand Grand Opening

Most small business owners don't think about having a grand opening. "Peter," they ask, "if I don't have a store, how am I supposed to have a grand opening? My business is washing cars, what am I supposed to actually open?" I hear this question a lot from new entrepreneurs. My answer is: The grand opening is for every business, not just those with storefronts. You grand opening should include the following:

- *A press release.* Use the sample one in the back of this book as a guide. Announce that a new business has just been started by a young entrepreneur. For most small newspapers, that alone is story enough!

- *A new-customer discount.* Give a BIG discount to your first 5, 10, or even 100 customers, whatever your business can handle. Say things like, "the first 15 people to call will get a free _____." People will scramble to make sure they are one of the first.
- *A photo shoot.* Even if this is a photo of you pushing a lawn mower across your first customer's yard, a photo shoot can provide great pictures for a press release or for future marketing materials.

The grand opening is simply an initial marketing blitz that will draw attention to your business. While you need to keep fixed costs down (so don't spend a grand on your grand opening), a few simple public announcements can really jump-start your new business.

You're ready! The next few chapters talk about how to improve an up-and-running business. The section after that has short summaries of more than 100 businesses that you can start; all of which satisfy the Five *S* Formula. You are now on your way to being an entrepreneur!

PART TWO

IMPROVING YOUR BUSINESS

Congrats! You have an up-and-running business. The question now is: What can you do to improve it? Whether by advertising on the World Wide Web or by making your business just a bit more environmentally friendly, these next few chapters will provide some tips on how to put some quick cash into your pocket!

CHAPTER 13

Web Wealth

The Internet is one of the greatest gifts given to young entrepreneurs in the last 50 years. The Internet instantly levels the playing field between young and older entrepreneurs, allows you to reach customers worldwide, lets your business appear larger than it actually is, and allows for the testing of ideas without spending a lot of money. Whether you sell software or organic eggplants, your business needs to make use of the Internet.

Web-Site Insight

Your Web site is the cornerstone of your Internet marketing. It's your storefront to the world. Whether your business is a technology business or not doesn't really matter. Every business needs a Web site. If you have a Web page, literally anyone in the world with an Internet connection can learn about you and your business. There are four basic types of Web sites:

- The landing page
- The static Web site
- The interactive Web site
- The blog

The Landing Page

The *landing page* is the first page that the visitor to your Web site sees. It is usually just one page. It can be a long page that folks have to scroll down to keep reading, but there are no other pages to click to on the site. If and when landing pages do allow *hyperlinks*, the links take you away from the landing page to a completely different Web site. Hyperlinks are simply virtual doorways that connect Web pages and Web sites. Landing pages are used to promote one product or service, so aside from the hyperlink, they are not interactive. If you want to promote multiple products or services, then you need multiple landing pages. Keeping it to just one product or service ensures that your landing page will rank high in *search engines* like Yahoo! and Google. (A search engine is a site on the World Wide Web that uses search software to locate key words at other sites.) A landing page promoting garden tools and fertilizer and tractors and gardening courses and flowers and hoses and sprinkler systems is going to have a tough time ranking high. If your business sells all these things, you should have a separate landing page for each product: one site for hoses, one for gardening courses, and so on.

DOLLARS & SENSE
Ranking high in the search engines is part art, part science. An easy way to succeed is to focus on one product or service per page.

Landing pages also force the customer to focus. Sometimes pages that sell everything turn away customers because the customer is distracted. If a customer is searching for a new garden hose and sees that your site is also selling gardening classes, he might suddenly remember that the library *also* has gardening classes and that those are free. He might then decide to not buy the hose until he takes the free gardening class from the library. In this case, your page put too many ideas into the customer's head, so he left.

The landing page is so easy to set up that there is little excuse not to have one. Even if it consists of your company name, your phone number, e-mail and mailing addresses, and a 100-word description of what it is you do, that's better than nothing.

The Static Web Site

The static Web site consists of multiple pages, but the customer cannot interact with the site at all. Its only function is to provide information. Unlike the landing page, the static Web site has multiple pages, to make it easier for customers to find what they want. Static Web sites can market multiple products and services. While they vary in size, most static Web sites have the following five pages:

1. *Home.* This is the main page of the Web site; it briefly tells the visitor what the company does.
2. *Bio.* This page tells the story of the company and its founder(s).
3. *Contact us.* This provides the e-mail, mailing address, and phone number of the company.
4. *Product and services.* This page tells the visitor more about the company's products and services. Sometimes it even includes a price list.
5. *Clients and testimonials.* This is your chance to brag about whom you have already worked with and post any testimonials that your current customers have given you. (Remember to get their permission before posting.)

Static Web sites are usually pretty easy to set up. Even though they consist of multiple pages, the programming is about the same as it is for a landing page, so the cost shouldn't be too much more.

The Interactive Web Site

The interactive Web site is almost identical to the static Web site, except for one big difference, which you can probably guess: Customers can interact with the interactive Web site. Perhaps they interact by buying something. Maybe they simply sign up for a newsletter by entering their e-mail address at the Web site. Interactive Web sites are the most difficult and most expensive to set up, but they are the most profitable, because they can actually receive information and money from a customer.

DOLLARS & SENSE
The interactive Web site is like having a 24-hour, seven-day-a-week employee who works for free!

Many interactive Web sites are connected to multiple landing pages. Imagine that my company sells a wide variety of gardening products through the mail. My interactive Web site tells the consumer all about my company, about me, and about what I sell. Customers can order all of my products directly from my interactive Web site. They can also sign up for my newsletter.

In addition to the interactive Web site, my business also has three landing pages. One landing page sells hoses, another sells seeds for roses, and another sells a gardening book for beginners. If customers come to my hoses landing page, they can read all about why they should buy hoses from me. At the bottom of that page is a link that goes directly to the hoses order page of my interactive Web site. Notice that the link doesn't take them to the home page—that would just be a distraction—it takes them directly to the place where they can buy a hose. The seeds landing page takes them directly to the order page for rose seeds. If we were to diagram how an interactive Web site works with landing pages, it would look something like Figure 3.

Oh, My Blog

A blog is like a newsletter, but with fewer rules. Blogs can be Web sites themselves, or they can be part of another Web site. You can get your blog hosted for free at Web sites like *www.blog.com*. Blogs typically aren't used to sell anything, unless the blog itself is the business. They are best used to establish relationships with your customers. If your business is selling your paintings, you probably want people to look online every time you have a new painting. That would mean you would have to send everyone a mass e-mail every time you finished one. That's a great way to annoy your customers.

If, on the other hand, you had a blog that was updated every week with new painting tips, people would want to visit your site every week, without you ever asking them. They are in search of great information. Because blogs are informal, they are pretty easy to set up. Sometimes, bloggers write one line. Other times, they write a two-page blog. Whichever type of Web site you have, consider adding a blog. It's a cheap way to stay in touch with your customers. What's more, some blogs have become so popular that people pay to belong to them. Yours could be next!

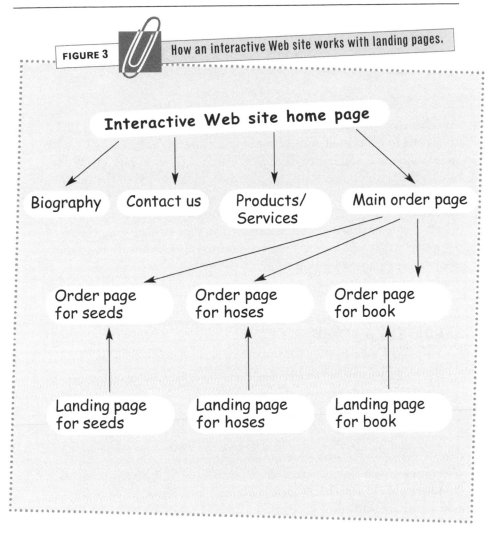

FIGURE 3 How an interactive Web site works with landing pages.

Setting up a Web Site

Setting up your Web site couldn't be easier. Many people delay having online exposure because they feel they have to start with a complete, interactive Web site. If you're able to do this, then do it, but don't feel bad in the least about starting with a simple landing page.

Your Web site should reflect your company's colors. Think of your favorite large companies and the colors associated with them. McDonald's are gold, white, and red. Coca-Cola's are white and red. Walmart's are blue and white. These major corporations make sure that all of their commercials, print advertisements, packaging, and signs always use the same colors. What colors represent your company best? Whichever you choose, be sure to use those as the background colors of your Web site.

Keep It Simple

Another reason businesses hesitate to create a Web site is that they feel they need to include all sorts of cool Flash programming with moving graphics, audio, and even video. Don't bother. The simpler the Web site is, the better. Remember, there are still millions of people who do not have a high-speed Internet connection. You don't want a page that takes a long time to load, and more complicated pages have larger files, which will load slowly if people don't have a high-speed connection. Skip the funky graphics and the long, boring explanations. Every page should come right to the point.

DOLLARS & SENSE

Sites that take a long time to load do nothing more than turn away millions of potential customers who don't have high-speed Internet access.

Open Your Wallet: Web-Site Costs

Web sites can cost anywhere from $100 to $100,000. Sometimes you don't get what you pay for. Regardless of total cost, there are a few basic fees associated with all Web sites:

- Design fees
- Domain registration
- Hosting fees
- Transactional fees
- Maintenance fees

Design Fees

Design fees are the one-time fees that you pay to have your Web site created. Many young entrepreneurs skip these fees by designing their Web sites themselves on a program like Microsoft Front Page. (In fact, you can find a mini-business plan in Part Four of this book, describing how to make money designing Web sites for others.) If yours will be a simple landing page or static Web site, designing it yourself is not all that hard. On the other hand, if you're planning on having a Web site that can accept customers' credit cards, you want to make sure that the site is technically sound. These sites need a ***shopping cart***, which is the virtual equivalent of a grocery store shopping cart. It allows customers to select products from your Web site, throw them into the virtual cart, and then take these products to the checkout and pay for them. You don't want to scare away customers because the site isn't working properly.

Domain Registration

Domain registration is the annual charge to register your Web site address or "domain." Choosing the right domain is key to having a Web site that is easy to find. Many smart entrepreneurs register several domains and have them all point to one site. Businesses often register their business name and then try to grab as many available domains as possible that relate to that subject. For my gardening business, I might register my business name *www.petersgardeningstuff.com* and as many other subjects related to gardening as I can find. I might try to grab *www.gardening.com*, *www.greenthumb.com*, *www.flowergarden.com*, *www.landscaping.com*, and so on. (Of course, we're just talking hypothetically here. These particular domains have been registered for a long time, because they're so good. Most of the more obvious names have already been taken. But think outside the box. You'll find something.) Domains cost about $8 to $15 a year to register. Two great sites to register your domain names on are *www.godaddy.com* and *www.namecheap.com*.

DOLLARS & SENSE

It's important to grab your domain name quickly! Some 70,000 domains are registered every *day*, so be sure you can get the domain you want before you make a final decision on your business name.

Hosting Fees

Hosting fees are like paying rent in cyberspace. Although your page is accessible to anyone on the World Wide Web, it is actually stored somewhere on someone's hard drive. This hard drive is often referred to as a ***server***. (Sorry if this is too basic for you techies, but the non-techies will thank me!) Large businesses can justify the expense of having their own server and paying their own technicians to maintain it. But for small start-ups, this is just too expensive. Web-site hosting can cost anywhere from $2 to $100 a month. The drastic cost difference comes from several factors, such as the actual size of the Web site (how many megabytes it is), and the amount of traffic expected to come to the Web site. Sites with large numbers of visitors need more *bandwidth*. Bandwidth determines the amount of transfer the Web site can handle. Think of transfer as traffic. If your site expects 1,000 visitors a month, it needs more transfer space (bandwidth) than a site that expects only 100 visitors a month. If too many visitors show up and there is not enough bandwidth, the Web site will crash, which is kind of like a Web-site traffic jam: Too many people are trying to get in, and there is not enough room. Keep in mind that you can always upgrade bandwidth from your hosting company as your site becomes more popular. But every time you buy more, it will cost more.

Hosting fees can also include features like a *POP3 e-mail account*, which gives you an e-mail address that uses your domain name. My POP3 e-mail is *peter@peterbspeaks.com*. (Write me an e-mail and say hello!) While I could save a bit of money using a gmail or Yahoo! account, it looks more professional to have my e-mail address include my domain name.

These extra features can make it difficult to make apples-to-apples comparisons among Web-hosting companies. My advice is to stick to our timeless theme of keeping those fixed cost down. As long as you can get a reasonable amount of bandwidth and your own POP3 e-mail address, go with the cheapest place. It's unlikely that your brand new business will have a large Web site with heavy traffic. Start small and upgrade later.

Transaction Fees

Transaction fees are costs that occur when a customer buys something from your Web site. This would make them part of COGS, because you don't pay transaction fees until a product is actually bought. In order to accept credit cards on your Web site, you'll need either a third-party company like PayPal or ClickBank, or you'll need your own *merchant account*. A merchant account is established with a credit-card processor that is linked to your bank account. Whether you have your own merchant account or you use a third-party company, you will have to pay transaction fees. You might sell a product for $10, but the third-party company will take 5% of the sales price as its service fee, so you wind up with only $9.50. Most interactive Web sites should establish an account through PayPal, as it is very easy to set up, requires no maintenance fees, and is such a popular and well-respected site. If you are going to be taking payments online, probably the best Web site to help you set up a merchant account is *2Checkout.com*. At the time of this writing, for a one-time fee of $50, you can set up everything you need in order to start accepting credit cards. While *2Checkout.com* doesn't have the cheapest transaction fees, they have no monthly maintenance fees. So once you cough up the initial $50 set-up fee, that's all you need to pay until you start selling. If you are under age eighteen, your parents might have to help with the set-up of the merchant account. It shouldn't cost them any money; companies simply require an "adult" to sign on the dotted line. Just ask.

Maintenance Fees

Maintenance fees are the occasional fees you pay to your Web designer to update the Web site. Perhaps your original site didn't have a "testimonials" page but, after a few happy customers, you are ready to add one. Your Web designer might charge a small fee to add this page. Of course, if you design your own site, there aren't any maintenance fees.

Often you can get a minimal number of maintenance hours wrapped into your Web-hosting package. Most designers also have hosting services that may not be the cheapest in town but may still be the best bet because of the inclusive maintenance.

Another tactic to cut down on maintenance fees is to have your designer make your Web site easily programmable. For example, even though I know as much about programming as I do about goat herding, my Web site can be easily changed by me, using a program my designer installed that works like Microsoft Word. This allows me to make changes to it, even though I am not familiar with programming languages.

Getting Started

The Web site creation process follows these steps, to describe it simply:

1. *Select your domain name.* Because tens of thousands of domains are snatched up every day, start with this step. It's best to make a list of several domain names, each a variation of your ideal domain. So if *www.gardening.com* is taken, maybe your list would include *www.easygardening.com*, *www.gardeningonline.com*, and so on. (Again, I am just using these names as an example. Smart businesses have already registered these names. Sorry.)

2. *Create the content of your site.* Whether you design your own site or hire someone to do it, it's best to write up the contents in a word-processing program, where you can easily check the spelling in the program. The fact that you have already created the content of the site will allow a designer and host company to give you a much more accurate cost estimate.

3. *Select your designer and host company.* Show them the site you created in your word-processing program so both designer and host company can give you an accurate idea of cost. Be sure to ask about a POP3 e-mail account and what your designer charges for ongoing maintenance. Also be sure to ask whether your designer can make your site easily programmable, so you can make minor changes yourself.

4. *Open a PayPal and merchant account.* You will need one one of these if your business is going to accept online orders. Remember that *2Checkout.com* requires only one $50 set-up fee, and then you don't pay a thing until you sell something.

5. *Total your online costs.* Design fees and domain registration fall under start-up costs, while hosting and maintenance fees are fixed operating costs. PayPal and merchant account fees are part of COGS. You'll need all of these to prepare your financial statements.

6. *Ask your friends and family to preview the site.* Your Web-site designer can help you create a secret Web address that only friends and family can access. This way it can be online but not yet accessible to the general public. Ask your friends and family to comment on the site's ease of use and to tell you about any spelling mistakes.

7. *Announce that your business has an up-and-running Web site.* Be sure to put your Web address on all of your marketing materials.

Adding Online Ads

Advertising on the Web is an advertiser's dream for three basic reasons: It has the best targeting of any advertising medium; it has a pay-per-click cost structure; and it allows for easy *micro-testing*.

As you know from Chapter 6, targeting is simply focusing on only those customers you want to reach. While newspapers, magazines, radio, and TV stations have been touting this for years, their targeting has been mediocre at best. A TV station might tell a business wanting to advertise to adult males that it should air its commercial on the sports show. But while men are strong sports-show viewers (Go, Patriots!), many women watch sports as well. Younger kids may be watching as well. Worst of all, when a television commercial comes on during a sports show, that's when people head to the bathroom or flip to another channel, so advertisers are airing their commercials when people are most likely not to watch them.

Compare that to someone's Facebook page. Not only does Facebook headquarters know exactly when you are online, but your page describes all of your interests and hobbies. Facebook knows your age, sex, and relationship status. If I want to only target 18-year-old African-American females from Texas who are interested in entrepreneurship, I can do that. In fact, before I even pay for the advertising, Facebook can tell me exactly how many members it has that fit that description. Now *that's* targeting.

The number-one drawback to traditional advertising is that you often pay money to advertise to people who either don't care or who aren't even watching or otherwise exposed to your ad. The Web overcomes this challenge not only by its targeting capabilities, but also through its pay-per-click system. Pay-per-click simply means that you don't pay until you know for sure that someone is interested, which they show by "clicking" on your advertisement. When they click, you pay. If they don't click, you don't pay!

Micro-testing is a fairly new term in the advertising world. "Test, test, test" has always been the motto of successful advertisers. Before you pay to run an ad for twelve months, run it for one month first to see if it is even remotely successful. Even though testing was done quite often in print, TV, and radio media, it took a long time and was still pretty expensive. There isn't really a cheap way to buy an ad in the *Wall Street Journal*. What's more, some magazines require the final version of the advertisement to be submitted months before the magazine is released. It can be expensive to wait that long.

The Internet, by contrast, allows someone to test her advertisement in a few hours. I can throw up an ad, wait three hours, and then see how many people clicked on it. If no one clicked, I can rewrite the ad in another hour, throw it back up, wait another three hours, and count the clicks. I can keep repeating that procedure until I find the ad I want. And the best part is that I don't have to pay until it is successful!

Here is an example of how I can use all three of these great features—targeting, micro-testing, and pay-per-clicks—in a simple campaign to sell my flowerpots made out of recycled rubber tires.

First, I create a landing page that just sells these pots. I write some attractive copy about how every time someone buys these pots, ten pounds of carbon dioxide is kept out of the atmosphere because the tires are being recycled to make them. Second, I mention that in stores these pots cost almost double what I charge. And last, at the bottom of the page is a link to the order page of my Web site that deals only with these pots.

So I have my landing page, which leads customers to my virtual store. Now all I need to do is get them here. I could advertise in gardening magazines, but many people aren't interested in flowerpots. Plus my ad can't run for five months. Instead, I decide to try my hand advertising on Google.

In the real world, where a business is located is very important. A grocery store located at the intersection of the town's two busiest streets will fare far better than the one at the end of a dirt road. Companies pay big money to be located in the best spots. But in cyberspace, location is irrelevant: What matters is *how* someone gets to your site. People don't want to pay for advertising space; they want to pay for advertising words, because most people "travel" the Internet using words. We type in the name of the Web site we want to go to, or we type the words that describe where we want to go into a search engine.

Google, the largest search engine of them all, sells these words through its **AdWords** program. When you buy an AdWord, you are buying the privilege of having your Web site come up first when someone types in that word. Pretend someone is searching for flowerpots on Google. If I bought the AdWord *flowerpots*, that person would see my Web site first on the right side of the page. (The Web sites on the left side of the page are those that naturally rank high in the search engines because of the content of their site.)

AdWords are sold by an auction system, so the price of an AdWord (or AdWords) is determined by how badly people want it. The AdWord *garden* is probably pretty popular, whereas the AdWords *sea slugs* are not so popular. When you bid on an AdWord, you decide what you want to pay, and depending on what others have bid for that same AdWord, that's how your Web site's rank will be determined.

Let me provide a simple example: Suppose I want to buy the AdWord *gardening*. I put in a bid of one dollar. That means every time someone searches for *gardening* and then clicks on my Web site, Google charges me a dollar. Suppose two other people bid on the word *gardening* as well. Jermaine was willing to pay $2 for that word, while Sheila was only willing to pay 50 cents. Whenever someone searches using the word *gardening*, Jermaine's Web site will be listed first, because he paid the most; mine will be listed second; and the Web site of Sheila, the lowest bidder, will be listed last.

When you buy AdWords from Google, you first set up an account, and you can set limits as to the total amount you want to spend. If you bid $1 per ad word and 10,000 people click on it one hour, you wouldn't want to be on the hook for ten grand! So Google allows you to set a limit. When you've used up your limit, your AdWords disappear from the Web page.

With this system, I'm only targeting people searching for stuff related to the word *gardening*. Someone searching for solar-powered kazoos won't find me. What's more, I'm paying only when these people actually click on my AdWords. And finally, I can test several AdWords in one afternoon. Within a day or two, I will know which ones work the best.

Unfortunately, marketing on the Web could fill a whole book. Also, the technology is constantly changing. However, I wanted to give you a taste of some of the really cool stuff you can do without spending a lot of money. It's worth picking up a book or two about online marketing. This is especially true for those of you whose business sells products or services that can easily be bought over the Web.

TALES FROM THE FRONT LINES

Don't overlook the power of the Internet. Devin Lazerine, founder of *Rap-Up*, a hip-hop magazine for teenagers, started his Web site when he was only fifteen years old. Devin always wanted to create a print magazine but figured he would have to spend years working his Web site before anyone would help him take his idea to print. But as Devin explained in an interview in *USA Weekend*, "My plan was to write for *Vibe* or *The Source* when I got older and work my way up to getting my own [magazine]. But a couple days after I launched the Web site, I pitched the magazine idea to a few publishers, thinking, *Hey, it can't hurt.* The next day, a publisher from H&S Media in Chicago called and was interested."

Things move very fast online. Remember: Web sites can start simply and cheaply as information-offering landing pages. From there, you can upgrade to interactive sites that give you a virtual storefront. The point is get something online, so the world can find you!

CHAPTER 14

Some Advice on How to Get Advice

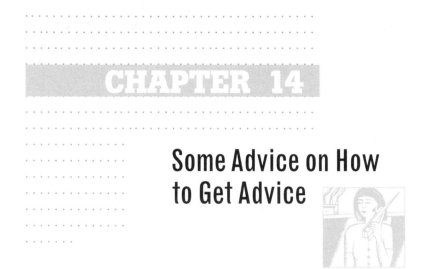

Smart business owners know they shouldn't go it alone. One-person businesses (the most popular of all start-ups) can be overwhelming: the owner feels she has to do everything herself. To a large extent, the owner *does* have to do many things herself. But although most start-ups can't afford to hire employees and can barely justify the expense of an independent contractor, there is little reason not to form an advisory council.

An advisory council is a group of individuals with varying areas of expertise that advises you on your business. Sometimes, entrepreneurs have scheduled meetings with their advisory council (monthly, twice a year, annually, etc.). Other times, the advisory council simply agrees to help out the business owner when and where it can. Most new businesses can't afford to pay their advisory council directly, so they often reward them in other ways. Perhaps your accountant is on your advisory board because he knows that the better your business does, the more business he will get from you. Perhaps your parents are on your advisory board, because they are investors in your company. Some people put their teachers on their advisory boards. Not only does the teacher get to help out, she also gets to use your business as a teaching tool for her classes. Whoever you choose, there are a few keys to assembling an advisory council, which I'll describe below.

- ***Clearly define the commitment level.*** The commitment level is up to you, but it's best to overestimate the amount of commitment you'll need from everyone. Also, define what you will be asking the council to do. Is it one hour on the phone? A monthly in-person meeting? Will people need a high-speed Internet connection? Must they listen to all the songs you wrote for your Birthday Party Polka business? These are all questions that potential council members will ask of you, so you need to be ready to answer them.

- *Only accept people who can make the commitment.* The commitment varies from business to business. Whatever the level of commitment your business requires, clearly state it to potential council members. Make it easy for them to say no to you. It's best to know up front if they can't do it.
- *Find some way to reward them.* Okay, so you can't afford to pay them. No problem, just find something else. Perhaps they get free products, or they get a "thank you" on your Web site. Whatever it is, make sure the council is taken care of.
- *Treat their time as precious.* Your council members might be business owners themselves, so you know how busy they can be. If you told them that serving on the council required one hour of phone time per month, don't chew up three hours of their time. They committed to one hour, not to three.
- *Don't pick them because they are your friends.* Your advisory council is not your "hang out" council. You want talented people who can add valuable advice to your business, even if it's painful advice to hear.
- *Pick people with varying talents.* It makes little sense to have five accountants on your advisory board—or five lawyers. You don't need the same advice five times. Strive to form as diverse a council as you can. Vary the ages, sexes, races, and talents of your council. Ideally, you'd like at least:

  - ☞ One person who is in your target market
  - ☞ One person who has experience with marketing
  - ☞ One person who has experience as an accountant or CFO
  - ☞ One person who has experience in running a small business
  - ☞ One person who has a legal background

The best time to set up an advisory council is *before* you start your business. The council can steer you clear from start-up pitfalls. It can help review your Web-site copy and your financial statements. Having a council is a back-door way to get lots of free professional advice, so

✔

TALES FROM THE FRONT LINES

On my council, one advisor I have is very tough on me, so tough that I often don't want his advice! However, he provides information I need to hear: facts that I'd like to ignore but that really damage my business for every hour I ignore them. My favorite thing to do in my business is create new products. I have a blast thinking up new book ideas and new audio CDs I can sell. But I'm not so good at the follow-through. For a while, I would create a new product but never try to sell it. My business started to slump, and this hard-line advisor pointed out that I was spending too much time on the fun stuff and not enough on the stuff that made money. "Have fun on your own time," he said. "But during office hours, you need to make sure you are making a profit." Ouch! But he was right.

don't feel that you need to put off forming one until you have an up-and-running business. Get started on it today. By the way, another good thing to get started on is saving the environment. Turn the page to find out how to do that.

CHAPTER 15

Make Some Green
Going Green

Going green is all the rage today. From celebrities to politicians to families, everyone is trying to do his part to save the Earth. I hope that you will be no exception. Entrepreneurs, however, have a second reason for keeping a close eye on their environmental impact, besides saving the planet. Going green can increase their bottom line! That's right, going green creates green. When a company makes a conscious decision to do its part for the environment, the financial reward can come back in three ways:

1. STRAIGHT TO THE BOTTOM LINE. There are the eco-friendly choices that you want to be sure your business is making, because they lead directly to higher profits. A friend of mine owns a rental property that had an old, inefficient furnace that burned up a lot of oil. His tenants had to pay their own heating bills, which, of course, were pretty high. One day he asked his tenants if he could raise their rent by $100 a month, but he promised he would install a new furnace. He estimated that a new furnace would lower their heating bills by as much as 40%. My friend bought the furnace on a payment plan of $75 a month. So he earned an extra $25 a month from increased rent, the tenants saved close to $120 a month in heating bills, and the property became more valuable because it had a brand new furnace.

2. MORE CUSTOMERS. People's concern for the environment varies widely. Some don't give it much thought, while others are hard core about making sure their money is only given to green companies. You'll never lose customers by going green, but you might gain several for this simple act alone. David Yudkin, one of the co-owners of Hot Lips Pizza in

Portland, Oregon, tries to use electric cars to deliver his pizzas. He reported to the media that people call and demand their pizza be delivered in an electric car. Many will even wait an extra fifteen minutes if they can be guaranteed it will be delivered in one of the electric vehicles.

3. INCREASED GOODWILL. *Goodwill* measures a company's regard in the eyes of the public. Companies with a high degree of goodwill are viewed favorably by the public. People want to do business with them. Other companies, like tobacco companies, have a low degree of goodwill; they have to spend more money on marketing to compensate. Going green has lately become a universal way to create goodwill.

There are countless steps your business can take to become more eco-friendly. Let's focus on the few that will put some cash on your bottom line:

- *Print double-sided.* This is a simple way to reduce your paper costs by half. If you have yet to purchase a printer, inquire about this feature. Even if the printer costs a little bit more, it might pay for itself in paper savings.
- *Ask, "Do I need this?"* I once worked in marketing for a company that catered to real estate agents. As one of our promotions, we delivered to these real estate agents a discount certificate for $50 off our service. The certificate came in a nice, professional-looking envelope. At one of our marketing meetings, Carol, the head of the company, asked, "Do we really need the envelope? Can we just give them the certificate on its own?" Everyone thought for a minute and then agreed we could. Not only did we save a few trees, we also cut down our marketing costs. Take some time and look at your business operations: Are there some things you could do without? Instead of mailing customers a DVD, can you send them to a Web site that has the video footage? Can you e-mail your invoices?
- *Switch to compact fluorescents.* These are those funky, spiral-looking lightbulbs that can cut down energy use by as much as $30 per bulb. They use 75% less energy than a regular lightbulb, and they last ten times longer. Even if you are using a home office and your parents pay the electric bill, suggest that the entire household make the slow switch to these energy savers.
- *Analyze your business's waste.* Bestselling author Harvey Mackay, owner of Mackay Envelope Corporation, recalls a

convention he went to early on in his career when his business was near bankruptcy. Sitting at a bar in the hotel, Mackay struck up a conversation with a person who was also in the paper-goods business. Mackay asked the man, "How the heck do you make any money in this business?" "Depends what you get for the scrap," replied the man. Until this little conversation, Mackay was paying to have his company's paper scrap removed. Little did he know that he could actually sell the scrap paper to companies who would recycle it.*

What is your business throwing away, and is there someone who can use it? Better yet, will that person pay you to use it? Maybe the wooden shavings from your hand-carved wooden doll business can be sold as kindling for fires. Maybe the peels from your lemonade stand can be sold as compost. Throwing something away is often the first solution that comes to mind. But think deeper. There may be far more profitable options.

Shannon Williams and Nicole Windhom of Elancee Clothing figured this out. Where do they get the fabric patterns to design their clothes? From old clothes!

Consider making your whole business about saving the environment. Garage sales are terrific for the environment, and they can bring in a lot of cash. The trouble is, most people are too busy to organize them. Enter Ben Weissenstein, the creator of Grand Slam Garage Sales *(www.grandslamgaragesales.com)*. Ben's company will handle the entire garage sale for you. He will even take all the unsold stuff to a Goodwill store and get you a donation receipt that you can use to save money on your tax return! According to his Web site, the most money made at one of his garage sales was $2,284.95! That would really motivate me to save the environment!

As I wrote this manuscript, the price of oil was at $135 a barrel. In 2001, it was less than $50 a barrel. There is a lot of talk going on right now that oil will hit $200 a barrel. Only time will tell if this will happen. Think about how difficult it is for a business to plan with prices going up like this. While you are probably not in the oil business, don't forget that most of the products we buy are oil-based. So when oil costs go up, everything from gasoline, to CDs, to the price of a loaf of bread goes up as well. The more businesses like yours can minimize their dependence on nonrenewable resources, the stronger your company will be.

Want another easy way to save money? Just turn the page.

*Harvey Mackay, *Swim with the Sharks without Being Eaten Alive: Outsell, Outmanage, Outmotivate, and Outnegotiate Your Competition.* Ballantine Books, New York, 1988.

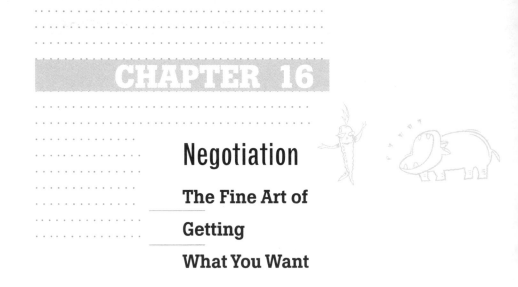

CHAPTER 16

Negotiation

The Fine Art of Getting What You Want

Every business owner needs to know how to negotiate. If you want the best prices, the best service, the best payment terms, you'll need to learn this art. Business owners are constantly negotiating with customers, employees, bankers, and vendors—and in your case, even teachers and your parents.

But what exactly is **negotiation**? Negotiation is the art of establishing a difficult relationship. Imagine I go to buy a used car, and all I want to pay is $10,000. If the used car salesperson will sell me the car I want for $10,000, then there is no need to negotiate; the relationship of car seller and car buyer is established automatically. But most likely, the used car salesperson wants to sell that car for $15,000. If I'm willing to pay no more than $10,000, then this relationship is not going to progress on its own. We'll need to negotiate.

So how do you negotiate? You could fill a whole book on the art of negotiation, but I can offer a few great pointers here. The first thing to understand is that negotiation is an art, not a science. What I mean is that since you are negotiating with people and since people are emotional creatures, the same techniques will have different effects on different people. Just because something worked the last time, that's no guarantee it will work the next time.

Basically, all negotiations boil down to four questions:

1. What do I want?
2. What do they want?

3. What do I have?
4. What do they have?

Smart negotiators continually ask these four questions over and over in a negotiation. Let's stick with the used car example:

1. What do I want? I want the car.
2. What do they want? They want $15,000.
3. What do I have? I have $10,000.
4. What do they have? They have the car.

Does this relationship work? Not with these four questions alone. So we just keep asking them:

1. What else do I want? I want a loan to buy the car.
2. What else do they want? They want more customers.
3. What else do I have? I have several friends who could serve as potential customers.
4. What else do they have? They have an in-house loan company.

Round and round you go until you each come up with a large enough list of haves and wants so that a relationship can be established. Really, it's this simple.

DOLLARS & SENSE
The reason so many people struggle with negotiation is that they focus solely on what they themselves want. First, figure out what you have that the other side wants and how to get it to them. It will then be far easier for them to help you get what you want.

Here are some other great tips to strengthen your negotiation skills.

- *Silence is golden.* One of the best things you can do in a negotiation is to shut up. Allow the other side to negotiate against itself. If they say they want $100, don't say anything. You'll be amazed how quickly they'll say, "Well, how about $75?"
- *Keep prices as consistent as possible.* While I have raised my speaking fee over the years, I try to keep my prices consistent from one customer to another. Maybe I could get client X to

pay $100 more, but what if client X finds out that client Y paid $100 less for the same speech? This will quickly create an angry customer. So, even if your negotiation skills could get you far more money, remember that your business is more than any one deal. If you cut prices for one client and raise them for another, be sure there is a clear justifiable reason for doing this. Maybe client X made a larger order and therefore got the bulk discount. Maybe client X is a repeat client. Whatever the reason for the price break, be sure it is evident, just in case other clients find out.

- *Take notes.* Often in negotiations, the note-taker wins. The note-taker writes down only the stuff that is important to her. When it comes time to review the negotiations, all of the note-taker's wants are accounted for.

- *Research, research, research.* The key to a winning a negotiation is information. What has the other side paid in the past? How many other products are they considering in addition to yours? How badly do they need yours? How soon do they need yours? What else do they need? The more you know about the other side, the better you will do.

- *Negotiate in stages.* Sometimes, if it's not working out, the best thing you can do is take a break. Or maybe the other side makes an offer that you'd like to consider. It's okay to excuse yourself from the room or even to suggest that you resume negotiations tomorrow or next week. These stages allow you to do more research, think over their offer, and ponder what else you could offer them.

- *Take it slow.* When people negotiate, they often jump straight to price. This instantly creates gridlock. Give yourself plenty of time to negotiate. You can also negotiate the small stuff first. Before you talk price, ask about shipping options or payment terms.

- *Don't be afraid to go to the extremes.* Don't worry about upsetting people. If your price is way too high or too low, they'll tell you.

TALES FROM THE FRONT LINES

A few years ago, when I first started my speaking business, a potential customer wanted to know my speaking fee. I had recently raised my fee by almost 30% in one year, and I was a little nervous about my new asking price. I swallowed hard and uttered my new fee. "Oh, that's all?" was the reply. I learned from that day on that it is dangerous (and expensive) to assume you know what your customers can afford.

To sum up, negotiation is an art, not a science. If you follow the suggestions in this chapter, you will have more money. But what to do with that money? Well, that's next.

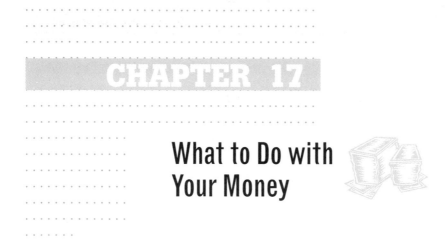

CHAPTER 17

What to Do with Your Money

The whole point of starting a business is to make a profit. If it's not making a profit, then it's a hobby. Or it's a hassle. I hope that this book has given you a pretty good set of tools to ensure that your entrepreneurship efforts are turning a profit. The question now is: What do you do with it? At the end of it all, there are only five things you can do with your money:

1. You can spend it.
2. You can save it.
3. You can donate it.
4. You can invest it back into your own business.
5. You can invest it in someone else's business.

Let's take a look at some of these options.

Spending Your Money

Let's start with the fun one: spending your money! I'm not going to tell you what to buy; it's your money, you earned it, so you should spend it where you want. But I can offer a few tips to make those dollars go a little bit further.

What Do You Want?

Probably the best thing you can do is write down your goals. Writing down your goals is not only a good idea for your business, but also for your personal life. Let's face it. It's hard to save money, even if you are saving it up for something you really want. You might have some money in your pocket and then you walk by a bakery selling warm chocolate chip cookies. They're only $2 each so you buy one. Now that $2 doesn't seem like much compared to the $600 you've saved so far to buy that guitar, but if you were to spend $2 three times a day for a year, you would be losing a lot of money to those impulse purchases.

The best way to fight back is to have a reason not to buy that cup of coffee or that cookie. That reason is your goal. So take a few minutes and write down some of your personal goals. Do you want to buy a car? Take a trip to Europe? Whatever it is, write it down. Keep your goals somewhere where you can see them. They'll remind you of why you're not blowing your money on all those little things: You're holding out for the big stuff.

Shop Around

Okay, so you have your goals. What else can you do to get the most mileage for your money? If you're saving for a big purchase, you should spend a lot of time doing your research. Often it's difficult to determine the best value simply by looking at price. I remember shopping for a computer printer a few years ago. I found one that was $100 cheaper than all the others. On the surface, this clearly looked like the best deal, but I knew I had better do a little more research. Later I discovered that though the printer was much cheaper, the ink cartridges were more expensive. Within the first year, the $100 that I would have saved on the cost of the printer would have been lost in the extra ink costs.

It's always a good idea to check the store prices with the prices online. While Internet shopping almost always adds a shipping cost, often the Web is a warehouse of good deals. Savings can even be found if you comparison-shop among stores. The old advice to shop around was, is, and always will be true in both your personal and business life.

Wait It Out

Prices are always going up and down, so if you can hold out just a bit longer, you can save some serious money. You can even ask the sales-people in the store when they will be having a sale. They will usually tell you. And if they won't, you can guess. After the holidays, everything is on sale. Skis are on sale in July, swimsuits are on sale in December, so plan as far ahead as you can to get those discounts.

Save It

You cannot, however, spend it all. You need to save at least some of your money. Typically, people save for two reasons. Either there is something they want to buy that they cannot afford yet, or they are saving for the all too familiar "rainy day." In other words, they are saving it for an unexpected emergency. Both are good reasons.

If you want to buy something right now, but you don't have the money right now, there are only two things you can do. You can save up for it or you can borrow money to buy it. The trouble with borrowing money is that someone may charge you interest (or your big sister may hassle you about the loan she made until you no longer enjoy that video game you bought with the money). A safer option is to save up for something.

When it comes to saving, I have only two pieces of advice. The first is to work backwards towards your goal. If you want to buy a $1,000 plasma TV within 12 months, you have to save $80 a month, or about $3 a day. When people think in terms of $1,000, they think, *Well, that's a lot of money*. But if they think about $3 a day, that's easy.

The second thing to remember when it comes to saving money is to make sure your money is earning the highest interest rate possible. Yes, you have a personal savings account if you are using my recommended five-account system. But ask your bank if it has a better deal, especially if you know that you won't touch $1,000 or so for a year. Banks reward people who agree not to withdraw their money for a certain period of time, like six months or a year. There's probably a better rate out there than the one you currently have; you just need to snoop around for it.

Donating Your Money

As Steve Mariotti, president of the National Foundation for Teaching Entrepreneurship, says, "doing good is good business." You know that the purpose of a business is to make a profit. Once it makes a profit, then what? Well, some of that money is going to be used to improve your life. However, improving the lives of those around you is not only the right thing to do; it's also good for business.

I'm going to skip over the morality thing. You don't need a book like this to remind you that billions of people in this world need your help, folks less fortunate than you. How much to give and when and to whom is up to you. It's your money, and I can't help you with advice in this area.

I can, however, show you ways to give back to society that will bene-
fit your business. Many people slam this as "selfish giving," but I feel
that the easier it is for entrepreneurs to give, the more they will give.
Below are some tips to maximize your contributions to society while
maximizing your bottom line.

- *Give away your products, not your money.* What happens to
  the cookies you don't sell? What happens to last year's
  T-shirts? You may have a ton of stuff that your business can't
  use but someone else would be thrilled to have. Find a charity
  that could use your products or unsold inventory. For
  instance, if you bake cookies, contact your local soup
  kitchens. They may be able to use any extra ones. Another
  advantage of giving away your product can be seen when you
  look at its COGS versus its price. Suppose a local homeless
  shelter badly needed blankets. You could donate $200 in cash
  so the shelter could buy maybe twenty blankets. The donation
  would obviously cost you $200. But if you are in the blanket-
  making business, it may only cost you $5 to make a blanket.
  Donating 20 of your product costs you $100. The shelter still
  gets the same number of blankets, but you save a lot of
  money! Dollars can go farther when products are donated.
- *Create a press release around your donation.* Often, people
  are shy about donating. Or they feel they are being chintzy by
  making a donation and then announcing it. But billion-dollar
  corporations do this all the time, because the donation comes
  back to them in the form of greater profits. And the greater
  the profits, the more they can donate! Don't be afraid to send
  out a press release announcing your donation! You may motivate others to give!
- *Tie your donation to your product sales.* You've seen this
  one before. "10% of our profits go to _____."
  You can do the same thing. By announcing that you will
  give a percentage of your business's profits to a certain
  charity, not only will you attract customers who are loyal
  to the product, but you will also attract customers who
  are loyal to the charity.
- *Ask the charity for help.* Maybe the charity has a monthly
  newsletter that goes out to 25,000 people. Will they mention
  your donation in the next newsletter? This can be a great way
  to get free advertising while donating to a worthwhile cause.

- *Make your entire business the charity.* Why not? One thing to remember about nonprofit companies is that you can still make money by paying yourself a set salary. If, after you pay yourself a salary and pay all your other expenses, your business still makes a profit, you simply must put all the profits back into the business or donate them, because you're a nonprofit company. Becoming a nonprofit can be an interesting option. Instead of giving some of your business's profits to charity, make charity your business!

TALES FROM THE FRONT LINES

Twelve-year-old Shennendoah Hollsten and her nine-year-old brother Bo Erik started a nonprofit corporation called NeuroKids. They raise money to educate kids about the human brain. They even designed a program called "Week of the Brain," which is a week-long (duh!) program that teachers use to teach about the human brain. Check them out at *www.neurokids.org.*

One final thought on the subject of donating money. Don't ask me how this works, but I believe money is always flowing. As we see money flow into our business, we are tempted to grab it and hold onto it as tightly as we can. We're worried it may one day stop flowing. While I do believe money stops flowing, I believe that happens to people who try to hoard it all. Letting money flow through your fingers to those who need it will bring in far more money down the road.

Investing Your Money

Many people lump *saving* and **investing** under the same definition, but these terms are significantly different. Remember, saving is only done for one of two reasons: to prepare against an emergency or to have enough money to make a purchase down the road.

Investing is the practice of risking your money in hopes that it will grow to a larger sum. The key word here is **risk**. When you save money, you put it in a super-safe place where it will never go down in value. If there is a chance that it will go down in value, that's not saving—that's investing.

So why invest then if there is a risk? Simple. There is a much larger reward. If you were to save money in a bank account, indeed the bank would pay you some interest, maybe around 3% per year. While that's not a great return, at least your money is not at risk.

But were you to invest that money in something like the **stock market**, you might be able to get a return of 12%, or four times what the bank would give you. However, there is a risk that your money will go down in value, maybe even to zero. So there is a relationship between risk and **reward**. Risk is defined as the probability that you will lose your money. Reward is the return you get for taking a risk.

DOLLARS & SENSE

The higher the risk, the higher the reward should be.

Compound Interest

The benefits of a higher reward become evident when you consider **compound interest**. Albert Einstein called compound interest "the eighth wonder of the world." Compound interest is interest that builds up both your principal and your interest. You know that when you borrow money, you pay interest. And you know that your principal is the original loan amount. If an investment pays **simple interest**, it pays interest only on the principal. If I loan out $1,000 at 10% simple interest per year, I get back $100 a year in interest plus a portion of the principal, until it is all paid back.

With a compound interest investment like the stock market, interest keeps piling on top of interest. The stock market has a 70-year average return of around 12%. Some years, it could return 30%; other years, it could *lose* 5% or more. But the overall average seems to be around 12% per year. So if, 70 years ago, I had invested $1,000 in the stock market, the first year it would have been worth $1,120 because

$$\$1,000 \times 12\% = \$120$$

$$\text{and } \$1,000 + \$120 = \$1,120$$

The second year, however, the 12% would have multiplied not only on the original $1,000, but on what my investment had grown to in the prior year. My investment would have been worth $1,254, because:

$$\$1,120 \times 12\% = \$134$$

$$\text{and } \$1,120 + \$134 = \$1254$$

Had I left my money in the stock market for all 70 years, I would have made $2.7 million, just from a $1,000 original investment.

A word of caution here: In shorter periods, the stock market does go up and down. Although the long-term trend is up, there are times when the market will be down, sometimes way down for a long time. But smart investors know they have not invested in the stock market to make a quick buck. They are in it for the long haul. You should be too. Watching the market fluctuations every day is the quickest way to a headache that I know of. While you are working hard on your business, you want your money to work for you. You do that by investing it some-place where you can get a compounded return. There are two basic places that entrepreneurs invest to get that kind of return:

1. Back into their own business.
2. Into someone else's business (via the stock market).

Selecting the Right Investment

If those are the two most common places to put your money, the question is, Which one do you choose?

Investment selection is based on two primary factors: ***diversification*** and ***return on investment (ROI)***. Let's start with diversification.

Diversification

Diversification is the act of spreading your money out over several different investments to protect yourself from risk. Imagine that I buy five investments, each for $100. One of them drops to zero, and I lose everything. Three of them drop by 20%. The last one triples in value.

At first glance, I don't look like a very intelligent investor. Four of my investments lost money, and one of those lost everything. But I'm still ahead because I had one great investment. The losers can go only so low, but the winners have no ceiling. This is why diversification is so important. It's next to impossible to tell in advance exactly which investments will do well, so to protect ourselves, we diversify.

DOLLARS & SENSE
When you buy any investment, you can lose only what you put in—but most investments have no limit as to how much you can make.

There are several ways to diversify, but I like to focus on six criteria to consider. These six criteria can be used to evaluate any investment, whether it's a $500 stake in your friend's lemonade stand or stock in Walmart. Before you buy an investment, you should ask these six questions:

1. *Risk.* What are the odds I'll lose money?
2. *Reward.* How much money am I likely to make?
3. *Control.* Do I have any say in what goes on? If you buy stock in Coca-Cola, you can't participate in the day-to day management of the company. If you own your own business, then YOU get to decide when to work, when to hire new people, and when to discontinue unpopular products. Much of the control is yours.
4. *Minimum investment and cost of investment.* How much does this investment cost? Do I pay any fees to own this investment? Do I pay any transaction fees to buy it? What do I have to pay in taxes? Taxes and fees cut into your profits. Also, the amount of money you need to put up to buy the investment affects its attractiveness. Real estate is a great investment, but its major downside is that you often have to put up a lot of money to buy it.
5. *Liquidity.* Can I get my money quickly, if I need it? Your bank account is an investment that is very liquid. You can get your cash at any time. Your business is an investment that is not very liquid; it can take months to sell a business and get your cash. Liquidity makes an investment attractive.
6. *Method of repayment.* How and when will I get my money back? Will I get it in stages over time or all at once at the end when I sell it? The sooner I get back my money, the better, because that means I can put it somewhere else. If I have to wait months or even years, that is a downside.

Unfortunately, there is no investment that scores high on all six criteria. You always have to give up something. An investment that pays a high reward usually has a high level of risk. An investment like your bank account is very liquid and very safe, but we all know bank accounts don't pay much in interest. There is always a tradeoff.

The six criteria point to areas where you can diversify. Some of your money needs to be liquid so you can get it for emergencies (or for that last-minute gift you have to buy for your friend's party). But liquid money doesn't pay much in the way of reward, so some of your money is going to be illiquid (meaning that you can't convert it to cash quickly), in exchange for a higher return. Some investments, like your own business, will require a lot of your time, because you are in control. You don't have time to control everything, so you want to invest in other companies in which you don't have to worry about day-to-day decisions.

Return on Investment

The next tool that investors use to select investments is a formula called return on investment (ROI). ROI measures how much money you will likely get back, compared to how much money you put in. While people can use it to evaluate stocks and real estate, it is actually most helpful to small business owners.

Imagine that you run a lemonade stand where you make lemonade out of fresh lemons. You cut and squeeze all the lemons by hand. During peak hours of your business, the line gets to be so long that you have to hire a student just to cut and squeeze the lemons, while you work the cash register. You pay that student $10 an hour for 6 hours per week. Over the course of a year, this person costs you $3,000, or 50 weeks at $60 per week.

Then one day you are reading a magazine and see an ad for an automatic lemon slicer/squeezer. It costs $1,000. If you were to buy it, you would no longer have to hire an assistant. The ROI calculation would tell you if it is worth it. Here is the calculation.

The machine would "earn" you $3,000 a year (the amount you would have spent on your assistant). It costs $1,000 to buy. So your profit on the machine in one year would be $2,000. To calculate ROI, just divide profit by the cost of the investment:

$$\$2,000 / \$1,000 = 2$$

Because ROI is always expressed as a percentage, multiply that number by 100. In this case, the lemon slicer/squeezer had an impressive ROI of 200%. Time to buy the lemon machine!

Suppose, however, the slicer/squeezer cost $2,500? What would the ROI be then?

$$\$3,000 - \$2,500 = \$500$$

$$\$500/\$2,500 = .20$$

$$20 \times 100\% = 20\%$$

An ROI of 20% is still a pretty good return, especially considering that the slicer will be fully paid for after the first year. Everything after that first year is pure profit. Obviously, the higher the ROI is, the more attractive the investment. But one problem with the ROI is that it doesn't calculate risk, and it doesn't talk about method of repayment. Suppose I told you the average lemon slicer/squeezer breaks down 50% of the time it's under operation? That makes calculations a lot more difficult. Or suppose the company had a year-long waiting list for the slicer and required 100% of the money to be paid up front? You would have to shell out $1,000 this year, but you wouldn't get a dime of it back until next year.

Still, ROI can be a great tool for entrepreneurs, especially since so many of our "investments" include concrete tools to make our businesses more efficient, tools like faster printers, electronic instruments, and software programs that have tested track records of how well they perform. The hard data on these tools make it fairly easy to calculate an accurate ROI.

So if your business is considering buying that Fry O-Lator, that high-speed printer, or even hiring that independent contractor, do a quick ROI calculation to see if it makes sense to shell out the extra cash.

While ROI is a great calculation to determine whether it is worth putting profits back into your business, never forget the first rule about doing this: Don't put 100% of your profits back into your business! Many entrepreneurs are tempted to do this. Their thought is, *Hey, my business is making a lot of money, so if I put more money in, I can make even more money!* While this may be true, there are times when your business will lose money. When those times come around, you'll be thankful you had some money in your savings and investments. You'll be glad you followed the first rule: Diversify.

So that's investing in your own business. But what about stocks? Turn the page to find out.

CHAPTER 18

Taking Stock

The law of diversification warns you not to put all your eggs in one basket. You already have some money invested in your own business, so how do you diversify outside of that? The good news is that you can invest in other businesses through the stock market.

How the Stock Market Works

The **stock market** is a market just like any other market, such as the supermarket or the flea market—it's a place where things are bought and sold. But in the stock market, we are not buying tomatoes or old comic books, we're buying and selling **shares** (or pieces) of companies. These shares of companies are often referred to as "stocks."

The entire impetus of the stock market is based on one simple fact: New companies always need to raise money. Believe it or not, that's all there is to it. Imagine that you owned a small company that specialized in drive-thru psychotherapy called Drivin' Me Crazy. Your business is chugging along, but you really could make some serious money if you opened ten drive-thru psychotherapy centers all over the country.

The trouble is that each drive-thru center costs $1 million to build. Where are you going to get $10 million? You know from Chapter 7 that businesses get their money through either owners or loaners. You also know that most start-ups can't borrow money because banks won't loan money to companies that have not established themselves. The old adage is true: A bank is a place that will loan you money as soon as you can prove you don't need it.

Most start-ups raise money by selling pieces of the business to owners. Investors buy those shares at $10 a whack in hopes that once you built the drive-thrus, your business would grow and those shares they bought will be worth a lot more.

Now, selling a $500 stake in your lemonade stand to your mom is one thing, but how the heck are you supposed to sell a million 10-dollar shares? Chances are you don't know enough people to sell the shares to. So you would go to someone who does, namely an ***investment bank***. Investment banks help companies raise money. The investment bank would sell the shares for you in what is known as an ***initial public offering*** or IPO. The bank charges a small fee per share to do this. After the IPO, investors own part of your company, the investment bank has made a profit by selling the shares for you, and you now have your $10 million to build your drive-thrus.

So where does the stock market fit in? Well, the investors who bought those shares need someplace to sell them. So they go to the stock market. After an IPO, your company is now ***public***, which means anyone can buy the shares. The stock market simply provides an easy arena for investors to unload or load up on shares.

The prices of shares in the stock market are set solely by investor demand. If everyone wants to buy shares in your company, your stock price will rise. If everyone is trying to sell your company shares, the stock price will go down. People buy and sell based on two emotions: fear and greed. These emotions spawn from their research into the company. For instance, if my publicly traded music label/fruit importing company Busta Limes finds itself in a major lawsuit tomorrow, investors might cram to sell their shares in Busta Limes because they are afraid the lawsuit will make the stock go down. Likewise, investors may scurry to get shares of another company that makes clothes for the sophisticated Ninja, after hearing that the Ninja look is coming back. (I am assuming, of course, that the look was actually once "in.") On any given day, some stocks rise in value, and some fall in value.

Of the thousands of companies traded in the stock market, how do you know which ones to buy? It is quite difficult to pick the handful of companies that will outperform all the others. Amateurs and professionals alike share in successes and failures. Fortunately, there is a solution. You can buy them all.

We're All in It Together: Mutual Funds

Imagine you had $500 to invest in the stock market. That $500 can't really get you much diversification. The financial industry quickly realized this, and they created a way for modest investors to diversify with little money. They created *mutual funds*.

A mutual fund is a money pool formed by a group of investors and headed by one manager. Thousands of investors throw their money into the fund, and the manager decides which stocks to buy. The investors don't own the stocks themselves; rather, they own shares in the fund. With thousands of investors pooling together thousands of dollars, these funds become quite large. It's not at all uncommon to see a fund valued at $1 billion or more. Because the fund's manager has access to such huge sums of money, she can buy shares in hundreds of different companies. This means great diversification. By the way, the manager does charge a fee to manage this money. (You didn't think she did this for free, did you?) This fee is an annual fee based on the amount of money in the fund. A manager may take a fee of, say, 1% of the money in the fund every year. So if the fund has $100 million in it, the manager's annual fee is $1 million, which pays for her research staff, office expenses, and the like.

There is one specific type of mutual fund that does not have a manager. It is called an *index mutual fund*. Instead of a living, breathing human being picking the stocks, stocks are selected based on a computer program. Because there is no manager, index mutual funds charge a much lower expense fee (something like less than 0.6%).

DOLLARS & SENSE

One of the six criteria for evaluating an investment is cost. Fees cut into your profits.

What's more, with index mutual funds, there really isn't much selection at all. The computer just buys every stock on the market. Index mutual funds take all the guesswork out of investing in the stock market. When you buy an index mutual fund, you buy everything: there is super diversification.

I'm not here to say this is the greatest investment of all time, but it is a great investment for all. People always ask me whether they should invest in real estate, or biotech companies, or whatever. The truth is, it depends on you. I know nothing about biotech, so I stay away from it. However, I do feel I have some advantages in real estate, so that is something I do invest in. Do what works for you, and if you're not sure, then just buy everything using an index mutual fund.

Duck Those Taxes with a Roth IRA

Now you know how the stock market works. The final thing to learn is how you are going to own the investment. When it comes to investing, it's not just what you own but how you own it.

If tomorrow you were to purchase shares in a mutual fund, then 100% of all profits you made off that mutual fund would be taxable. (Yep, they tax mutual funds too.) Wouldn't it be nice if you could keep those extra dollars instead of giving them to the IRS? You can if you buy your mutual fund shares inside a *Roth IRA*.

An *IRA* is an Individual Retirement Arrangement. The word *Roth* comes from the name of the United States senator who proposed the idea, William Roth. (By the way, if you're reading this, thanks, Bill.) The purpose of the Roth IRA is to encourage people to save for their retirement. The enticement is that any investments inside a Roth IRA are exempt from taxes.

Picture the Roth IRA like a suitcase. In it, you can put investments like your index mutual funds. Whatever is inside that suitcase is protected from taxes. So, in order to protect our index mutual fund from taxes, we're going to buy the shares of that fund inside the Roth suitcase.

Doing this is easy. You simply open up a Roth IRA account at any major investment firm, such as Charles Schwab, Fidelity, T. Rowe Price, Vanguard, or E*TRADE. The IRS doesn't care if you are eighteen when you open the Roth IRA; you just need earned income. (In other words, your parents can't give you the money.) However, most brokerage companies will require the parents to step in once you start buying investments inside the Roth. So it's best to get Mom and Dad on board with this from Day One. (Trust me, though, they will be on board with it. A good time to talk to your parents about this is right after you get a speeding ticket.) When you open the Roth IRA, you have to deposit cash into it. Once the cash is inside the Roth, it is protected from taxes. You now use that cash to buy investments that are also exempt from taxes. Easy.

There is only one catch to the Roth. Any profits you make must remain in the account until you reach age 59½. I know what you're thinking, but it isn't as bad as it sounds. Although your *profits* have to stay in the Roth, your *contributions* can come out at any time.

Imagine you invest $500 into a Roth IRA and within a year your investment swells to $550, a 10% return. Now, let's say the gang's having a road trip, and you want in. If you wanted to take cash from your Roth IRA, you could, but only $500, because your earnings (the $50) must remain in there until you turn age 59½; otherwise, the government takes a HUGE chunk of it as a penalty. But remember, if you didn't have this money in the Roth, you'd lose it anyway to taxes.

So you're buying stocks via an index mutual fund, inside a Roth IRA, using dollar-cost averaging. Not so hard, right? The final decision is: Which company do you choose to handle your investments? Some companies will let you open a Roth with as little as $500. Some firms require a lot more. If you have more money (like $1,000), you probably can find more firms. Nearly all firms will let you get started with $2,000.

I suggest asking your bank or credit union if it can help. I like the idea of having all your money in one place because then it is easy to manage. Also, ask your family whom they use, and look around online. This will help you double-check your bank's fees. The point is not so much which company (as you can always switch at any time) but a company. Getting started is half the battle.

PART THREE

TIPS FOR PARENTS AND TEACHERS

Time to hand this book off to your teacher or Mom and Dad. I mean, you can read these chapters too, if you want. Actually, it couldn't hurt to read what your parents and teachers are reading, because then it will be easier to a) get extra credit in school or b) get money for start-up costs. But even if you don't want to take the time, insist that Mom and Dad check out these next chapters. Then flip to Part Four of this book, 101 Businesses You Can Start, on page 157. *Parents and teachers:* In this part of the book there are a few chapters to help you help the new entrepreneurs in your life. Please take time to read them. They can save you a lot of sleep.

CHAPTER 19

Running the Bank of Mom and Dad

Two factors that have tremendous influence in the success of young entrepreneurs are the support of their parents and the support of their teachers. I came from entrepreneurial parents, so the spirit of working for yourself was touted as long as I can remember. At times, when I pondered getting a "real job," I was actually discouraged by my folks. My father ran the numbers with me, proving that if I got just two more landscaping clients, I could earn in a day what would take me an entire week to earn at a movie theater. For me, the choice was always easy.

Here's What to Do, Mom and Dad

For some parents, the idea of entrepreneurship doesn't come so naturally. This is especially true if you are not an entrepreneur yourself, or if you once tossed your hat into that ring and it didn't work out so well. Whatever your past, for the sake of your children's future, I urge you to fuel whatever entrepreneurial sparks you may see. If you don't see any sparks, I urge you to ignite them. If that's tough for you to swallow, consider the four points discussed below.

1. YOUR CHILD WILL VERY LIKELY MAKE MORE MONEY AS AN ENTREPRENEUR THAN HE OR SHE WOULD AT A PART-TIME JOB. Remember, employees earn, pay taxes, and then spend. Entrepreneurs earn, spend, and then pay taxes. So $10 an hour to an entrepreneur is often worth more than $10 an hour to an employee. What's more, most jobs for students have a salary ceiling. Whether they switch from Walmart to Lowe's, to

McDonald's, or to Applebee's, it is unlikely that young people will be able to find a job for more than $15 an hour. To a young entrepreneur, $15 an hour might be closer to the salary floor than to the salary ceiling.

2. RUNNING A BUSINESS IS AN EDUCATIONAL EXPERIENCE IN WHICH TEENS ARE FORCED TO LEARN NEW SKILLS. Accounting and bookkeeping are the obvious ones, but your children will also learn how to sell, edit, and market. They will develop communication, organization, and budgeting skills. Often kids who can barely stay awake in school can't get to sleep at night because they are looking over their income statements or rereading their latest newsletter before it goes out. If you've tried everything to motivate your child, but have had little success, suggest that she start her own business.

3. COLLEGES, GRADUATE SCHOOLS, AND EMPLOYERS VALUE ENTREPRENEURSHIP. Even if your child isn't going to business school, running a business is an extracurricular activity that colleges will look upon favorably. If you're worried the business will chew up a lot of precious résumé-building time, don't be. The business *is* résumé-building time.

4. IN THIS NEW GLOBAL ECONOMY, ENTREPRENEURSHIP MAY ACTUALLY BE THE SAFEST CHOICE. It's no longer just the manufacturing jobs that are being outsourced. *No one* is safe, save for the entrepreneurs. Until now, starting your own business was viewed as the risky option in comparison to working for a large company. While we're not there yet, we are getting very close to a time when the opposite might be true. Let's face it, you could be a stellar employee whom everyone—be it customer or co-worker—loves; your job is *still* in danger if someone in Bangalore can do it reasonably well and for one-quarter of your salary. (Although don't feel so bad. The Bangalore guy is worried that someone in Bangladesh can do it for one-quarter of *his* salary.)

So I hope I've convinced you to fuel or ignite the entrepreneurial flame. The question now is: How do you do that? There are several ways parents can jump in to help.

- *If you are an entrepreneur, show your child your business.* Even though I grew up in an entrepreneurial world, it was years before I learned how my father's business worked. As soon as you can, invite your child to join you for a day in the life of you. Explain why you run your business the way you do. Tell him about the obstacles you face, and ask him to come up with solutions. Ask his opinion about your Web site and your newest marketing materials.

- *If you're not an entrepreneur yourself, introduce your child to one of your friends who is.* In *Rich Dad, Poor Dad*, bestselling author Robert Kiyosaki's "poor" dad was smart enough to realize that he couldn't help with his son's entrepreneurial dreams. However, he knew someone who could (the "rich dad" in the books). Kiyosaki's father suggested that he and his friend Mike meet with Mike's dad to learn about running a business. That seems to have worked well for Kiyosaki.

- *When it's time for a part-time job, suggest entrepreneurship.* Depending on a student's other commitments—sports, theater, community service—she might not get a part-time job for some time. I've even run across students who've never had a part-time job. After graduation, their first full-time job is also their first job. Whatever the case for your child, when the job search starts, if entrepreneurship doesn't pop into her head automatically, it needs to be you who suggests it.

- *Promote education as an investment.* The one danger of childhood entrepreneurship is that it will cut into grades. As a parent, it is tough to argue back. "Study hard so you can get into a good college, then get a good job and earn a lot of money," you say. "But Mom," your child will reply, "I already have a job that earns me a lot of money." He may even pelt you with tales of Internet millionaires who dropped out of college to focus full-time on their businesses. (Bill Gates, by the way, will be his most powerful argument.) Instead of giving the standard spiel on grades, tell your child that his education is an investment, just like his investment in his business or in his mutual funds. If this doesn't work, you can put good grades on the deal-making table. If your child wants to keep using the garage to store products for free, he needs to hit the books. Or, if he is seeking family financing for the first time, make the loan interest-free as long as your child maintains a 3.0 average.

- *Bankroll your child using realistic and fair terms.* One of the biggest hurdles for any business start-up is getting the start-up funds. The overwhelming majority of small businesses are financed with some combination of self-financing and financing from family and friends. If your child's biggest roadblock is the money, chip in. It's fair and proper for you to create realistic terms that are equitable to both you and your child. In other words, feel free to charge your child an interest rate or require that all money be paid back in five years, or even that you are entitled to a portion of the profits. The Body Shop, the search engine Excite, Mrs. Fields Cookies, and thousands of other businesses were funded by family investors. It's best to get this agreement in writing and hold to it, even if your kid's business bombs. Offer a way for him to repay you, even if he can't do that out of business revenue; perhaps through larger household chores. Make the loan or the ***venture capital*** (money available for investing in a new business) subject to certain tasks and benchmarks. Maybe your young entrepreneur has to prepare a complete financial statement (income statement, cash-flow projections, and a balance sheet) before he can get the money. It's your money; you set the terms.

- ***If you can't be an investor, be a cosigner.*** If your entrepreneur is under the age of eighteen, she will run into many problems because of her age. Technically, a minor cannot own any property (stocks, etc.) and cannot borrow any money. If she runs a landscaping business, she probably won't be able to rent a lawn mower unless you cosign. So if you're short on cash, you can contribute in a big way by offering to be the over-eighteen partner.

- ***Introduce your child to good candidates for his advisory board.*** Most professionals are busy people, and they might not respond to a cold call from your child. But you might be able to make the introduction that your child needs. If no one comes to mind, ask your child who he would love to have on his ideal advisory board and help to find that person.

- ***Constantly ask how you can help them.*** In many areas of your children's life (dating, to name just one), they want you to stay out. But if they run their own business, they might actually approach you, asking for help. Give all that you can; if it's outside your area of expertise, introduce your children to someone who can help.

Running a business at a young age can give your child a sense of confidence, maturity, motivation, and responsibility that's tough to re-create anywhere else. Entrepreneurs learn and adapt fast because they have to. They won't pick up a book and learn about accounting because someone tells them to; they do it because they know if they procrastinate one more day, they'll be out of business. This is the effort level that parents dream of, and entrepreneurship can deliver it.

CHAPTER 20

Teaching the Business Leaders of Tomorrow

Steve Mariotti, the founder of the National Foundation for Teaching Entrepreneurship, began his teaching career as a math teacher in an inner city school. Frustrated as a first-time teacher in a classroom environment where kids were used to goofing off, Mariotti began searching for ways to make his classes interesting to students. He looked back on his past math lessons and recalled that kids were most interested when he used real-life examples of how businesses worked. He increased his entrepreneurship lessons and found that classroom interest and attendance increased right along with them. His classes became so successful that he started the foundation, which has taught entrepreneurship to more than 60,000 students.

Perhaps what's most interesting is that Mariotti realized that the lessons learned reached far beyond math and economics. He watched racial tensions ease when students learned that a minority business in their neighborhood was making only 5 cents of profit for every dollar that came in, as opposed to the 95 cents of profit the students thought that the business was making. Until Mariotti's lesson, students believed that the business owner was fleecing the neighborhood with his prices. Mariotti proved to them that the business owner was barely staying afloat and, almost overnight, the animosity toward the owner dwindled. He watched quiet students begin to become pros at the sales pitch. He saw self-proclaimed math haters prepare a business ledger. And it was all because students had learned something that they could immediately apply to their lives.

If you are a teacher reading this, no doubt you have heard this classic complaint, "When are we ever going to need to know this?" The classic teacher response has always been, "You need to know it if you want to graduate." While this is true, you've probably spent some time trying to come up with a better answer. Entrepreneurship might be that answer.

When I do presentations for educators, I often hear them complain that their subject doesn't allow for entrepreneurship. But with a little creative thinking, entrepreneurship can be brought into almost any subject. Most teachers think entrepreneurship is appealing to students because it teaches them how to make money. I think that's only half of it. Entrepreneurship is appealing because it can very quickly be applied to students' everyday lives. It's this immediacy that can help make all of your lessons more interesting. Here are some tips to incorporating entrepreneurship into the classroom:

- *Make problems real-world.* A math word problem aimed at teaching percentage calculations might be about arbitrary situations, like "Susie wants to give 30% of her cake to Jill and 20% of her cake to Timmy." Although these problems teach about percentages, they don't do much else. It would be better to make these problems about something like taxes, which will not only teach kids about the math at hand, but will also introduce a valuable business concept.

- *Take the entrepreneurship option.* If you're an English teacher who is teaching students how to do research using a book's index, you can teach them using any book that has an index. Why not have them use the index in Publication 17 to look up a few IRS regulations? During tax time, you can get as many free copies of Pub. 17 as you need from your post office or library. Or your students can search online at *www.irs.gov.* Which questions do you use? Look at your own tax return! You'll have a room full of tenth-grade accountants doing your work for you, while learning about research and personal finance.

- *Find some amazing financial facts.* The world of commerce has a stunning history. Did you know that in 1932, during the Great Depression, people bought U.S. Treasury Bills, knowing that they paid a *negative* interest rate? People were so desperate for something safe, they accepted the guaranteed small loss over a potentially unknown larger loss. Did you know that one of the most successful start-ups in the 1980s, ZZZZ

Best (pronounced ZEEE Best!) Carpet Cleaning Service, was "cleaning" money for the Mafia? Keep in mind that the birth of this country began over a dispute about taxes. Whether the subject is history, English, science, or math, there is room for a financial education, even if it is stuck in covertly.

- *Offer your class's assistance to a real-world entrepreneur.* Many college classes do this, but high schools can too. Most small, cash-starved start-ups would be glad to have an army of 20 student assistants working for free to help solve their business's problems. While businesses will be hesitant to share some data (for example, their COGS), your students could help by conducting a survey, designing new marketing materials, editing existing marketing materials, or even acting as a young-person focus group. How happy will your students be when the entrepreneur actually takes their advice? They'll be able to say, "Hey, I gave him that idea!"
- *Get some help.* If you're still stuck, check out the Web site *www.adoptan-author.com.* This free program helps teachers get students excited about reading and learning by having the actual author of the book assist in classroom activities. I just happen to be one of the authors, and the Web site has a complete curriculum for this book.

According to a recent survey by the student peer-to-peer lending company Duck9, financial problems are now the number-one reason for college dropout. Students are prepared to learn in college; they just aren't prepared to pay for college. Every teacher can chip in to help, not by adding more business lessons to the curriculum, but by making little tweaks to existing curriculums so they have more of a business focus.

CHAPTER 21

Keeping Them Safe

If your child or student is starting a business, safety might actually be the last thing on his mind. Most budding entrepreneurs (regardless of their age) are willing to take money from just about anyone who will to give it to them. The desire to keep the cash flowing might blind some young entrepreneurs to making the right choice. While the customer is always right, not every customer is right for your business.

Fortunately, keeping a business safe couldn't be easier. All one really needs to do is follow three simple steps:

- Choose a safe business.
- Conduct safe practices with customers.
- Conduct safe practices with your accounts.

Let's examine how your child or student can effectively accomplish each of these goals.

Choosing a Safe Business

If your young entrepreneur followed the Five *S* Formula, we can hope that she is starting a safe business. As tempting as a paintball camp may be, the insurance risks are probably too high. As a parent or teacher, be sure to ask your child exactly what the business does, because sometimes seemingly safe businesses can have some dangerous requirements. House painting might be a good example. There's little harm in swinging a brush, but consider that for two-thirds of the house paint-ing, people are up on ladders.

It's a good idea, for reasons well beyond safety, that entrepreneurs write down all the tasks they are likely to perform in running the busi-ness, from typing sales letters to climbing ladders. As their unpaid safety consultant, you should review the list and identify ways that risky jobs can be made safer, outsourced to someone else, or scrapped altogether.

If you are a parent, I don't need to tell you that sometimes your kids won't listen to you. That's why it can help to have a family friend who is a lawyer go over the business plan with your child. Or, perhaps you know an entrepreneur who is in the very business your child wants to start. It's one thing for Mom to say, "Honey, I don't like the idea of you climbing those ladders." But, it's far more powerful for a successful painting contractor to say, "My insurance is $5,000 a year."

If your child is insistent upon starting a reasonable but potentially dangerous business like house painting, it's well worth the investment to set up a limited liability company. If your child can't or won't spring for it, then I have just given you a suggestion for the perfect birthday gift. Most teen entrepreneurs start as *sole proprietorships*, which means that they personally are legally responsible for everything the business does. However, if your teen is under eighteen, that means *you* are now legally responsible for everything your teen's business does. For about $500, you can sidestep all of this by forming a limited liability company or LLC. Under an LLC, customers can't sue you or your child; they must sue the LLC. If the customer wins, you don't pay—the LLC pays. If you're worried about your child running a sole proprietorship, $500 to set up an LLC could preserve more sleep than a $2,000 mattress.

Conduct Safe Practices with Customers

Many businesses, big and small, make the colossal blunder of trying to attract as many customers as possible, without ever realizing that not all customers are worth having. Some customers cost a company far more money than they bring in, and for young entrepreneurs, some cus-tomers can be outright dangerous. Here are a few tips to make sure your child or student deals safely with customers:

- *Use a buddy system for meeting new customers.* If your young entrepreneur is meeting a new customer, ask that he take a buddy along. Perhaps that buddy is you. If the customer is someone he doesn't know, don't let him go alone.

- *Don't make house calls; instead, set up meetings in a public place.* You probably don't have the time to accompany your child or all your students to every initial meeting they have with customers. So, in addition to the buddy system, suggest that all meetings with potential customers be conducted in a public place.

- *Have your child check out and check in with you.* Perhaps after a few meetings with a new customer, you feel comfortable with your child going to that customer's house. Even then, it's still a good idea for her to check in with you. The customer could be the next Mother Theresa, but things can still go wrong. So ask for updates.

- *Invest in a cell phone.* I'm going to take your kid's side on this one. I know he has been asking forever, but if there was ever a good reason to get your kid a cell phone, this is it.

- *Have a code word.* When I used to sell real estate, I would have to meet clients in their homes at night all the time. My office had a code sentence in case those situations ever proved dangerous. If I called the office and said, "Can you look up something in the red file for me?" that meant, "Something is wrong, call the police." Make up a code word or sentence with your child in case she needs to call you without being able to explain exactly what is going on.

- *Ask the teen to write down a safety policy.* Maybe your daughter has a babysitting business, and your policy is that you accompany her to meet all her new clients before she agrees to a deal. But then the phone rings with a last-minute request by someone who is willing to pay double if your daughter can help out that night. She desperately wants the money, but you're concerned about safety. Your argument is a lot stronger if you can refer to the written safety policy.

Conduct Safe Practices with Your Accounts

Statistically, your child is most likely to become a victim of identity theft. While this crime rarely leads to physical danger, it can shut down a business in a matter of days. This can be a difficult defeat for a young entrepreneur. Fortunately, it is one of the easiest crimes to protect against. Here's what you can do:

- *Be sure your young entrepreneurs review their bank and credit card statements every month.* They should be doing this anyway, but be sure they are on top of it every month. The whole key to identity theft is catching it quickly.
- *Consider getting a locking mailbox.* It's a misconception that most identity theft crimes happen over the Internet. You're most vulnerable through the mail. Suggest that your child get a mailbox at the post office and have all her business mail sent there. (And, here's a tip: Don't have her put "P.O. Box 613" as part of her business address. Instead, use "Suite 613." Mail will still get delivered, and it makes the business look a little bigger than it really is.)
- *Have your young entrepreneurs check their credit report at www.annualcreditreport.com.* In most cases, you're not supposed to have a credit report unless you are over the age of 18. But mistakes can happen, which means anyone can have a credit report by mistake. You can check your credit reports (and you have three of them) once per year, for free on this Web site.

Sometimes the fear of lawsuits and potential dangers can make a parent or teacher want to scrap the whole idea of encouraging entrepreneurship altogether. However, that may be the most dangerous move of them all—to rob a would-be entrepreneur of one of the most rewarding experiences there is. By following the steps in this chapter, you will drastically reduce your young entrepreneur's chances of becoming derailed due to a safety issue.

PART FOUR

101 BUSINESSES YOU CAN START

If you've read this far and you still can't decide what business to start, then help has arrived! Here are more than 100 ideas to inspire you. One thing to keep in mind about these businesses: While nearly all of them meet the Five S Formula and some can be started for literally nothing, there are always those hidden costs. In many of the businesses, I recommend you print up flyers for advertising. I also recommend that your business develop a Web site. These costs, however, are not accounted for in the Cost to Start section, simply because you can get started without them. You can add these items later when you have some cash coming in.

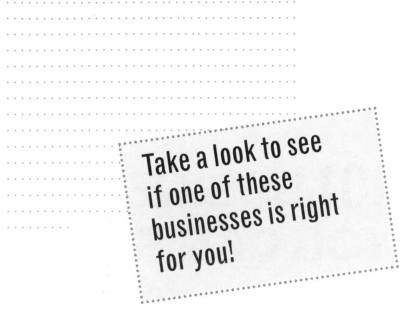

Take a look to see if one of these businesses is right for you!

1. ASTROLOGER/TAROT CARD READER

WHAT IS IT? People will pay good money to have their fortunes read. There are several ways you can do this. You can send out weekly horoscopes to clients that subscribe. Or you can set up a booth at a county fair, flea market, or even on the sidewalk and do astrology charts or read fortunes using tarot cards.

WHAT YOU NEED TO START:
- Books on astrology (under $50)
- Optional course in astrology (under $200)

Cost to Start: Under $50
Time to Get Started: Under ten hours
Skills Needed: Reading and writing, interest in New Age subject matter
Potential Customers: Anyone, but flea markets, country fairs, and parents with children are great places and people to start with.

HOW TO GET STARTED:
1. Research different astrology techniques. Learn how to map out the stars in order to divine the future. Practice coming up with weekly horoscopes for each sign.
2. Set a price for people to subscribe to a weekly horoscope. You can call or e-mail them to notify them of their horoscope each week.
3. Also inquire about the costs of county fairs and local flea markets.
4. Post flyers around your neighborhood and in local stores and schools.

For More Information: *www.astrology.com*

2. BABYSITTER

WHAT IS IT? As you can guess, this business involves taking care of children when parents have no one else to watch them. It could also include a standing appointment to pick the children up after school and watch them for a few hours until the parents get home.

WHAT YOU NEED TO START:
- No materials
- CPR course ($50; optional but highly recommended)

Cost to Start: $0
Time to Get Started: Under five hours
Skills Needed: Good with children, patience
Potential Customers: Neighbors, family

HOW TO GET STARTED:
1. Practice babysitting a sibling or neighbor. It is recommended that you get your CPR (cardiopulmonary resuscitation) certification from the American Red Cross. Ask your parents for tips on controlling children. Most hospitals also have a babysitting course that includes everything from first aid to diaper changing.
2. Set an hourly wage.
3. Post flyers around your neighborhood. Spread the word through friends; let it be known that you are available. Ask for referrals!

For More Information: *www.urbanext.uiuc.edu/babysitting; www.redcross.org*

3. BAKER

WHAT IS IT? Some people love to cook and will never be your customers. But others hate to cook or are just too busy; baking for them can be a great business. Bakers can either bake "on spec," which means they bake their own stuff and try to sell it at flea markets and county fairs, or they can bake stuff that others request, like birthday cakes.

WHAT YOU NEED TO START:
- Oven and pans (borrow from your parents)
- Baking supplies (varies)

Cost to Start: Varies
Time to Get Started: Under four hours
Skills Needed: Cooking, following directions, cake decorating
Potential Customers: Neighbors, your school, busy parents

HOW TO GET STARTED:

1. Research different recipes. Find a few that you enjoy making. Practice making them until you get them perfect. Have your parents taste test them and give you advice.
2. Set a price per baked good. Also create a menu of common treats you can bake, like birthday cakes.
3. Inquire about the cost and rules for selling baked goods at your local flea market.
4. Post flyers in your neighborhood and at grocery stores, to advertise your availability for parties and events.
5. Remember that during the summer and the holidays, people go to a lot of parties, and they often wish to bring a baked good. But many people just don't have the time to bake. Be sure to think of your parent's busiest friends and target them the hardest.

For More Information: *www.joyofbaking.com; www.verybestbaking.com; www.baking911.com*

4. BALLOON ANIMAL MAKER

WHAT IS IT? Kids love balloon animals. They add a lot of fun to parties, flea markets, and county fairs. Sometimes you make and sell the animals and sometimes people pay you an hourly wage to make them.

WHAT YOU NEED TO START:

- Balloons (under $10)
- Book or video about making balloon animals (borrow from library)

Cost to Start: Under $10
Time to Get Started: Under four hours
Skills Needed: Good with kids
Potential Customers: People having celebrations

HOW TO GET STARTED:

1. Learn how to make various animals out of balloons. Practice until you are able to make them quickly and easily. (Of course, if you have zero experience making balloon animals, your start-up time will be more than four hours.)
2. Set an hourly wage to go to parties and create balloon animals.
3. Inquire about having a booth at local flea markets. Often flea markets will pay you to come simply because balloon animals attract kids, and kids bring their parents.
4. Post flyers around your neighborhood, parks, and at party-supply stores advertising your business.

For More Information: *www.ziggosballoons.com; www.balloonanimals.com*

5. BETA TESTER

WHAT IS IT? Beta testing means testing computer software for companies and then giving them notes on how to improve the product. Believe it or not, software companies will pay big bucks for people who can do this well.

WHAT YOU NEED TO START:
• Computer with Internet connection (borrow from your parents)

Cost to Start: $0
Time to Get Started: Under four hours
Skills Needed: Computer skills
Potential Customers: Video game creators, software companies

HOW TO GET STARTED:
1. Practice using a few kinds of computer software. Learn how they work and what could be fixed on them. Write a sample report that you can send to companies to show off your skills.
2. Look online to find companies that need people to test their computer software or game software (they will set the price). You may have to do a few tests for free before you can start charging, but this is a cheap way to let companies sample your services.
3. Post flyers around local businesses in case companies in town have software they would like you to test.

For More Information:
http://en.wikipedia.org/wiki/Beta_testing#Beta_testing;
www.youtube.com/watch?v=vinHZ46pETI

6. BICYCLE REPAIR

WHAT IS IT? Repairing bicycles for customers, including tune-ups and tire replacements.

WHAT YOU NEED TO START:
• Bicycle repair kit (under $30)
• Bicycle to practice with (use yours or borrow from a neighbor)
• Book or video on bicycle repair (borrow from library)

Cost to Start: Under $30
Time to Get Started: Under five hours
Skills Needed: Good with tools, patience
Potential Customers: Friends, neighbors, bicycle shops

HOW TO GET STARTED:
1. Practice fixing many different problems that bicycles have. Learn how a bicycle works so you repair any type of problem. You may even want to inquire about doing an internship at a bicycle repair store for a few months.

2. Set an hourly wage in addition to cost of parts to repair the bike. Set up shop in your garage with easy access to the street for kids to stop in. You might be able to outsource yourself to bicycle shops, which probably have a ton of business in the spring, when people start biking again.

3. Post flyers around your neighborhood and in local bike shops advertising your business.

For More Information: *www.bikewebsite.com*

7. BIKING TOUR GUIDE

WHAT IS IT? You can make money taking people on bike tours. Tours can be through the city or even through the woods. If you have a bike, you are in business.

WHAT YOU NEED TO START:
- Bike (use your own)
- Helmet (use your own)

Cost to Start: $0 (assuming you already own the bike and a helmet)
Time to Get Started: A day
Skills Needed: Good biking and speaking skills
Potential Customers: Biking clubs, tourists, families looking for a fun way to spend a Saturday

HOW TO GET STARTED:

1. Decide what your basic tour path will be. It could be through your city or town, outlining all the historic sites, or it could be a tour through the woods. During the tour, you'll need to stop a few times to rest and point out the highlights, so it's best if you do some research on them.

2. Set a price per tour. To meet the "safe" rule of the Five S Formula, you should insist that everyone bring his or her own bike and helmet.

3. Drop off flyers at bike shops and offer to pay them a referral fee for anyone they send your way.

For More Information:
http://www.entrepreneur.com/businessideas/248.html

8. BILL REVIEWER

WHAT IS IT? Helping clients find the best companies and deals for their utility, phone, Internet, and cable services.

WHAT YOU NEED TO START:
- Computer with Internet connection (borrow from parents)

Cost to Start: $0
Time to Get Started: Under five hours

Skills Needed: Reading and research
Potential Customers: Family and neighbors

HOW TO GET STARTED:

1. Research different companies that offer phone, heating, electricity, cable, and other services. Compare prices and services. Many oil and gas companies give neighborhood discounts.
2. Set an hourly wage to go to people's homes and look over their bills to make sure people are with the companies that give them the best deals.
3. Post flyers around your neighborhood and at local businesses, offering your services.

For More Information: *www.lowermybills.com;* contact your local utility providers

9. BIRDHOUSE BUILDER/DESIGNER

WHAT IS IT? Constructing unique and custom birdhouses for clients.

WHAT YOU NEED TO START:
- Wood and nails (under $30)
- Saw and hammer (borrow from your parents)

Cost to Start: Under $30
Time to Get Started: Under four hours
Skills Needed: Being good with tools, following instructions
Potential Customers: Family and neighbors

HOW TO GET STARTED:

1. Learn the basics of making a birdhouse. Research what works and does not work when it comes to birdhouse designing.
2. Practice building your birdhouses. Ask your parents for their opinions.
3. Set a price per birdhouse and birdhouse design (be sure to set a price on the design and your time if you are selling your design and showing others how to build the birdhouse).
4. Post flyers around your neighborhood and at local garden supply stores to advertise your business.

For More Information: *www.freebirdhouseplans.net*

10. BLOGGER

WHAT IS IT? Maintaining a blog on just about any topic you wish that people will subscribe to.

WHAT YOU NEED TO START:
- Computer with Internet connection (borrow from your parents)

Cost to Start: $0
Time to Get Started: Under six hours
Skills Needed: Computer skills, research skills
Potential Customers: Everyone, but focus on the folks that would be most interested in the subject matter of your blog

HOW TO GET STARTED:

1. Pick a topic that you either know a lot about or you wouldn't mind learning a lot about. Your goal is to find a deep enough niche that people will actually pay to subscribe to your blog. The more of a niche you have, the better. For example, rather than reviewing electronics, maybe you only review flat screen TVs.
2. Create a blog and start giving it away for free. In the blogging world, you can earn money through either advertising or subscriptions. Most bloggers, however, have to start out offering their service for free. You might want to start with a basic blog that is free, but which offers the chance to upgrade at any time to a premium blog for a price.
3. Spend a few hours on the Internet, posting on blogs in your subject area. If you review flat screen TVs, you can post something on all the electronic blogs like, "I actually just reviewed this TV on my blog. Find the article at: _____."

For More Information: *www.blog.com*

11. CALLIGRAPHER

WHAT IS IT? For special occasions, including weddings, birthdays, graduations, and anniversaries, people will pay extra to have their invitations handwritten in beautiful script by a calligrapher.

WHAT YOU NEED TO START:
- Calligraphy set (under $30)
- Paper for practicing (under $5)

Cost to Start: Under $35
Time to Get Started: Under five hours
Skills Needed: Practice and patience
Potential Customers: People celebrating special occasions like weddings, families with graduating children, and wedding and event planners

HOW TO GET STARTED:

1. Learn how to do calligraphy (with either a kit, a DVD or a book, or by taking a class). Practice this art until you can do it easily and well. Have your parents look over your work and give you advice on how to improve.

2. Set a price per job or per unit.
3. Post flyers advertising your talent around your neighborhood, especially in card shops and art stores. Also contact bridal shops and wedding and event planners.

For More Information: *www.studioarts.net/calligraphy/*; check out library books on calligraphy

12. CAR WASHER

WHAT IS IT? Uhhhh . . . guess.

WHAT YOU NEED TO START:

- Soap (under $10)
- Bucket (under $10)
- Brush (under $20)
- Sponge (under $10)
- Vacuum (optional; borrow from parents)

Cost to Start: Under $50
Time to Get Started: Under three hours
Skills Needed: Eye for detail
Potential Customers: Anyone with a car

HOW TO GET STARTED:

1. Practice washing your parents' car. Be sure to make it sparkling! Ask for tips on how to do a more efficient job. Be sure to time yourself so you know roughly how long it takes.
2. Set a price, either an hourly wage or a flat rate. Determine what you are going to include with a cleaning. Will you vacuum too? Will you wash the inside of the windows? You might want to have a price menu for each task and then offer a discount if people buy the complete inside-and-outside cleaning package.
3. Post flyers around your neighborhood. You can offer to go to the car or to have the car come to you.

For More Information: *www.chemicalguys.com*

13. CARE-PACKAGE MAKER

WHAT IS IT? Sending boxes full of food products, gifts, and toys from parents and relatives to family members in the military or to children who have gone to camp, boarding school, or college.

WHAT YOU NEED TO START:

- Nothing. Only buy materials for the care packages once you have a customer who has put down a deposit.

Cost to Start: $0
Time to Get Started: Under three hours

Skills Needed: Eye for detail, creativity
Potential Customers: Military families, parents with kids at camp, college, and boarding school.

HOW TO GET STARTED:

1. Practice making a care package for children that are away at camp or college. Ask your friends if it includes things they would like. Photograph sample packages and post these photos online.
2. Set a price per package including cost of supplies, packaging, and shipping. Offer to do customized care packages for parents who request special supplies.
3. Post flyers around your neighborhood and at local stores to advertise your business. Most camps and colleges won't give you their mailing list, but you can always ask.

For More Information: *www.customcarepackage.com*

14. CHAUFFEUR BUSINESS

WHAT IS IT? Driving people to specified locations, including airport drop-offs and pickups, car drop-offs, errands; driving people around on their vacation

WHAT YOU NEED TO START:
- Chauffeur license ($25–$50)
- Chauffeur insurance (over $300 a year, but it may not be required)
- Map of covered area (under $25)

Cost to Start: Over $375
Time to Get Started: Over five hours
Skills Needed: Driving
Potential Customers: Family, neighbors, any of your parents' friends who have a long commute, elderly people

HOW TO GET STARTED:

1. Go to your local Department of Motor Vehicles and obtain a chauffeur's license and find out if chauffeur's insurance is required in your state. It is good to get chauffeur's insurance, in case you are involved in an accident while driving another person's vehicle.
2. Set a price list: a minimum cost, as well as per mile. You may charge a flat fee for airport drop-offs and pickups. Include price of your return travel if you are dropping off a vehicle.
3. Practice driving to common locations like airports. Find alternative routes in case of traffic.
4. Create flyers with a description of your business. Distribute them around your neighborhood and local airport, as well as to retirement homes (for driving elderly people on errands in their own cars).
5. Remember to ask for referrals! Ask your parents where their

friends work. If several of them have a long commute, you might be able to sell three of them on having a personal chauffeur! You can drop off and pick up everyone. They can work or even sleep in the car, and they save money on gas!

For More Information: *www.dmv.org*

15. CHEF FOR HIRE

WHAT IS IT? Cooking a meal for clients when they want a special dinner or are not able to cook themselves. This could be on request, weekly, or on a daily basis.

WHAT YOU NEED TO START:
• Cooking education ($100)

Cost to Start: $100
Time to Get Started: Over three hours, depending on your current culinary expertise
Skills Needed: Cooking, following instructions
Potential Customers: Busy professionals, families, and friends

HOW TO GET STARTED:
1. Somehow you need to hone your cooking skills. Perhaps you watch cooking shows on TV and try their recipes. Perhaps you take a cooking class or two. Or perhaps you just watch your parents and you practice, practice, practice. The point is you have to be fast and good at it.
2. Find a local grocery store that has all the potential materials you will need.
3. Create estimated costs for a meal, including food supplies, as well as a flat rate per meal. Consider what it would cost the family to go out to eat. If you can beat that price, you'll have more customers.
4. Post flyers detailing your business around town and in local markets.
5. When meeting with potential clients, be sure to find out which tools will be available to you in their kitchen.
6. Remember to ask for referrals! Focus on busy people with kids.

For More Information: *www.allrecipes.com*

16. CHILDREN'S CHAUFFEUR

WHAT IS IT? Driving children to lessons, to school, and on errands when parents are not able to.

WHAT YOU NEED TO START:
• Car (borrow from your parents)
• Insurance (over $300). Ask your parents' insurance company what kind they recommend you buy.
• Chauffeur license ($25–$50)

Cost to Start: Over $350.
Time to Get Started: Under four hours
Skills Needed: Good with children, driving
Potential Customers: Parents who need children driven to school and to activities, businesses that have a lot of kids as customers, such as karate schools and ballet schools

HOW TO GET STARTED:
1. Practice driving around your town to learn where many things are located.
2. Set a price; either an hourly wage or price per trip (include price of gas).
3. Post flyers around your neighborhood, advertising that you are available to drive people's children to different activities.
4. Market to businesses. A karate school might have twenty kids in one class, all of whom need a ride to class. Offer a referral fee to the owner of the school if he will mention your service.

For More Information: *www.dmv.org;* be sure to talk to your parents' friends about what their children's chauffeur needs are

17. CHILDREN'S LUNCH MAKER

WHAT IS IT? Making tasty and nutritious lunches for children going to school or day camp who need to bring a meal. This is a great business, because parents are busy and kids need a lunch every day!

WHAT YOU NEED TO START:
• Nothing (don't buy any food until you have a customer!)

Cost to Start: $0
Time to Get Started: Under three hours
Skills Needed: Sandwich making
Potential Customers: Parents in your neighborhood with school-aged kids

HOW TO GET STARTED:
1. Practice making lunches that children can bring to school. Be sure to make them healthy and include a treat like a cookie (if the parents approve). It's a good idea to post menus on your Web site so parents can pick the lunches they want for their kids.
2. Set a price per lunch. Have parents let you know ahead of time of any special dietary needs of the child. You will have the lunches brought to their home every morning.
3. Post flyers around your neighborhood and at school.
For More Information: *www.cooks.com*

18. CLEANING SERVICE (GENERAL)

WHAT IS IT? Cleaning the houses of clients. The type and level of cleaning would be up to the client: It could be anything from vacuuming to deep cleaning a house.

WHAT YOU NEED TO START:
- Nothing (borrow cleaning materials from your parents or client)

Cost to Start: $0
Time to Get Started: Under five hours
Skills Needed: Cleaning, eye for detail
Potential Customers: Any adult with a home

HOW TO GET STARTED:
1. Practice cleaning three rooms in your house. Do a kitchen, a bathroom, and the living room. Practice vacuuming, dusting, and washing anything dirty. Make sure to pay attention to detail.
2. Have your parents evaluate the job you have done and give you pointers on how to improve.
3. Set an hourly wage.
4. Post flyers around your neighborhood, including grocery stores and hardware stores.
5. When accepting a job, be sure to confirm that the client has the necessary cleaning supplies. If not, you'll either have to buy them and charge the client or borrow them from your parents.
6. Ask your parents if they will "rent" you cleaning supplies if you "pay" them by offering to clean the whole house once a month.

For More Information: *http://www.cleanisnotenough.com;* look online for your state's house-cleaning association

19. CLEANING SERVICE (SPECIFIC)

WHAT IS IT? Cleaning only certain places, like a bathroom or kitchen, instead of a whole house. There are some things that people just hate to clean, namely bathrooms and kitchens. Focusing on just those might make you stand out from all the other cleaning services, which usually won't take a job unless they can charge for a whole house.

WHAT YOU NEED TO START:
- Nothing (borrow supplies from your parents or your customer)

Cost to Start: $0
Time to Get Started: Under three hours
Skills Needed: Cleaning, eye for detail
Potential Customers: Any adult with a home

HOW TO GET STARTED:

1. Clean both a kitchen and a bathroom; practice cleaning these rooms until you can make them sparkle.
2. Set an hourly wage to go to someone's house weekly to clean the specified room. (Make sure the client has all the cleaning supplies you will need. Otherwise, you'll have to borrow from your parents or buy the supplies and charge them to the client.)
3. Post flyers around your neighborhood and in local stores, offering to clean kitchens or bathrooms.

For More Information: *www.cleanisnotenough.com*; look online for your state's house-cleaning association

20. COMPANION TO ELDERLY PEOPLE

WHAT IS IT? Many elderly people live alone, and busy sons and daughters want someone to keep their parents company for a couple hours every day. You may have to do some small cleaning and cooking chores.

WHAT YOU NEED TO START:

• Nothing

Cost to Start: $0
Time to Get Started: Under four hours
Skills Needed: Good with people; cleaning and cooking skills
Potential Customers: Family and neighbors

HOW TO GET STARTED:

1. Practice by catering to your grandparents' needs. Cook them meals, bring them drinks, do their laundry, and above all, just keep them company.
2. Set an hourly wage for your services.
3. Be sure to get medical emergency numbers from all clients.
4. Post flyers around your neighborhood and in nursing homes and retirement communities.

For More Information: *www.aging-parents-and-elder-care.com*

21. CRAFT MAKER

WHAT IS IT? Creating craft items to sell at country fairs or online.

WHAT YOU NEED TO START:

• Craft supplies ($25–$50)
• Scissors (borrow from your parents)

Cost to Start: About $25–$50
Time to Get Started: About three hours
Skills Needed: Ability to follow instructions
Potential Customers: Everyone

HOW TO GET STARTED:
1. Find a craft that you enjoy, such as candle making, decoupage, or jewelry making. Before you go out and make anything, ask local craft stores what they might want to buy.
2. Go to your local craft-supply store and buy enough materials to make ten of your chosen craft: five for practice and five for sale.
3. Practice making your craft and decide how much to sell completed projects for, based on the cost of materials used in each project as well as the time and energy put into each object.
4. Open an eBay account. Take photographs of all your crafts and post them online. Set an online price for each one and be sure to include eBay's fees as well as shipping and packaging costs.
5. Inquire about where you can sell your crafts locally, such as at craft fairs, craft stores, and flea markets. Maybe you can find outsource work by talking to vendors at craft fairs. You make 'em; they sell 'em.

For More Information: *www.enchantedlearning.com/crafts*

22. CRAFT/HOBBIES TUTOR

WHAT IS IT? Not only can you make money making crafts, you can also make money teaching someone how to make crafts. Parents may hire you to teach them how to craft or to teach their children as a fun project. You can also teach "make and take" crafts at kids' birthday parties. Children make the project at the party and then take it with them.

WHAT YOU NEED TO START:
- Craft-making supplies ($25–$50)

Cost to Start: Under $50
Time to Get Started: Under five hours
Skills Needed: Ability to work well with others
Potential Customers: Parents with young children; friends; nursery schools, and kindergartens

HOW TO GET STARTED:
1. Research different crafts and pick five you enjoy doing.
2. Practice making five different crafts and teaching your parents to make these crafts, so you will be able to teach it to potential clients.
3. Be sure to have enough supplies to make a sample craft and to have materials for your students.
4. Set a price list, including the cost of materials for different crafts, as well as an hourly wage.
5. Create flyers advertising your business and post them around your neighborhood and in local craft supply stores.
6. You could offer to teach one of your crafts to a kindergarten

class. The kids will then take their crafts home, and parents will know it was you who showed them how to do it!

For More Information: *www.enchantedlearning.com/crafts*

23. DATA ENTRY

WHAT IS IT? Even though we live in a digital world, there is still a ton of information transmitted on good old paper. This information needs to be entered into a computer somehow. That's where you come in. Salespeople might have a stack of business cards they need entered into a database, or old data from a noncompatible computer system needs to be entered into the company's new system.

WHAT YOU NEED TO START:
- Computer (use parents' computer or borrow from customer)
- Internet (also supplied by parents)

Cost to Start: $0
Time to Get Started: Under three hours
Skills Needed: Computer skills, typing
Potential Customers: Parents, businesses, neighbors, small business owners, data-entry companies

HOW TO GET STARTED:
1. Practice typing quickly and efficiently. Take online typing tests to determine your words per minute.
2. Learn how to use databases such as Excel, Access, and Act.
3. Come up with an hourly wage; however, many places will set their own salary.
4. Prepare fliers advertising your typing speed and knowledge of different programs. Post them at local businesses and around your neighborhood.

For More Information: *www.typingtest.com*

24. DECORATION MAKER

WHAT IS IT? Creating homemade decorations for holidays and birthdays. Of course, people can always go to a store to buy a decoration, but many times, people want something unique and homemade.

WHAT YOU NEED TO START:
- Ribbon ($5)
- Stencils of varying shapes (under $10)
- Construction paper ($5)
- Markers or paints ($5)
- Scissors (borrow from your parents)

Cost to Start: Under $25
Time to Get Started: Under five hours
Skills Needed: Artistic skills, ability to follow instructions
Potential Customers: Everyone

HOW TO GET STARTED:

1. Learn how to make holiday shapes with your stencils on construction paper. Paint or color designs onto the shapes to customize them.
2. Make bows out of the ribbon.
3. Get creative! Make new and different decorations that someone would not be able to buy in a store.
4. Price the varying decorations based on cost of materials and time spent on them.
5. Post flyers in your local neighborhood, advertising your decorations for birthday parties and holidays.

For More Information:
www.amazingmoms.com/htm/christmas_crafts.htm;
www.christmas-decorations-gifts-store.com; visit your local crafts store for books on making decorations

25. DESKTOP PUBLISHER

WHAT IS IT? Companies need help creating and mailing their newsletters, online magazines, and blogs. While it is crucial for small businesses to stay in touch with their clients every week or every month, it is a pain in the butt for a small business to do this itself. You can help them to: create topics for their newsletter or blog, format it (perhaps even write the article for them), and e-mail it to all their clients.

WHAT YOU NEED TO START:
- Computer (use your parents' computer)
- Some sort of publishing computer program like Microsoft Publisher (over $100)
- Some sort of database management program (like Act) and an e-mail program (like Swiftpage Email or Constant Contact)

Cost to Start: Over $100
Time to Get Started: Over four hours
Skills Needed: Computer skills, typing
Potential Customers: Small businesses, schools

HOW TO GET STARTED:

1. Become familiar with all the programs necessary to create and manage a newsletter or blog.
2. Practice making newsletters, blogs, and e-zines.

3. Create an hourly wage or a flat rate per project. Remember, what's great about this business is that if you can create a decent newsletter for a company to send every month, you will have cash flow every month. Once companies start sending newsletters, they can't stop. They need to keep going.

4. Post flyers at local businesses and around your neighborhood promoting your skills. Remind your customers of their problem. Have your fliers read something like this: "Has your business considered publishing a newsletter but thought it would be too time-consuming and expensive?"

For More Information: *www.blog.com*

26. DINNER MAKER

WHAT IS IT? Making a dinner that you precook and sell with heating instructions. The client then takes the meal, returns home, heats it up, and serves it.

WHAT YOU NEED TO START:
- Food supplies to make a dinner you are good at (price varies, but you don't buy anything until you actually have a customer)
- Pots, pans, oven (use parents')

Cost to Start: $0
Time to Get Started: Under four hours
Skills Needed: Cooking, ability to follow instructions
Potential Customers: Friends and neighbors

HOW TO GET STARTED:
1. Learn how to make dinners for families or for a couple's special night. Practice cooking ten different recipes, and have your parents taste-test them and give you advice. Ask them to pay for the ingredients.

2. Set a price per dinner, including the cost of food and your time.

3. Post flyers around your neighborhood and at local grocery stores, advertising your business. Focus on busy people and remind them of their problem: "Would you love to give your family a home-cooked meal but don't have the time to cook it? I'll cook it, you heat it!"

For More Information: *www.allrecipes.com*

27. DISC JOCKEY

WHAT IS IT? Playing music at parties and special events

WHAT YOU NEED TO START:
Starting a DJ business requires equipment that is very expensive (like in the realm of $5,000 for used equipment). However, you are best off renting the equipment after your first client has given you a deposit. You will need:

- Speakers
- Sound system with mixing board
- Microphone
- Lights
- A large music collection

Cost to Start: $0 (Avoid purchasing or renting anything until your first client has given you a deposit)
Time to Get Started: Under three hours
Skills Needed: Ear for music
Potential Customers: Parents, friends, people having celebrations, hotels and function halls, event and wedding planners, as well as high school prom committees

HOW TO GET STARTED:

1. Find a company that will rent you all of the above equipment. See what they require for insurance.
2. Become acquainted with many different types of music. Remember, you might love hip-hop, but your client might need a DJ for a dance for senior citizens. So learn a little bit about music with which you are not familiar.
3. Set an hourly wage. Always ask your clients for a play list. Remember, you might have to buy or borrow music that you don't have. You may have to subscribe to an online service that allows you unlimited access to as many songs as you like. The cost of music needs to be incorporated into your fee.
4. You might be able to find outsource work with established DJs. After all, they can only be in one place at a time.
5. Post flyers in your school as well as around your neighborhood. Contact event and wedding planners. Make yourself available for parties.

For More Information: *www.dj-tips-and-tricks.com*

28. DOG WALKER

WHAT IS IT? People who work full-time often want their dogs walked while they are at work or while they are on vacation. You can actually walk several dogs at once.

WHAT YOU NEED TO START:

- A pair of good walking sneakers (look in your closet)
- Dog treats (under $10)
- Leash (borrow from clients)

Cost to Start: $10
Time to Get Started: Less than an hour
Skills Needed: Good with animals
Potential Customers: Friends and neighbors who work full-time and have a dog

HOW TO GET STARTED:

1. Read up on tricks to make dogs heel. Practice making a dog obey you with your dog or a neighbor's. Find a good place to walk dogs, like a local dog park.
2. Set a price per walk.
3. Post flyers in your neighborhood to advertise your availability.

For More Information: *www.FabJob.com/DogWalker*

29. DRINK STAND OPERATOR

WHAT IS IT? People always need a cold drink on a hot day. While this business is often associated with selling lemonade, you can actually sell anything you think people will drink.

WHAT YOU NEED TO START:

- Folding table (borrow from your parents)
- Pitcher (borrow from your parents)
- Plastic glasses (under $10)
- Lemons (under $5 per pound)
- Poster board ($2)
- Markers (find around your house)

Cost to Start: Under $20
Time to Get Started: Under three hours
Skills Needed: Practice
Potential Customers: Friends, neighbors, businesses, local stores

HOW TO GET STARTED:

1. Make enough lemonade to fill the pitcher and extra lemonade for when it runs out.
2. Set up the table at the corner of your street with the cups and lemonade.
3. Set a price per glass of lemonade, about $1 or $2.
4. Make a poster with the name of your lemonade stand and the price per glass.
5. Post flyers around your neighborhood that give directions to your lemonade stand.
6. Try experimenting with different drinks and even different locations. Can you set up shop at a soccer game? On the baseball field? Near the town playground?

For More Information: *www.wikihow.com/Make-Lemonade*

30. ENTERTAINMENT CENTER INSTALLER

WHAT IS IT? Installing entertainment centers and video equipment in the homes of clients. These days people aren't just buying a TV, they are buying an entertainment package. So they need help connecting the TV to the stereo and the DVD player to the speakers. They even need help programming the remote. They also need help putting together the furniture to house the entertainment center. Some people will ask you to do all the work; others will just want a helper.

WHAT YOU NEED TO START:
• Nothing

Cost to Start: $0
Time to Get Started: Under three hours
Skills Needed: Ability to lift heavy objects and follow instructions
Potential Customers: Friends, neighbors, and store clients

HOW TO GET STARTED:
1. Ask your parents if you can take apart and then reassemble their entertainment center. (Be sure you still have the manual! You don't want to say, "Mom, about the entertainment center . . . yeah . . .") Browse through some of the manuals you have on the electronics in your home. Have your parents test what you did to make sure everything works correctly.
2. Set an hourly wage to put together entertainment centers.
3. Post flyers around your neighborhood and at local electronics and furniture stores.

For More Information: Your local media supply stores; read the manuals from your own entertainment center

31. ENVIRONMENTAL CONSULTANT

WHAT IS IT? Oil prices are on the rise, and every day, people are becoming more and more concerned about the environment. So this business has two powerful forces working for it. As an environmental consultant, you would be helping people become more energy efficient and green in their households. You would examine their heating bills, appliances, insulation levels, even their gardens, and then prepare a report on ways they could save.

WHAT YOU NEED TO START:
• Nothing

Cost to Start: $0
Time to Get Started: Five or more hours
Skills Needed: Research skills
Potential Customers: Friends and neighbors

HOW TO GET STARTED:
1. Research different ways that houses can become more energy efficient. Spend a lot of time finding out about new products that can be easily installed into houses to make them more environmentally friendly. Look into the LEED System, which helps people

constructing houses make their home energy efficient. LEED also suggests ways you can renovate an existing home.

2. Remember Return on Investment (ROI)? (Look it up in the index of this book if you don't remember.) That is what people are going to be most interested in. They want to know: If we replace our furnace today, how long will it take for us to make back that money in oil savings?

3. Charge a flat rate to walk through people's homes and give advice on ways to make updates and improve their energy efficiency.

4. Post flyers around your neighborhood and at construction sites and get referrals!

For More Information: *www.goodtobegreen.com, www.usgbc.org/LEED*

32. ERRAND RUNNER

WHAT IS IT? Running errands for busy people. This may include grocery shopping or picking up dry cleaning, taking cars to get washed, and getting the mail.

WHAT YOU NEED TO START:

- Car (borrow your parent's car)
- Map ($5–$10)

Cost to Start: Under $10
Time to Get Started: Under two hours
Skills Needed: Driving
Potential Customers: Friends, family, and neighbors

HOW TO GET STARTED:

1. Practice driving to grocery stores and pharmacies. Acquaint yourself with your neighborhood.

2. Set a price, either an hourly wage or a flat rate. Remember to include the cost of gas.

3. In order to keep your fixed costs down, it is best to bunch multiple client orders into one trip. Rather than going to the pharmacy three times for three clients, try to make one trip for all three. A good way to do this is to set errand hours. Maybe every Saturday and Tuesday night you run errands for a few hours. Let people know they can call you at the last minute.

4. Post flyers in grocery stores, in nursing homes, and around your neighborhood.

For More Information: Ask friends and family what tasks they would like to have help in completing throughout the day.

33. EVENT PLANNER

WHAT IS IT? Planning different events, such as birthday parties, graduation parties, or baby showers. You create a party theme, order the catering, create and send out the invitations, and then supervise the party itself.

WHAT YOU NEED TO START:
- Nothing! (don't buy any party materials until you have your first client)

Cost to Start: $0
Time to Get Started: Three hours
Skills Needed: Organizational skills, working well with people
Potential Customers: People planning celebrations, family, and neighbors, businesses that have holiday parties

HOW TO GET STARTED:
1. Ask your parents to let you plan their next party as practice. Find local stores that supply cakes, decorations, and food. Find a DJ that is willing to work at your parties.
2. Create a price list, including the cost of supplies for each party and a flat rate.
3. Post flyers around your neighborhood and at party supply stores to advertise your services.
4. Remember, the summer and the holidays are the times for heavy partying!

For More Information: *www.partypop.com*

34. FACE PAINTER

WHAT IS IT? Painting faces at birthday parties and other special events, such as county fairs and flea markets.

WHAT YOU NEED TO START:
- Face-paint kit (under $20)
- Photo paper for computer (under $15)
- Digital camera (borrow from parents if necessary)
- Computer and printer (optional; borrow from parents)

Cost to Start: Under $35
Time to Get Started: Under four hours
Skills Needed: Drawing, an eye for detail
Potential Customers: Schoolchildren, flea markets, neighbors, friends

HOW TO GET STARTED:
1. Create designs and pictures of animals that you can paint on people's faces.
2. Ask your parents to let you practice on them. (Mom's going to

look great with a tiger face!) When you paint one to your satisfaction take a picture of it. Print the photograph to show clients what you are able to do, if you have access to a computer; or get them printed at a local copy shop.

3. Create a price list based on cost of paints and an hourly wage.
4. Post flyers around your neighborhood and at local parks and schools to advertise your skills.
5. Flea markets often pay face painters to set up shop, because they need ways to make the flea market fun for kids.

For More Information: *www.facepaintingbusiness.com*

35. FISH TANK MAINTENANCE

WHAT IS IT? People love having fish tanks in their homes, but fish tanks are a pain in the butt to clean. You can jump in there and help, and then look forward to repeat business all year long.

WHAT YOU NEED TO START:

• Nothing (borrow from clients. Most will already have the gear to clean their fish tank. If not, you can always buy supplies and charge them to your customer)

Cost to Start: $0
Time to Get Started: Under four hours
Skills Needed: Cleaning, an eye for detail
Potential Customers: Fish owners, restaurants, and doctors' offices

HOW TO GET STARTED:

1. Go to your local pet-supply store and research how to maintain a fish tank, including scrubbing the sides, cleaning the filter, testing the water, and stirring up the rocks. Offer to work for a month free of charge if the store owner will teach you.
2. Practice cleaning someone's fish tank; ask for any tips the fish keeper may have.
3. Set a weekly wage to clean the fish tanks.
4. Post flyers around your neighborhood and at local doctors' offices and restaurants, advertising your business.

For More Information: *www.ratemyfishtank.com*

36. FLYER DISTRIBUTOR

WHAT IS IT? Ever come back from the mall and find a flyer on your car? How did it get there? Probably someone has a flyer distribution business. You can make good money posting flyers for other businesses.

WHAT YOU NEED TO START:

• Nothing

Cost to Start: $0
Time to Get Started: Under three hours
Skills Needed: None
Potential Customers: Businesses and charities

HOW TO GET STARTED:
1. Find areas in town that are high traffic and where people are likely to read flyers. Inquire about the rules of posting flyers. (Many businesses won't let you post anything, and in some places, it is flat-out illegal.)
2. Set an hourly wage to distribute someone's flyers.
3. Advertise with your own flyers, saying something along the lines of: "You read this flyer, now let me advertise your business on it!"
4. A great way to get customers is to collect flyers from other businesses and ask whom they hire to distribute their flyers and how much they charge. Maybe you can beat their prices.

For More Information: Find flyers that have been passed out and study them

37. FOCUS GROUP ORGANIZER

WHAT IS IT? Before a company releases a product, it is tested on a "focus group." A focus group is a collection of similar individuals (all kids, all moms, etc.) that are asked to comment on a new product or service. As a young entrepreneur you can specialize in focus groups for companies wishing to connect with young people. Tell companies you can compile a group of young people to act as a focus group for their new product or service.

WHAT YOU NEED TO START:
• Nothing, just your friends

Cost to Start: $0
Time to Get Started: Under three hours
Skills Needed: Communication skills, writing
Potential Customers: Entrepreneurs, businesses

HOW TO GET STARTED:
1. Post flyers around town advertising a child or teen focus group. Your group will test products and give feedback to the companies.
2. You can also go online and pitch to major corporations. This may take a while, but you could become the source for companies wishing to connect with young people.
3. Submit yourself to focus-group companies. Not only will you get paid, but you will also see exactly how they do it!
4. Set a flat rate for your services. Remember that you must pay your friends for their time to participate in the focus group.

For More Information: Look in the paper for ads for other focus groups and see what they charge

38. GARAGE CLEANER

WHAT IS IT? The garage is a room in the house that sometimes goes for years without being cleaned. When people do get around to cleaning it, it is a daunting project, and they will often hire someone to help. You'll probably help them with cleaning, organizing, and even hauling away stuff.

WHAT YOU NEED TO START:
• Nothing (get materials from clients)

Cost to Start: $0
Time to Get Started: Under an hour
Skills Needed: Cleaning
Potential Customers: Homeowners

HOW TO GET STARTED:
1. Clean your own garage to see how long it will take you to do a thorough job.
2. Create a price based on an hourly wage. Confirm that clients have their own cleaning supplies.
3. Consider partnering with someone who runs a yard-sale business. He might work for free to help you clean the garage if he gets first access to the stuff he wants to sell.
4. Post flyers around your neighborhood to advertise your skills. Make sure to do a thorough job at each house, and ask for referrals!

For More Information: *www.ClosetPlace.com; www.aBetterAbode.com*

39. GARBAGE REMOVAL

WHAT IS IT? Removing all the garbage from someone's home and taking it to the dump or even just taking it out to the curb. (Sometimes people don't even want to carry their garbage out of the kitchen to the end of the driveway!)

WHAT YOU NEED TO START:
• Extra-large garbage bags (under $5)
• Car if taking trash to the dump (borrow from parents)

Cost to Start: Under $5
Time to Get Started: Under an hour
Skills Needed: None
Potential Customers: Everyone, especially homeowners in your neighborhood

HOW TO GET STARTED
1. Learn when the pickups for garbage are in different areas of town. If you are taking stuff to the dump, find out when it is open.
2. Set a price to have you come and take out all of the garbage throughout someone's house.
3. Post flyers around your neighborhood to advertise your business.
For More Information: Look at your town's Web site; talk to neighbors

40. GARDENER

WHAT IS IT? Starting and maintaining a garden in a client's yard.

WHAT YOU NEED TO START:
• Nothing (you can probably borrow everything you need from your parents or from your customers)

Cost to Start: Under $50
Time to Get Started: Under five hours
Skills Needed: Gardening skills, plant knowledge
Potential Customers: Homeowners, schools, and businesses

HOW TO GET STARTED:
1. Research plants, herbs, and flowers that grow in different environments. Find plants that grow well with other types.
2. Practice planting a garden. Rake the ground, dig holes, and plant the seeds or seedlings. Practice weeding your parents' garden in case a client wants you to come back and maintain her garden.
3. Set a flat rate (including the cost of plants) for the first planting and an hourly rate for weekly maintenance.
4. Post flyers around your neighborhood and at garden supply stores.
For More Information: *www.thegardenhelper.com*

41. GIFT-WRAPPING BUSINESS

WHAT IS IT? People are especially busy during the holidays. They need help anywhere they can get it, and one thing you can do is wrap all their gifts for them.

WHAT YOU NEED TO START:
• Scissors (borrow from your parents)
• Transparent tape ($3)
• Five different kinds of wrapping paper ($5 each)
• Bag of bows ($5)
• Two different colors of ribbon ($3)

Cost to Start: $36
Time to Get Started: Under three hours

Skills Needed: Wrapping gifts
Potential Customers: Family, friends, neighbors, and local stores

HOW TO GET STARTED:

1. Wrap five practice presents for your parents. Have them evaluate your technique.
2. Set a price list for both your hourly wage and the cost of supplies per gift. Maybe you charge $8 an hour plus supplies, or you simply charge a flat fee per gift. It's up to you. Use the five practice gifts you wrapped for your parents to determine how long it takes and how much it costs.
3. Make up flyers with your prices and a description of your services. Distribute them throughout your neighborhood. (You could go to local nursing homes or elderly housing communities and hang flyers there too.)
4. See if gift stores will outsource their business to you. Maybe you can set up a table in the back of the store to wrap gifts for people.
5. Do a great job wrapping every gift and always ask your customers for referrals! Remember, the holidays are the time to ramp up your marketing.

For More Information: *www.papermart.com*

42. GRAPHIC DESIGNER

WHAT IS IT? Creating brochures, flyers, logos, stationery, and cards on your computer. This is a great business for young entrepreneurs because young people can keep their fixed costs down.

WHAT YOU NEED TO START:
- Computer (borrow from your parents)
- Printer (borrow from your parents)
- Graphic design computer software (over $100)
- Paper ($15)

Cost to Start: Over $115
Time to Get Started: Five hours
Skills Needed: Computer skills
Potential Customers: Businesses, family, and neighbors

HOW TO GET STARTED:

1. Practice using the design software on your computer until you feel comfortable making brochures, cards, etc. Ask your parents to have you create something for them as a test.
2. Set an hourly wage.
3. See if you can get outsourced work from a local print shop. While the shop may already have an in-house graphic designer, I bet you can offer better prices.

4. Create flyers advertising your skills and post them at local businesses and around your neighborhood. Make sure your flyers have a unique design. If the flyer catches someone's eye, he will want to make his own flyers as attractive as yours.

For More Information: *http://graphicdesign.about.com*

43. HOLIDAY CARD MAKER

WHAT IS IT? During the holidays many individuals and businesses will send out the same card to hundreds of people. Many of the cards, however, look similar. You can offer people a unique set of cards that cannot be bought in stores. You can even offer to address and mail them.

WHAT YOU NEED TO START:
- Computer (borrow from your parents)
- Printer (borrow from your parents)
- Graphic design or image software for computer (over $100)
- Paper to practice on ($5)
- Paper (card stock and envelopes; don't buy until you have your first client)

Cost to Start: over $105
Time to Get Started: Under four hours
Skills Needed: Computer skills
Potential Customers: Everyone, but small businesses are more motivated

HOW TO GET STARTED:
1. Practice making holiday cards on your computer. After printing them out, write in personalized messages. Have your parents look over the cards and give you advice on how to make them better. You can also create handmade cards and sell them for a higher price than computer-generated ones.
2. Set a price to make cards for someone else.
3. Post flyers before the holidays, advertising your business.

For More Information: *www.myfreeclipart.com*

44. HOLIDAY YARD DECORATOR

WHAT IS IT? Everybody hates hanging holiday lights. What's more, not many people are good at it. Decorating a client's yard for the holidays with decorations they already own can be a simple and safe business.

WHAT YOU NEED TO START:
- Nothing (use client's ladder and materials)

Cost to Start: $0
Time to Get Started: Under four hours

Skills Needed: Creativity, attention to detail, some electrical knowledge

Potential Customers: Homeowners, businesses, and churches

HOW TO GET STARTED:

1. Practice decorating your own yard for different holidays. Ask your parents to critique your work. Take photos of your work for marketing purposes.
2. Set an hourly wage to decorate someone's yard with decorations that the homeowner supplies.
3. Post flyers around your neighborhood before the holiday season to advertise your work.

For More Information: Next holiday season, drive around your town and see what people have done to decorate their yards. Look on Internet at prior years' holiday decorations. Make note of creative decorations.

45. HOMEWORK CHECKER

WHAT IS IT? Homework checkers spend most of their time reading over homework that is already done. If they find mistakes, they often teach the student how to fix any problems. Homework checkers also proofread term papers and even critique oral presentations.

WHAT YOU NEED TO START:

- Pens or highlighters (borrow from your parents)

Cost to Start: $0

Time to Get Started: One hour

Skills Needed: Knowledge of a subject, attention to detail, patience

Potential Customers: Schoolchildren, friends, and parents of students

HOW TO GET STARTED:

1. Find a subject that you excel in, one in which you feel comfortable helping other students.
2. Create a price based on an hourly wage or a flat rate per assignment.
3. Post flyers around your school that offer your services. Be careful not to do the homework for other students, but only to check over what they have already done.

For More Information: *www.wikihow.com/Become-a-Tutor*

46. HOUSE SITTER

WHAT IS IT? Maintaining a house while its occupants are out of town. This includes tasks such as watering plants, feeding pets, and taking in the mail.

WHAT YOU NEED TO START:
- Nothing

Cost to Start: $0
Time to Get Started: One hour
Skills Needed: Safety skills, sense of responsibility
Potential Customers: Homeowners

HOW TO GET STARTED:
1. Offer to "pretend" house-sit for your neighbors. Even though they are home, you can get their mail, water their plants, and feed their pets. Ask them to critique your work.
2. Create a daily wage. You might charge extra if there is a lot of additional work in watering plants and feeding pets.
3. Be sure to get the homeowners' emergency numbers.
4. Post flyers around your neighborhood to advertise your availability. Ask for referrals! Remember that people tend to go away during holidays, the summer, and school vacations. That is your top marketing time.

For More Information: *www.housecarers.com*

47. IRONING SERVICE

WHAT IS IT? Ironing is one of those tasks that everyone needs to do but very few people enjoy. Most families would love to outsource some of their ironing to you.

WHAT YOU NEED TO START:
- Iron (borrow from your parents)
- Ironing board (borrow from your parents)
- Starch (borrow from your client)

Cost to Start: None
Time to Get Started: Under three hours
Skills Needed: Ability to play the tambourine. (Only kidding, you need ironing skills, of course!)
Potential Customers: Businesspeople and parents

HOW TO GET STARTED:
1. Practice ironing your clothes; be sure to fold or hang them well. Ask your parents for advice on how to do this correctly. Remember, different fabrics need to be ironed at different temperatures.
2. Set a price, either an hourly wage or per item.
3. Ideally, people drop off their ironing at your house or you pick it up from them and work at your home. This way, you can work on your own schedule. It's also a little safer to do it this way, as you won't be inside other people's homes. A client may insist you do the ironing at his house, but be sure you only do this for a person you know.

4. Post flyers around your neighborhood to advertise your availability. Often self-service laundries have places to post flyers.

5. There may also be outsourcing opportunities from self-service laundries and dry cleaners.

For More Information: Your first client is your family. Offer to take over all the ironing duties. Mom and Dad will love you for it!

48. KNITTER

WHAT IS IT? Knitting products such as hats, scarves, and even sweaters to sell.

WHAT YOU NEED TO START:
- Practice yarn (under $5)
- Knitting needles (under $10)
- Pattern book and knitting basics book (under $20, or try to borrow some from people you know who knit, or from the library)

Cost to Start: Under $35
Time to Get Started: Under four hours (unless you are totally clueless about how to knit. Then this will take some time)
Skills Needed: Knitting/sewing skills
Potential Customers: Family, neighbors, friends, and parents

HOW TO GET STARTED:
1. Learn how to knit. Practice making different items such as scarves, hats, baby sweaters, and afghans. Visit your local yarn store (some of them give lessons), or ask a friend or relative who knits to teach you the basics. Look on the Internet for demonstrations in real time.
2. Set a price per item.
3. Post flyers around your neighborhood and at local fabric supply stores to advertise your items. Go to local stores and ask if they are willing to sell your item.
4. The best way to start this business is to knit custom orders. That way you won't spend a lot of money knitting things that people may not buy. Feel free to sell your "practice" items, but don't knit too many until you know someone will buy your finished products.

For More Information: *www.theyarnco.com*

49. LANDSCAPER

WHAT IS IT? While gardeners are considered creators who tend to focus on planting and plant care, landscapers focus more on yard maintenance. When they do plant, it is often much larger stuff, such as entire lawns or small trees. There can be good money in landscaping because even people who do take care of their yard need a little help with the bigger projects.

WHAT YOU NEED TO START:

- You can borrow most of the materials you need from your parents if they have a house, or from your clients. Plan on slowly buying your own equipment, especially the equipment no one else has.

Cost to Start: $0
Time to Get Started: Four hours
Skills Needed: Landscaping skills, such as edging, lawn mower operation, and raking
Potential Customers: Homeowners and businesses

HOW TO GET STARTED:

1. Practice mowing your parents' lawn, trimming the hedges, pulling weeds, and spreading bark mulch.
2. Set an hourly wage for your services. If all you are doing is mowing a lawn, you might want to charge a flat fee for the lawn.
3. Post flyers in your neighborhood and at your local garden supply and hardware stores. Be sure to confirm with potential clients that they have all the materials needed to work in their yard.
4. As a former landscaping company owner, I'll give you a tip here. Often clients will hire you for the dirtiest jobs. Riding around on a mower is nice, but you'll probably be asked to do things like weeding and digging up rocks. That's okay, though. Do a good job with those tasks, and clients will hire you for bigger stuff.

For More Information: *www.greatlandscapingideas.com*

50. LAUNDERER

WHAT IS IT? This business consists of washing and drying clothes for customers, either at your home or theirs, or offering to take their clothes to the local self-service laundry.

WHAT YOU NEED TO START:

- Washing machine and dryer (borrow from your parents or client or use machines at the self-service laundry)
- Laundry detergent and fabric softener (under $10, but don't buy them until you get a customer)

Cost to Start: Under $10
Time to Get Started: Under three hours
Skills Needed: Skilled at operating washer and dryer
Potential Customers: Homeowners and hotels, people who live in apartments that don't have washer and dryer facilities on site

HOW TO GET STARTED:

1. Practice washing your laundry and drying it. Be sure to pay attention to washing instructions on tags! Practice ironing clothes, which you could do upon request.
2. Set a price per load. Include cost of detergent, fabric softener, and laundry fees.

3. If you are using your parent's washer, it is only fair to pay them for wear and tear, water, and electricity use.

4. Be sure to set aside some money as your "insurance fund" just in case you ruin someone's new blouse!

5. Post flyers around your neighborhood and at grocery stores to advertise your business.

For More Information: Ask your parents to show you how to do laundry, if you haven't asked already. Also consider reading your washing machine's manual

51. LAWN MOWER

WHAT IS IT? Mowing the lawns of multiple clients. You can do this weekly or simply fill in for them when they are out of town.

WHAT YOU NEED TO START:
• Nothing (borrow the equipment from your customers)

Cost to Start: $0
Time to Get Started: Under three hours
Skills Needed: Ability to safely operate large machinery
Potential Customers: Homeowners and businesses; look for people you know who go on vacation every year

HOW TO GET STARTED:
1. Practice mowing your parents' lawn.
2. Set an hourly or weekly wage.
3. Post flyers around your neighborhood to advertise your business.
4. Be sure that each client has a lawn mower, or borrow one to start.
For More Information: *www.allaboutlawns.com*

52. LEAF RAKER

WHAT IS IT? Maybe you don't have the time in your schedule to be a full-blown landscaper. You're just looking for some quick cash! Specializing in raking leaves can be a great business. Landscapers have to charge a lot for leaf raking, because they have a lot of overhead from the other landscaping things they do (such as lawn mowing and land clearing). But you can run this business with no overhead.

WHAT YOU NEED TO START:
• Rake (borrow from your parents or customer)
• Tarp (borrow from your parents or customer)
• Leaf bags (don't buy until you have a client)
• Gardening gloves ($5)
• Dust mask (optional)

Cost to Start: $5
Time to Get Started: Under two hours
Skills Needed: None
Potential Customers: Homeowners and businesses; landscapers

HOW TO GET STARTED:
1. Practice raking your parents' yard. Put all of the leaves either into a pile or into garbage bags upon request.
2. Set either an hourly wage or a flat rate based on the size of the yard. Be sure to ask about where to dump the leaves. (I bid on a leaf raking job once, thinking I could dump the leaves in the woods behind the lawn. But the customer expected me to haul them away. Needless to say, I didn't make so much off that job.)
3. Post flyers around your neighborhood and at your local garden supply store. Be sure that all potential clients have their own rakes for you to use.
4. When leaves fall, they fall on everyone at the same time, so landscapers need some extra help. This can be a great opportunity for outsourcing. Tell landscapers you are available to help on their bigger jobs.

For More Information: *www.wikihow.com/Rake-Leaves*

53. MAGICIAN

WHAT IS IT? You can get paid to do magic shows at birthday parties and special events.

WHAT YOU NEED TO START:
- Magician's kit (under $30)
- Top hat (under $20, optional)

Cost to Start: Under $50
Time to Get Started: Five hours
Skills Needed: Practice
Potential Customers: Parties, friends, and neighbors

HOW TO GET STARTED:
1. Learn and practice magic tricks. Ask to perform them in front of your parents and have your parents give you advice on how to make your routine better. The best tricks to know are ones that don't require you to buy any expensive equipment.
2. Set a price, either hourly or per job.
3. Post flyers in your neighborhood and at local schools to advertise your magic show.
4. For magicians, the single best way to get business is to do a free presentation. Find places where you can demonstrate your act. Ask to come to a kid's camp, library, or a kindergarten class or to perform at one of your parent's parties.

For More Information: *www.magicgeek.com*

54. MAIL-ORDER BUSINESS

WHAT IS IT? A mail-order business specializes in selling a product that the business does not make. It finds a product (literally, it can be anything) and sells it through the mail.

WHAT YOU NEED TO START:
- Envelopes ($7)
- Stamps (varies)
- Computer (borrow from your parents)
- Paper (under $10)
- Printer (borrow from your parents)

Cost to Start: About $20
Time to Get Started: Five hours
Skills Needed: Working with people
Potential Customers: Businesses and neighbors

HOW TO GET STARTED:
1. Find a product that you would like to sell. Okay, so of the millions of products out there, how do you find the right one for you? Ideally you want a product that meets one of the following criteria:
   - It cannot be found easily in stores.
   - You can sell it cheaper through mail order than most stores can.
   - People simply would prefer to have the product delivered than to go pick it up.

2. Go online and look up "drop ship" companies. These are companies that will ship a product in their warehouse directly to your customer. They make it, store it, and ship it; you simply sell it. The product never touches your hands.
3. Write up a one-page leaflet with a lot of pictures advertising your product. Make it appealing to others. Put your contact info on the leaflet.
4. Set a price for each product, including the cost of shipping.
5. Determine your target market. Remember, mail-order companies can send their products to anyone in the world. So this might be a good time to make use of Google AdWords and micro-testing (see index of this book to look these up).

For More Information: *www.howtoadvice.com/MailOrderStartup*

55. MESSENGER SERVICE

WHAT IS IT? Sometimes even overnight mail is too slow. Many companies need same-day delivery. Bike messengers are a big business in big cities, but small companies in smaller communities need messenger services too. While errand runners have the luxury of following a set schedule, messengers are on call from 9 a.m. to 5 p.m. (or even later). Clients' "desperation" means big bucks for you!

WHAT YOU NEED TO START:
- Car (borrow from your parents)
- Bike (use your own)
- Helmet if biking (use your own)
- Map of town ($5)

Cost to Start: $5
Time to Get Started: Under three hours
Skills Needed: Driving or bike riding
Potential Customers: Businesses, e.g., local stores, and law firms

HOW TO GET STARTED:
1. Practice driving or biking around town until you know how to get to most places.
2. Think of businesses that need stuff delivered instantly. Law firms are a great source and so are real estate closing companies. Many stores need someone to make daily bank deposits. You can also pick up the daily lunch order.
3. Make a list of all the things you can deliver for businesses.
4. Set a price per delivery or deposit.
5. Post flyers around town and at local businesses to advertise your availability to make bank deposits and deliver small packages within certain town limits.

For More Information: *www.couriermagazine.com*

56. MOBILE CONCESSION STAND

WHAT IS IT? Selling concession items at local parks and beaches

WHAT YOU NEED TO START:
- Concessions cart (over $500)
- Food (under $50)
- Concessions license (depends on your town, about $50)
- Place to store food

Cost to Start: Over $600
Time to Get Started: Under two hours
Skills Needed: Food preparation
Potential Customers: This depends on where your concession stand is at the time. Don't think about potential customers; think about potential locations that will have a lot of customers.

HOW TO GET STARTED:
1. Find a food that you feel comfortable making or a drink you can sell. The simplest way for you to start is to sell food and drinks

that require no preparation at all, such as prepackaged candy and bottled drinks.

2. Find a location to sell your food, for example: sports fields, farmers' markets, local parks, and beaches.

3. Set a price for each item, including the cost of the food and preparation time, if any.

4. Start walking around selling your item! If people ask for items that you don't have, make a list of such items. If you get enough requests for something you don't carry, you need to start carrying it.

For More Information: *www.vendingconnection.com*

57. MUSICIAN

WHAT IS IT? There's just something about live music. If you have a talent with a musical instrument, many people will pay to have you play. The type of instrument you play often determines the events you can play at.

WHAT YOU NEED TO START:
- Instrument (cost varies, over $200, but you probably already own one). If it's an old instrument, you can always start by renting a better one every time you get a gig)
- Sheet music (under $15)

Cost to Start: Over $215
Time to Get Started: Over five hours
Skills Needed: Musical talent, practice
Potential Customers: Family, friends, and people having parties

HOW TO GET STARTED:
1. Find an instrument you enjoy playing and that you are good at. Practice playing the instrument until you are able to play many songs well. Think of the events you will be playing at. What songs do the attendees most often want to hear? If you are playing guitar at birthday parties, be sure you know how to play "Happy Birthday to You" on the guitar!
2. Set a price for each gig. Will you charge hourly or per event?
3. Post flyers at your school and around your neighborhood to advertise your availability for parties.
4. Be sure to network with other musicians!

For More Information: Go to your library to find music instruction books

58. ONLINE CONSIGNMENT RETAILER

WHAT IS IT? The Baby Boomer generation will be slowly downsizing over the next ten years. They will be getting rid of all the furniture in their four-bedroom houses and moving into smaller, two-bedroom condos. They have stuff to sell, but many of them are too busy to sell it. You can help sell their products online, charging a fee to do so.

WHAT YOU NEED TO START:
- Web site (under $50) or use an established site like eBay or craigslist
- Book about selling online ($25); see below

Cost to Start: About $75
Time to Get Started: Under three hours
Skills Needed: Marketing skills, computer skills, Web-site design
Potential Customers: Everyone

HOW TO GET STARTED:
1. Create a Web site to list all the products. Also, open up accounts on eBay and craigslist.
2. Open a merchant account and a PayPal account. Be sure to factor in these transaction fees when calculating your COGS (cost of goods sold).
3. Contact your friends and neighbors and let them know you can help them sell their stuff online.
4. The best people to target are those who are downsizing. Real estate agents often know when someone sells a big house and then buys a smaller one. Ask local realtors who is downsizing in your area, and target these customers. And, as always, ask for referrals!

For More Information: *www.craigslist.com; www.eBay.com.*
For help with eBay sales, read *Three Weeks to eBay Profits* by Skip McGrath or *How eBay Really Works* by Brad and Debra Schepp

59. ONLINE MAGAZINE PUBLISHER

WHAT IS IT? You may have always wanted to start your own magazine. The trouble is it often costs millions of dollars to print and mail magazines out. Enter the Internet. For almost nothing, you can create a magazine and people can subscribe to your online magazine or e-zine. E-zines make money in three ways: through paid subscribers, by charging for ads, or both. Unlike blogs, e-zines are far more formal and elaborate, with photos and regular columns written by multiple authors.

WHAT YOU NEED TO START:
- Computer with Internet connection (borrow from your parents)
- Publishing software (over $100)

Cost to Start: over $100
Time to Get Started: Under five hours
Skills Needed: Computer skills
Potential Customers: Family and friends

HOW TO GET STARTED:

1. Research what you would write in your magazine; make it appealing to others. Your best bet is to start with an ultra-niche magazine. There are already thousands of online magazines, and many of the major topics (business, politics, health, family, gardening, etc.) have already been taken. So think how you can be different. While there are many entrepreneurship e-zines, perhaps yours could target teenage females.

2. Price out the cost of creating and marketing your own online magazine. Talk to some Web designers. I'd start by figuring out not the best—but the cheapest—way to do it. As your subscription base grows, you can always upgrade your Web site. Also determine your revenue structure. Will you charge people to subscribe? Will you sell advertisements? A great way to start is to offer the magazine for free, but then offer a "premium" issue that people pay for.

3. If you are having trouble getting paid advertisements, you could try offering an affiliate program: Offer retailers free advertising space, but charge them a fee every time someone clicks on their ad. Or, you receive a percentage of the sale every time someone buys the retailer's product. It doesn't cost advertisers anything until they actually get a live customer!

4. Test out some Google AdWords (look up AdWords in the index of this book) to get subscribers. Offer to write free articles for other magazines like yours. If your magazine is for surfers, maybe you could write an article for a water sports magazine. Be sure to mention your own magazine in all the articles you write.

For More Information: *www.subhub.com*

60. OPENER AND CLOSER OF VACATION HOMES

WHAT IS IT? Many people have second homes, which they only use three months out of the year. It takes a lot of work to get a house ready for the summer and to close it down for the winter. When people are on vacation, they don't want to think about work. If you can have their vacation home ready for them when they arrive and close it after they leave, that means they have a few extra days of vacation! Opening and closing a home can include cleaning the place, setting the room temperature, either locking or unlocking all windows and doors, stocking the fridge, and even doing landscaping.

WHAT YOU NEED TO START:
- Cleaning supplies ($0; get from client or get money from client to purchase)

Cost to Start: $0
Time to Get Started: Under five hours
Skills Needed: Practice, knowledge of heating systems and thermostats
Potential Customers: Family, friends, neighbors, real estate agents

HOW TO GET STARTED:

1. Practice closing your parents' house. Clean the entire house, wash the sheets (do not put them back on the beds), do the dishes, cover valuables with a sheet, set the house temperature at 50 degrees Fahrenheit, and lock all windows and doors. Be sure when doing this for real that you notify the town that the house is empty before you leave.
2. Practice opening your parents' house. Dust the house, open windows to air it out, make beds, and turn up the heat (if applicable). Be sure to time yourself to see how long it takes to open and close a house.
3. Set a price for opening and closing someone's home.
4. Post flyers around your neighborhood and wherever vacation homes are located, to advertise your business.
5. Real estate agents in vacation towns often have a large vacation–rental-property business. You can probably find some outsourcing business through them.

For More Information: *www.vacationhomes.com*

61. OPEN-HOUSE SITTER

WHAT IS IT? Many real estate agents hold open houses every weekend for the homes they are trying to sell. Of course, they can only be in one house at a time, so they often need someone to sit in the open house while it is going on. In some states you may need a license to do this, but as long as you are over eighteen, you can get one. Other states might not require a license at all. You can also help the real estate agent set up the open house, by hanging balloons, turning on lights, and putting up signs.

WHAT YOU NEED TO START:

• Nothing (unless your state requires you to get a real estate license, in which case the cost of the license test and instructional course will be around $500. Perhaps the real estate agent you are working for will pay that)

Cost to Start: $0 (unless you need a license, then $500)
Time to Get Started: Under three hours
Skills Needed: Punctuality, good communication skills
Potential Customers: Real estate agents, especially the top salespeople, who have many open houses at once

HOW TO GET STARTED:

1. Call your state's real estate commission and find out if you need to be licensed to "sit" in open houses. In many states, you don't need a license, as long as you are not actually "selling" real estate (answering questions about the property).
2. Also find out how one goes about getting a license in your state. It may not be that hard and may be well worth it.
3. Spend a Sunday afternoon visiting open houses in your area. See what interesting marketing tricks realtors do to sell the house. (For instance, I've been to some open houses where real estate agents have cinnamon rolls baking in the oven. You walk in and the smell alone makes you want to buy the house. You could offer to supply such services to the agent.)
4. Print up some flyers and distribute them to local real estate agents.
5. Most offices have a monthly or even weekly sales meeting. Ask the managing broker if you can speak at their next meeting.

For More Information: *www.realtor.org*

62. PAINTER (ART)

WHAT IS IT? Painting pictures that you can then sell. You may offer to paint portraits or other requested subjects.

WHAT YOU NEED TO START:

• Canvas (under $5)
• Paint set (under $20)
• Brushes ($20)

Cost to Start: Under $45
Time to Get Started: Under seven hours
Skills Needed: Artistic talent
Potential Customers: Family, friends, neighbors, and art stores

HOW TO GET STARTED:

1. Practice painting different subjects. Find something that you enjoy painting. Have your parents critique your paintings to help you improve. Sign up for an art course in school or at your local community center.
2. Set a price for each painting, based on size. You can also be commissioned to paint a picture at someone's request (arrange pricing with the person).
3. Travel to galleries and stores, asking them to sell your work.
4. Set up a Web site with photos of your paintings. Mention that you do customized paintings as well.
5. Think about who would buy a customized painting. New families? Parents with graduating students? Remember, you always want to do target marketing!

6. Post flyers around the town and in your neighborhood, advertising your works of art.
For More Information: *www.painteasy.com*

63. PAINTER (EXTERIOR)

WHAT IS IT? Painting the outside of houses, porches, or fences for customers

WHAT YOU NEED TO START:
- Outdoor paint and brushes to practice with (under $25)
- Ladder (borrow from the customer)
- Scraper ($5)
- Dust mask ($5)

Cost to Start: Under $35 (charge any additional supplies to client)
Time to Get Started: Under four hours
Skills Needed: Practice
Potential Customers: family, friends, and neighbors

HOW TO GET STARTED:
1. Practice painting either a fence or porch outside. Make sure to do a thorough job, and have your parents critique it. Ask your parents to pay for the supplies.
2. Set an hourly wage.
3. Discuss with your parents the idea of your climbing ladders to paint the second or third floors of houses. This is a family decision and may require you to carry additional insurance.
4. Remember that houses built before 1978 may contain lead paint, which can be dangerous if it is sanded incorrectly. Be sure to inquire about the age of the house and ask your state's lead-paint agency for information about painting houses that may contain lead paint. Ask the client to test for lead before starting.
5. Post flyers around your neighborhood and at local hardware stores.
For More Information: *www.painteasy.com,*
www.behr.com/behrx/expert

64. PAINTER (INTERIOR OF HOUSE OR APARTMENT)

WHAT IS IT? Painting the ceiling, walls, and trim inside of people's houses is a great business. Sometimes people will hire you just to work alongside them. Remember, when you paint the inside of a house, it kicks up a lot of dust and temporarily removes rooms from use. Because of this, people want the job over with quickly, so even if they plan to do it themselves, they might hire you to assist them.

WHAT YOU NEED TO START:
- Paintbrushes (wide and narrow)
- Interior paint
- Painter's tape
- Rollers and roller sticks
- Rolling tray
- Tarp
- Sandpaper
- Dust mask
- Patching compound to fix cracks

Cost to Start: $0 (of course, you will need the above supplies, but you can charge them to the client)
Time to Get Started: Under three hours
Skills Needed: Practice
Potential Customers: Homeowners and businesses

HOW TO GET STARTED:
1. Read online or in a book about how to paint a room. Visit a local paint store for tips.
2. Ask your parents if you can paint one of the rooms in their house for practice. Be very careful not to drip any paint and to do an even job. Get them to pay for the supplies. Have them inspect your work.
3. Remember that houses built before 1978 may contain lead paint, which can be dangerous if sanded or disposed of incorrectly. Be sure to inquire about the age of the house and ask your state's lead-paint agency for information about painting in houses that may contain lead paint. Ask the client to test for lead before starting.
4. Set a price based on an hourly wage or size of room. Don't forget to include cost of supplies.
5. Post flyers around your neighborhood and at local hardware stores, advertising your availability. Be sure that each client has all the materials needed, such as brushes, etc. If they don't, you'll have to buy them and charge them to the client.
6. Be sure to also market yourself as a painter's assistant. Again, many people want to paint their own rooms, but they want to do it quickly and may pay you to help them.
For More Information: *www.behr.com/behrx/expert*

65. PAINTING/REFINISHING FURNITURE

WHAT IS IT? Older furniture was built to last forever. And it will. It just needs an occasional touch-up. This business involves sanding, painting, or staining a piece of furniture so that it looks new and improved. You can also offer to stain or paint unfinished furniture.

WHAT YOU NEED TO START:
- Paint or stain (under $25)
- Varnish, if using stain ($15)
- Brushes ($10)
- Sandpaper (under $5)
- Dust masks ($5)
- Rags ($0)

Cost to Start: Under $60
Time to Get Started: Under five hours
Skills Needed: Practice and patience
Potential Customers: Family, neighbors, local stores and businesses

HOW TO GET STARTED:
1. Ask your parents for a piece of furniture that you can sand and then repaint or re-stain to make it look better. Ask your parents to pay for the supplies. Be sure to wear a dust mask when sanding. Practice on this piece of furniture and make sure to cover every inch. Take before and after photos for marketing your work.
2. Research different techniques to make the furniture have an artistic look.
3. Set either an hourly wage or a price based on the size of the piece of furniture and difficulty of the job.
4. Post flyers around your neighborhood and at hardware stores. Also post them at stores that sell unfinished furniture.

For More Information: *http://thefurnituredoctor.net/business.htm*

66. PARTY ASSISTANT

WHAT IS IT? Helping to plan and assist at a party. You might be serving snacks, picking up the catering, or setting up the decorations.

WHAT YOU NEED TO START:
- Nothing

Cost to Start: $0
Time to Get Started: Under four hours
Skills Needed: Shopping, organizational and decorating skills
Potential Customers: Family, friends, neighbors

HOW TO GET STARTED:
1. Ask your parents to let you help them plan a party. Take care of all of the little details for your parents, like setting up decorations and food. Ask them to pay for the food, etc., and critique how you did.

2. Set either an hourly wage or have a flat rate per party.
3. Post flyers around your neighborhood at grocery stores and party-supply stores. Ask for referrals from your parents. Get the word out there that you are available!
4. Consider your marketing strategy. Maybe your parents go to several holiday parties every year. Contact the people hosting these parties and offer your services. Most people have parties during the summer or over the holidays. That's your time to market!

For More Information: *www.partycity.com*

67. PERSONAL ASSISTANT

WHAT IS IT? Helping a person maintain his or her life by doing things such as organizing files, helping with mailings, and updating the daily planner. Busy people always need extra help, and you will find a lot of customers who need a personal assistant just for one day a week or a month.

WHAT YOU NEED TO START:
- Notepad (under $5)
- Daily planner ($5)
- Pens (borrow from your parents)
- Cell phone ($50 a month, but it's possible to charge clients for this)
- Means of transport (car, bike, or other)

Cost to Start: Under $10 (plus cost of cell phone)
Time to Get Started: Under an hour
Skills Needed: Organizational skills, driving, or bike-riding
Potential Customers: Businesses, family, and neighbors

HOW TO GET STARTED:
1. Play the role of personal assistant to one of your parents for a day. Whatever you are asked to do, do it. This will give you a good idea of what it's like being a personal assistant.
2. Set an hourly wage. Be sure to include your expenses such as gas (if you drive) and cell phone costs.
3. Post flyers at local businesses and around your neighborhood to advertise your availability. Let friends of your parents know about your services. Be sure to mention it if you can run errands for them with a car.
4. Some good people to target are self-employed folks like real estate agents. Many people need a personal assistant but cannot afford to hire one full time. Offer your services for just a day or even for a few hours.

For More Information: *www.personalassistantpro.com*

68. PERSONAL SHOPPER

WHAT IS IT? Holidays are a very busy time. Malls are crowded, especially during nights and weekends. Personal shoppers act like professional gift buyers. They ask their clients to describe whom the gift is for, the recipient's interests and dislikes, as well as the price range of the gift. Then they shop and purchase the present.

WHAT YOU NEED TO START:
- Car (borrow from your parents) or other means of transport

Cost to Start: $0
Time to Get Started: Under an hour
Skills Needed: An eye for value, creativity
Potential Customers: Family, neighbors, local businesses

HOW TO GET STARTED:
1. Ask to help your parents with their gift shopping. Have them describe the people for whom they are buying gifts. Think of several gift ideas for these people. Don't buy anything. Just compare prices and report back to your parents. Ask them to critique your choices.
2. Set an hourly wage and don't forget the cost of gas if you use a car. Sometimes gift shoppers add a percentage onto the price of the gift. You might add a fee of 20% to any gift you buy. So if you buy a $100 gift, you just made twenty bucks!
3. Post flyers around your neighborhood and at local businesses. Think of busy people who don't have the time to do their own shopping. You can also offer an office discount. Take lawyers, for instance. They are busy people. Pitch to an entire law firm to do all of their holiday shopping and offer a discount.

For More Information:
www.ehow.com/how_15306_become-personal-shopper.html;
www.BecomeaPersonalShopper.biz

69. PET CAGE CLEANER

WHAT IS IT? Going to the homes of clients and cleaning the cages of their pets. This certainly is a dirty job, but that's why folks will pay big bucks for you to do it for them!

WHAT YOU NEED TO START:
- Rubber gloves ($2)
- Garbage bags ($5)
- Cleaning soap or detergent ($3)
- Paper towels ($2)

Cost to Start: $10
Time to Get Started: Under three hours
Skills Needed: Good with animals
Potential Customers: Veterinarians, animal shelters, and pet owners

HOW TO GET STARTED:

1. Practice cleaning an animal's cage. Throw out the newspaper or chips that the animal has been living in, clean the base and bars, and reassemble the cage (adding new paper/chips). Put in new water and food.
2. Set a weekly price to do this at someone's house. Be sure to include the cost of your supplies.
3. Post flyers around your neighborhood and at local pet supply stores.

For More Information: Contact your local veterinarian office or animal shelter or visit the Web site for the ASPCA *(www.aspca.org)*

70. PHOTO EDITOR

WHAT IS IT? Retouching and editing photos for clients.

WHAT YOU NEED TO START:
- Computer (borrow from your parents)
- Photo editing software (about $50)
- Scanner and printer (borrow from parents)

Cost to Start: About $50
Time to Get Started: Under five hours
Skills Needed: Computer skills, practice
Potential Customers: Family, friends, neighbors, and photography studios

HOW TO GET STARTED:

1. Practice editing photos on your parents' computer. Learn how to retouch, crop, change the exposure, and fix the photos.
2. Set a price, either hourly or per photo.
3. Post flyers around your neighborhood and anywhere that photos are printed, advertising your business. Offer yourself as an outsource option to print shops.

For More Information: *www.lunapic.com*

71. PHOTOGRAPHER (PORTRAIT, SPECIAL EVENTS)

WHAT IS IT? Taking pictures of special events or portraits.

WHAT YOU NEED TO START:
- Digital camera (over $200 or borrow from your parents)
- Computer (use your parents')
- Printer (use your parents')
- Blank CDs (under $15)

- Photo-editing software ($50 or more)
- Photo paper (bill to customer)

Cost to Start: About $265 or more
Time to Get Started: Three hours
Skills Needed: Experience with photography, computer skills
Potential Customers: Family, friends, neighbors, pet owners, wedding planners

HOW TO GET STARTED:

1. Practice taking pictures of your family in different lighting situations. Shoot both inside and out. Most photographers also work with an apprentice. Try to get some free training by offering to work for free as an apprentice to a local photographer.
2. Transfer the pictures onto your computer; learn how to edit them to create the best possible picture. Then burn the best ones onto a CD to give to your clients.
3. Set a price, either an hourly wage or flat rate.
4. Post flyers around your neighborhood and at local drugstores (near picture-printing areas).
5. Think of all the special events you can photograph: weddings, birthday parties, bar mitzvahs, graduation parties, new parents and their baby, and office parties.

   For More Information: *www.photographytips.com,* books like *Capture the Portrait* by Jenni Bidner and *Digital Portrait Photography: Art, Business & Style* by Steve Sint

72. PHOTOGRAPHER (PRINT)

WHAT IS IT? You can photograph newsworthy events or do nature photos and sell these photos to newspapers, magazines, and even to individual customers.

WHAT YOU NEED TO START:

- Digital camera (over $200 or borrow from your parents)
- Computer (use your parents' computer)
- Photo-editing software ($50 or more)
- Blank CDs (under $15)

Cost to Start: About $265
Time to Get Started: Three hours
Skills Needed: Experience with photography, computer skills
Potential Customers: Magazines and newspapers, frame shops

HOW TO GET STARTED:

1. Practice taking pictures in various lighting situations and locations. Shoot both inside and out. Most photographers work with an apprentice. Try to get some free training by offering to work for free as an apprentice to a local photographer.

2. Transfer the pictures onto your computer; learn how to edit them to create the best possible picture. Then burn the best ones onto a CD to give to your clients.

3. Visit local frame stores and ask what photos are the most popular.

4. Call up your local newspaper and ask what photos they are looking for. Mail them one of your CDs and let them know you are available as a freelance photographer.

5. Set a price, either an hourly wage or flat rate.

6. Post flyers around your neighborhood and at local drugstores (near picture printing areas) and framing shops.

For More Information: *www.photographytips.com; The KODAK Most Basic Book of Digital Nature Photography* by Russell Graves; *Digital Nature and Landscape Photography* by Mark Lucock (books)

73. PLANT CARETAKER

WHAT IS IT? Most people love having plants, but taking care of them can be a pain. Watering plants on a consistent basis inside and outside people's homes can be a great business, because if people want to go away for a weekend or for a vacation, they have to hire someone to water the plants. That's you!

WHAT YOU NEED TO START:
- Watering can and hose (borrow from customer)
- Plant fertilizer (borrow from customer)

Cost to Start: $0
Time to Get Started: Under two hours
Skills Needed: Knowledge of plants
Potential Customers: Neighbors, local businesses

HOW TO GET STARTED:
1. Research different types of plants and how much water they prefer. Check with the customers also about how they usually water.

2. Set a weekly wage to water all the plants in a person's home and garden.

3. Post flyers around your neighborhood to advertise your business.

For More Information: *www.lewisgardens.com/watering.htm; www.gardening.about.com*

74. PLANT/FLOWER SELLER

WHAT IS IT? Selling plants that you have grown from seedlings or selling bouquets that you have created using flowers from your garden.

WHAT YOU NEED TO START:
- Garden space
- Soil
- Fertilizer
- Seeds
- Gardening tools
- Small pots for transplanting
- Container for cut flowers

Cost to Start: Varies; under $100 (try to borrow as much equipment as you can from your parents)
Time to Get Started: Under three hours
Skills Needed: Gardening
Potential Customers: Family, neighbors, local stores and businesses

HOW TO GET STARTED:
1. Learn about what plants can thrive in your garden. Also find out what types of plants people are buying. Decide on the top two to five plants you are going to grow. Unsure of where to start? Ask your customers! Find out how to transplant plants. Visit a local nursery to get more information.
2. Let all your neighbors know you will be growing plants right in your own backyard. Your yard is your store. If you need more places to sell, inquire about selling at your local farmers' market (if doing this, you need a special permit and must grow your own flowers).
3. Set a price per bouquet or per plant.
4. Post flyers around your neighborhood to let people know when to go to your yard to buy fresh flowers or plants. Remember, businesses often order plants as gifts.

For More Information: *www.gardeningclub.com; gardening.about.com*

75. POET

WHAT IS IT? Buying the perfect gift for someone is always a challenge. You never know if the person already has it, or if it will be the right size. A great business is to offer an easy, one-size-fits-all gift for everyone. If you have a knack for writing, you could offer people the chance to give a personalized poem as a gift.

WHAT YOU NEED TO START:
- Nothing

Cost to Start: $0
Time to Get Started: Under five hours

Skills Needed: Writing, love of poetry
Potential Customers: Family and friends

HOW TO GET STARTED:

1. Practice writing poetry. Ask your parents and teachers to critique your work. Get inspiration by reading as much poetry as you can.
2. Set a price per poem. Offer to write a poem for your customer on a certain subject, like a daughter's graduation or the arrival of a new baby.
3. Think about special occasions when people would need a poem. Graduation? Weddings? Anniversaries? The birth of a baby? Find a way to market to these people.
4. Post flyers around your neighborhood, advertising your business.
5. Remember, anyone can buy this gift, so you might want to look into creating a Web site and AdWords campaigns (see index of this book for more info. about AdWords).

For More Information: *www.rhymer.com*

76. POOL CLEANER

WHAT IS IT? You would clean motorcycles. No, just kidding. Of course, you clean pools. This could include skimming the top for leaves, adding chemicals to keep it clean, and even vacuuming the bottom of the pool.

WHAT YOU NEED TO START:

- Nothing (almost all pool owners have their own cleaning materials)

Cost to Start: $0
Time to Get Started: Over three hours
Skills Needed: Knowledge of pool cleaning equipment and chemicals
Potential Customers: Homeowners, hotels, and apartment buildings

HOW TO GET STARTED:

1. Practice cleaning someone's pool. Learn the amount of chlorine to put in and how to use the vacuum, clean the filters, and remove debris floating on top.
2. Set an hourly wage or flat rate based on the size of the pool.
3. Make a list of all the people you know who have a pool. Be sure to include hotels, motels, and apartment buildings. Create a flyer and give one to each of them.
4. Consider creating a second flyer to give to people who don't own a pool but can refer you to someone who does. Offer a hefty referral fee for their help.

For More Information: *www.pooltechguy.com*

77. PRODUCT TESTER

WHAT IS IT? The majority of companies out there aren't run by teenagers, but many of them sell their products to teenagers. Before they make a sale, they often give a product to a teen to try out. A product tester may have the product for several months, testing things like its durability and reliability. Sounds cool, doesn't it?

WHAT YOU NEED TO START:
• Computer (borrow from your parents)

Cost to Start: $0
Time to Get Started: Under two hours
Skills Needed: Good communications skills
Potential Customers: Businesses that manufacture or market products to teenagers

HOW TO GET STARTED:
1. Go on the Internet and search for product testers. Find Web sites that will ship you free products in return for your feedback.
2. Beware of scams! Many companies sell information on how to become a product tester. Some of it is good; some of it is outright garbage. Be aware. Do not give out your personal information unless you are sure you are dealing with a safe Web site. Always consult your parents before providing any personal information.
3. Make a list of the top 25 companies for which you could test products. Put their names on a mailing list and start contacting them. Mail to them enough times, and they will have to respond to you.
4. When you receive the product, be sure to leave a lot of feedback!

For More Information: *www.zoompanel.com*

78. PROFESSIONAL ORGANIZER

WHAT IS IT? Remember when we discussed the E Myth? Just because you are good at making sandwiches doesn't mean you are good at running a sandwich shop. Likewise, many people are good at their job but need help with the little stuff, like staying organized. You can organize something as simple as a file cabinet, or an entire house or office building!

WHAT YOU NEED TO START:
• Nothing

Cost to Start: $0
Time to Get Started: Under three hours
Skills Needed: Cleaning and organizational skills
Potential Customers: Family, friends, neighbors, local businesses and other entrepreneurs

HOW TO GET STARTED:

1. Practice organizing your parents' offices, garage, attic, or any room that is overcrowded. Offer to organize all their files. Have them critique your work.

2. Compile a list of good questions to ask before you take on an organization job. Most people are unorganized not because they never took the time to do it, but because they never thought about the best way to do it.

3. Set an hourly wage.

4. Post flyers at local businesses and around your neighborhood, advertising your organizational skills for any type of room. Ask your parents about their messiest friends. These are the people to start with.

5. This can be a business in which sampling yields big rewards. Offer to organize just one file cabinet for someone. When he sees how good you are, he'll sign you up to do everything.

For More Information: *www.orgsolutions.net*

79. PROOFREADER

WHAT IS IT? Everyone needs a proofreader. Students need their term papers double-checked. Companies need someone to edit their brochures and Web sites. If you have a good eye and a firm grasp of grammar, this one is for you.

WHAT YOU NEED TO START:

- Computer (borrow from your parents)
- Colored pens (borrow from home)
- Style guide (such as *The Chicago Manual of Style*, $55)
- Dictionary (borrow from parents or use online dictionary)

Cost to Start: Under $60
Time to Get Started: Under three hours
Skills Needed: Computer skills, grammar and reading skills
Potential Customers: Friends, schools, and businesses

HOW TO GET STARTED:

1. Become familiar with the common proofreading symbols (see the Web site listed below).

2. Find two people you can practice on. One might have a small business that has a new brochure or Web site. The other might be a writer with a book or a student with a long term paper. Ask them to critique your work.

3. Set an hourly wage.

4. Post flyers around your neighborhood and at local businesses, advertising your attention to detail and editing skills.

5. A great way to get business is simply to proofread company Web

sites. If you find a mistake, e-mail the company about it. They'll be surprised you caught it.

For More Information:
www.unc.edu/depts/wcweb/handouts/proofread.html;
http://webster.commnet.edu/writing/symbols.htm;
www.thewritersbag.com/writing-techniques/proofreading-tips

80. RECREATIONAL VEHICLES WASHER

WHAT IS IT? While people can take their cars to a car wash, they can't do that with a motorcycle. Or a boat. Or an RV. Owners of these have to have their vehicles washed by hand.

WHAT YOU NEED TO START:
- Soap (under $5)
- Towels (under $5)
- Brush ($20)
- Bucket ($5)

Cost to Start: Under $35
Time to Get Started: Under five hours
Skills Needed: Attention to detail
Potential Customers: Neighbors and businesses, including boat marinas and RV dealers

HOW TO GET STARTED:
1. Practice washing boats, four-wheelers, and motorcycles. Research any special cleaning required for certain vehicles (like cleaning the bottoms of boats).
2. Set an hourly wage, and don't forget the cost of supplies.
3. Post flyers around your neighborhood and at parks, advertising your business.
4. Think about your target market. A boat owner is a good target, but a boat marina is better. Offer a discount to every boat in the marina. Offer the marina a referral fee for every boat it sends your way. Or maybe you could target campgrounds. People can park their RVs and then go on a hike for the day. When they come back, their RV has been cleaned!

For More Information:
www.docksidereports.com/washing_down.htm

81. RESEARCHER

WHAT IS IT? Researching topics for people when they cannot do the research themselves. You research the topics thoroughly and then turn in notes on the subject to the client. Assignments range from market research for an advertising company to historical research for a writer. In short, you get paid to learn.

WHAT YOU NEED TO START:
- Computer with Internet connection (borrow from your parents)
- Printer (borrow from your parents)
- Paper ($5)
- CDs ($10)

Cost to Start: $15
Time to Get Started: Under three hours
Skills Needed: Computer and reading skills
Potential Customers: Family, neighbors, businesses, and schools

HOW TO GET STARTED:
1. Find someone to act as your first client. You won't charge her; you simply want to practice your research skills. Ask very specific questions as to what she is looking for. Do the research, present it, and ask the client to critique your work.
2. Make a list of people you know who could use a professional researcher. Do you know any writers? College professors? Small business owners? All these people need help with research.
3. Set an hourly wage.
4. Post flyers around your neighborhood, at the local college, and at businesses. Researching is a great business for using sampling as a marketing strategy. Sampling doesn't cost you anything, aside from your time.

For More Information: Find specific Web sites or go to your local library for books on your subject. Two great research sites are *www.google.com* and *www.wikipedia.org*

82. SHOE SHINER

WHAT IS IT? Shoe shiners can either have a pickup service or an actual stand. Of course, they can do both. What I like about this business is that it really hasn't changed in a hundred years. It's safe and simple, and new technology is not going to force you out of business.

WHAT YOU NEED TO START:
- Shoeshine kit (under $50)

Cost to Start: Under $50
Time to Get Started: Under three hours
Skills Needed: Practice
Potential Customers: Family, neighbors, and businesses

HOW TO GET STARTED:
1. Practice shining five pairs of your parents' shoes. Make sure you do a detailed job.
2. Set a price per pair of shoes.
3. Post flyers around your neighborhood and at local businesses,

offering to shine people's shoes if they drop them off at your house. (You could even do a delivery service.)

4. Think about the big target markets. Some hotels offer a service in which folks can leave their shoes outside the door and have them shined for free. The hotel would pay you to provide this service. Or you could do all of someone's shoes at once, twice a year. Think about what will get you the most clients the fastest.

For More Information: *www.wikihow.com/Shine-Shoes*

83. SHOPPER FOR ELDERLY PEOPLE

WHAT IS IT? Shopping for groceries and other supplies for elderly clients if they can no longer do it.

WHAT YOU NEED TO START:
• Car (borrow from your parents) or bike

Cost to Start: $0
Time to Get Started: Under an hour
Skills Needed: Driver's license, organizational and bargain-hunting skills
Potential Customers: Family and neighbors

HOW TO GET STARTED:
1. Go shopping with your parents to learn the best products to buy and how to bargain shop.
2. Set a price for your service, either an hourly wage or a flat rate per errand.
3. Post flyers around your neighborhood, at retirement communities, and at nursing homes, advertising your business.

For More Information: *www.wikihow.com/Bargain-Shop*

84. SNOW SHOVELER

WHAT IS IT? When it comes to snow shoveling, there are three types of people: those who pay a snow-plowing company to do it all, those who do it all themselves, and those people who hire a plow for the big stuff like the driveway but choose to shovel their own walkways and steps. These last two groups are the ones you target. Sometimes, even the folks who want to do it all themselves need help during a big storm. And most snow-plowing companies charge way too much money to hand-shovel the walkways. You may have to get up really early, but this is a super business.

WHAT YOU NEED TO START:
• Snow shovel (borrow from your parents or customer)
• Bags of sand (free if you get them from your town)
• Bags of salt (charge to customer)

Cost to Start: $0
Time to Get Started: Under three hours
Skills Needed: Heavy lifting
Potential Customers: Homeowners, local stores and businesses

HOW TO GET STARTED:

1. Practice shoveling your parents' driveway and sanding or salting it.
2. Set an hourly wage or flat rate per driveway. Don't forget to include the price of salt. Offer to lay down salt or sand if your clients ask for it.
3. Post flyers around your neighborhood and at local hardware stores.
4. Snow-plowing companies can make a great outsourcing market. Most plow drivers won't bother to hand-shovel, even though they know most of their customers want it. That's where you come in!

For More Information: *www.wikihow.com/Shovel-Snow*

85. SONGWRITER

WHAT IS IT? People are constantly in search of a unique gift to give to their spouse, girlfriend or boyfriend, child, or other relative. Birthdays and the holidays come every year. Every year, people must dream up something new and different. A personalized song can be a great gift.

WHAT YOU NEED TO START:

- You'll need the instruments to play and to record your music, but you can bill this to clients when they hire you ($0)
- Ruled music paper if you're writing sheet music to give to the customers ($10)

Cost to Start: $10
Time to Get Started: Under six hours
Skills Needed: Writing music, playing a musical instrument, writing poetry
Potential Customers: Family, friends, party and wedding planners

HOW TO GET STARTED:

1. Practice composing music. To market your services, you will probably need to make a demo tape, showing samples of two or three of your songs.
2. Create a Web site at which people can listen to the demo songs online.
3. Get a price list from a recording studio to find out how much it costs to rent it for a few hours. Most likely this will be very expensive, so inquire about other ways to record songs for people. Keep in mind that many people might not want the recording, just the

sheet music for their song. Have a menu of services ranging from just the sheet music, to a "rough" recording using semiprofessional equipment, all the way up to a professional recording.

4. Practice writing lyrics to go along with your music. Ask your parents to give you a critique.

5. You can also write corporate jingles. These are songs that companies use to sell a product. Often companies have bigger budgets than individuals.

6. Post flyers around your neighborhood and at local music clubs, advertising your talent.

For More Information: *www.rhymer.com*

86. SPORTS TUTOR

WHAT IS IT? People tutor math on a one-on-one basis; why can't they teach soccer like that too? Or lacrosse? If you are particularly good at a sport, become a sports tutor.

WHAT YOU NEED TO START:
• Use your own sports equipment or borrow from your client

Cost to Start: $0
Time to Get Started: Under three hours
Skills Needed: Athletic ability, good communication skills
Potential Customers: Parents and friends

HOW TO GET STARTED:
1. Pick a sport that you are particularly good at. Write up some drills and exercises that you would have someone do to get better at the sport.

2. Set an hourly wage.

3. Post flyers around your neighborhood and at local sports venues, advertising your skill at said sport. Make sure that potential clients have all the supplies for that sport.

4. Talk to all the coaches for your sport in town. Oftentimes, kids are upset when they don't make the team. Parents are willing to spend money to make sure that doesn't happen next year. Coaches can tell you who those kids are!

For More Information: *www.howtosports.com*

87. TOY ASSEMBLER

WHAT IS IT? You know by now that the holidays are a busy time. Parents need all the help they can get. Whether it is assembling that bike so it will be ready Christmas morning or helping a child set up her new princess castle, there can be great money over the holidays helping parents put together toys. You can even help stores assemble toys for display models.

- Screwdriver and other tools (borrow from your parents or from your client)

Cost to Start: $0
Time to Get Started: Under two hours
Skills Needed: Ability to follow instructions
Potential Customers: Family, neighbors, and local stores

HOW TO GET STARTED:
1. Practice putting together toys that your parents have bought for others.
2. Set an hourly wage.
3. Post flyers around your neighborhood and at local toy stores around Christmastime, advertising your availability to put presents together.

For More Information: Carefully follow the instructions that come with the product

88. TRANSLATOR

WHAT IS IT? Can you speak a second language? If so, you might be able to find work as a translator. Businesses sometimes need help dealing with clients who don't speak English, or they might want to create a foreign-language version of their Web site. Sometimes adults want a bilingual person to accompany their elderly parents, who may not speak fluent English, on errands.

WHAT YOU NEED TO START:
- Nothing

Cost to Start: $0
Time to Get Started: Varies
Skills Needed: Fluency in a foreign language and reading ability in that language
Potential Customers: Businesses, first generation Americans

HOW TO GET STARTED:
1. Find a language that you love. Learn to speak it, if you have not already done so.
2. Remember that translators must be fluent in their second language. A general knowledge of the language is not enough.
3. Set an hourly wage.
4. Post flyers at local businesses, offering to help them with meetings conducted with people who speak your target language. You can also offer to translate documents.

5. Often there are ethnic clubs you can investigate, such as the Polish American club. These make great places to post flyers.

For More Information: Your local library probably will have many language tutorials on tape or CD to help you learn. Also visit *www.rosettastone.com*

89. TRAVEL AGENT

WHAT IS IT? With the introduction of online travel sites like Travelocity, many people think that the travel agent is a dying breed. On the contrary, this is a booming business for many people. Lots of money can be saved if a travel agent is watching the fares closely every day. Most people don't have the time to do that, so using an agent can actually save them time and money.

WHAT YOU NEED TO START:
• Computer with Internet connection (borrow from your parents)

Cost to Start: $0
Time to Get Started: Under five hours
Skills Needed: Computer and reading skills
Potential Customers: Family and neighbors, church and youth groups

HOW TO GET STARTED:
1. Research Web sites where you can book flights, reserve rooms in hotels, and rent cars. Find highly recommended places. Book a pretend vacation for your parents as practice.
2. Consider paying to join a travel-agent franchise, like Dugan's Travels. Although these can be expensive (like $500), you can earn a commission for putting someone into a hotel or rental car. (Airlines, unfortunately, no longer pay commissions.)
3. Set a flat rate for your services.
4. Post flyers around your neighborhood and at grocery stores and airports. Make sure to get referrals from friends!
5. Focus on groups and people who travel a lot. Ask your parents which of their friends are frequent travelers.

For More Information: *www.travelocity.com; www.kayak.com; www.duganstravels.com; www.hotels.com*

90. T-SHIRT DESIGNER

WHAT IS IT? You can never have enough T-shirts. T-shirt designers can make their own standard designs or offer to do custom designs around a specific event like "the Johnson Family Reunion."

WHAT YOU NEED TO START:
- T-shirts (under $5 per shirt, buy as you need them)
- Computer and printer (borrow from your parents)
- Iron (borrow from your parents)
- T-shirt transfer paper (under $20)
- Silkscreen machine ($1,000, don't need to purchase at start)

Cost to Start: Over $1,000 (if you buy a silkscreen machine)
Time to Get Started: Over three hours
Skills Needed: Computer skills
Potential Customers: Everyone, including sports teams, family groups, businesses, and rock bands

HOW TO GET STARTED:
1. Create several designs and ask your friends and family which ones they like best.
2. Print your design onto the transfer paper. Read the transfer paper instructions so you know what to do. Iron it onto the T-shirt.
3. Create a Web site with photos of all your T-shirt designs. You don't need to actually make the shirts; you can make the designs on your computer and explain that any of these designs can be transferred to a shirt.
3. Set a price per T-shirt, including the price of the shirt and paper used.
4. Post flyers around your neighborhood and at school, advertising the shirts. Sell them at town events (a license may be required to do this).
5. Eventually your T-shirt business should look into buying a silkscreen machine, which costs around $1,000. You might be able to rent one or get a few "free" hours on one by working in a T-shirt shop in exchange for the hours. Silk-screening creates much higher quality designs than the iron-ons.
6. The key to a T-shirt business is to get those large orders. Making and selling one T-shirt at a time is tough. Doing all the T-shirts for a baseball team or all the T-shirts for a rock concert or class reunion is the way to go.

For More Information: *www.thompsontransfers.com*

91. TUTOR

WHAT IS IT? Most parents will pay just about anything to make sure their kids succeed. You can get paid to help students with certain school subjects. Unlike a homework checker, who arrives after the work is done, a tutor is there while the work is being done.

WHAT YOU NEED TO START:
- Nothing

Cost to Start: $0
Time to Get Started: Under two hours
Skills Needed: Advanced knowledge of a subject, reading ability, working well with people
Potential Customers: Family, friends, neighbors, schools, and teachers

HOW TO GET STARTED:
1. Find a subject in which you excel. Research and study that topic to a greater depth. Find a child to practice-tutor for free. Ask that child's parents to critique your work.
2. Set an hourly wage for your services.
3. Post flyers advertising the subject in which you can help others around your school and neighborhood. Tell all the teachers in town that you are a tutor.

For More Information: *www.wikihow.com/Become-a-Tutor*

92. TYPIST

WHAT IS IT? Typing up reports or any other data that a client wants processed with speed. Some executives also dictate their notes into a machine and then send the files off to someone to be typed. Even in this high-tech world, many people still hate typing.

WHAT YOU NEED TO START:
- Computer (borrow from your parents)

Cost to Start: $0
Time to Get Started: Under three hours
Skills Needed: Computer skills
Potential Customers: Family, neighbors, businesses, and schools

HOW TO GET STARTED:
1. Practice typing on your computer until you become efficient at it. Take an online word-per-minute test to show your speed.
2. Set either an hourly wage or a flat rate per project.
3. Post flyers around your neighborhood and at local businesses, advertising your speed and offering to type various things for clients.
4. Offer this service to your fellow classmates that hate typing. Also, post flyers at local colleges. Many students still love to handwrite their notes, and you can offer to type them so they are easy to read later.

For More Information: *www.typingtest.com*

93. USED-BOOK SELLER

WHAT IS IT? Books are durable products that never really go out of style. People have such a large respect for books that they typically won't throw them away. But they will give them away, which means you can get products to sell for FREE! This is a great business because you can set up an account on eBay to sell your books and then you can take your most popular titles to flea markets and garage sales.

WHAT YOU NEED TO START:

- Various used books (cost is under $100, but also feel free to ask for donations)
- Folding table (borrow from your parents)

Cost to Start: Under $100
Time to Get Started: Under four hours
Skills Needed: Customer service, interest in literature, good sales skills
Potential Customers: Everyone

HOW TO GET STARTED:

1. Ask your parents, friends, and neighbors for donations of books.
2. See if one of your local town recycling centers has a book swap. Remember, one person's trash is another person's treasure. You might be able to get your inventory for free.
3. Set up an interactive Web site at which people can e-mail you and request titles. Next time you are scanning your local book swap, be sure to take the list of titles you are looking for.
4. Set up an eBay account listing all of your books and their prices.
5. Inquire at local flea markets about the cost of selling books. If you live on a busy street, you might even open a stand at the end of your driveway.
6. Price the various books you sell based on condition and cover. Offer to buy books as well, in order to sell them again. You can check your used book prices against the prices at online book retailers.
7. Post flyers around your neighborhood that list the hours that your stand is open. Remind your neighbors that you are happy to take their used books off their hands. That means free inventory for you!

For More Information: Check out used book prices at used book stores and online. Visit eBay to learn how to set up an account (*www.ebay.com*)

94. VIDEO GAME TESTER

WHAT IS IT? Yes, you read that correctly. Some people get paid to play video games. This, of course, is a much sought-after job, so I can't instantly give it the "simple" stamp of approval. But if you are passionate about it, go for it.

WHAT YOU NEED TO START:
- Computer with Internet connection (borrow from your parents)
- Video game console (use one you have or buy one for under $300)

Cost to Start: Under $300
Time to Get Started: Under three hours
Skills Needed: Video game skills, writing and communication skills
Potential Customers: Family, friends, neighbors, and local stores

HOW TO GET STARTED:
1. Bar none, the easiest way for this to work is to get ranked on one of the gaming Web sites or to win a video game tournament (either an online tournament or a live one). Then you won't have to market to video game companies. They will come to you.
2. If you don't have the amazing skill for that, you can simply start playing games you like, write very detailed reports on them, and send those reports free of charge to the companies that make the games. With luck, they will notice your attention to detail and ask you to write more of them and pay you for them!
3. I want to stress that this is not an easy business to start because so many people want to do it. But if you want to try, don't let the competition stop you!

For More Information: *www.gamestester.com*

95. VIDEOGRAPHER

WHAT IS IT? Every time there is a special event, people want it videotaped. But if they videotape it, they can't fully participate in the event at the same time. That's why they hire you!

WHAT YOU NEED TO START:
- Digital video camera (over $300 or borrow from your parents)
- Computer (borrow from your parents)
- Editing software (over $50)
- Blank DVDs (over $20)

Cost to Start: Over $370
Time to Get Started: Over four hours
Skills Needed: Video camera and computer skills
Potential Customers: Businesses, weddings, parties, and schools

HOW TO GET STARTED:

1. Learn how to use the video camera and the editing software. You can start by borrowing your parents' stuff; however, eventually you'll want to graduate to professional equipment. This you can rent on a per-job basis, but it should be in your business plan to slowly accumulate your own stuff.
2. Practice making a video of a family event like a wedding or graduation. Ask your parents to critique it.
3. Make a list of all the events you could videotape, like weddings, birthdays, graduations, and bar mitzvahs.
4. Set a price, either a flat rate or an hourly wage.
5. Post flyers around your neighborhood and let event planners know about you.

For More Information: *www.videomaker.com/learn/*

96. VIRTUAL ASSISTANT

WHAT IS IT? Rather than assisting clients in person, a virtual assistant helps someone over the phone or over the Internet. As long as a task can be done remotely, it can be done with a virtual assistant. With many people having high-speed Internet connections, this business is booming.

WHAT YOU NEED TO START:

• Computer with an Internet connection (borrow from parents)

Cost to Start: $0
Time to Get Started: Under three hours
Skills Needed: Computer skills
Potential Customers: Family, neighbors, and businesses

HOW TO GET STARTED:

1. Ask your parents to make you their virtual assistant for the day. Practice doing online research, editing, database upkeep, and typing. You will be available to the person only through the Internet or phone, so all tasks assigned to you will be things done on the computer.
2. Set an hourly wage. However, the person you will be working for may have another wage in mind, so you'll have to negotiate about the wages.
3. Post flyers around your neighborhood and at local businesses to offer your services. Have your parents spread the word at their place of business and among their friends.
4. Remember that being a virtual assistant means you can literally have clients in Tokyo. So you will definitely want to put up a Web site and maybe do a quick Google AdWords campaign to find customers.

For More Information: *www.elance.com; www.assistu.com*

97. WAKE-UP CALL SERVICE

WHAT IS IT? Are you an early riser? If so, you can make money waking people up! While alarm clocks are nice, some people want the extra comfort of knowing that a living, breathing human being is going to call them.

WHAT YOU NEED TO START:
- Phone (borrow from your parents)
- Two reliable alarm clocks (use your current one and borrow another from your parents)

Cost to Start: $0
Time to Get Started: Under three hours
Skills Needed: None
Potential Customers: Family, friends, and neighbors

HOW TO GET STARTED:
1. If you are an early riser, this is no problem for you; but if you are not, you should practice waking up early.
2. Set your alarm clock for various times, making sure that it is reliable. (Remember, these people are relying on you!)
3. Set a price per wake-up call.
4. Post flyers around your neighborhood and at local businesses, offering to wake people up for important appointments.

For More Information: *www.wakerupper.com*

98. WALKING TOUR GUIDE

WHAT IS IT? This is a simple, fun business. Many people make big bucks as walking tour guides. You don't need a giant tour bus or a boat; people can simply follow you on foot as you point out local points of interest. Some tour guides don't even walk with their group. They stand at the entrance of a tourist attraction (such as a historic gravesite) and sell pamphlets that highlight the most noteworthy sites. Some tour guides don't even sell the pamphlets; they give them away and simply display a tip jar.

WHAT YOU NEED TO START:
- Nothing

Cost to Start: $0
Time to Get Started: Over three hours
Skills Needed: Reading, work well with people
Potential Customers: Tourists, neighbors, and schools

HOW TO GET STARTED:
1. Find a site or a path that would make a good walking tour. Think outside the box. Many of the obvious tours have been taken. For

example, there are countless tours that point out the highlights of New York City. How about a tour that tells the history of crime in New York City? Or follows the rise to fame of a celebrity? Or spotlights famous ghost sightings?

2. Research your tour at your local library or online.
3. Take your parents on a sample tour and ask them to critique it.
4. Set a price for each person per tour. Be sure to offer a group rate!
5. Post flyers around town and at the town tourism and information center. Advertise what is special about your tour and some of the places you will visit.
6. Focus on marketing to people in charge of groups, like teachers leading field trips and summer camp counselors.
7. Optional: Once you get a tour well planned, make up a simple handout listing the places your tour covers, including short descriptions.

For More Information: Go to your local library and find travel books for your hometown

99. WEB DESIGNER

WHAT IS IT? Building and designing Web sites for companies or individuals

WHAT YOU NEED TO START:
- Online Web-design tutorial (under $30)
- Computer with Internet connection (borrow from your parents)

Cost to Start: Under $30
Time to Get Started: Over five hours
Skills Needed: Computer skills
Potential Customers: Businesses, local stores, and schools

HOW TO GET STARTED:
1. Take an online Web-design tutorial to learn how to build a Web site. Build a practice Web site through a free domain company. Remember, the better you get at this, the more you can charge!
2. Set a price for each Web site, based on the amount of detail asked for. Offer such things as photos, HTML, and JavaScript capabilities to potential clients.
3. Post flyers around your neighborhood and at local companies to advertise your skills. Be sure to put the URL of your test Web site on the flyer so people can see what you are capable of creating.
4. A great way to get customers is to figure out which businesses in your town have Web sites. Just look online. If they don't, call them up and pitch your services.

For More Information: *www.virtuallyignorant.com*

100. WINDOW WASHER

WHAT IS IT? Washing the windows of houses and buildings for clients

WHAT YOU NEED TO START:
- Window cleaner (under $5)
- Paper towels or regular towels (under $5)
- Squeegee (under $8)
- Window washing brush (under $10)
- Bucket (under $10)
- Ladder (borrow from client)

Cost to Start: Under $40
Time to Get Started: Under three hours
Skills Needed: None
Potential Customers: Homeowners, automobile owners, businesses, and local stores

HOW TO GET STARTED:
1. Practice washing windows inside and out at your parents' home. Make sure to do a thorough job. Ask your parents for a critique.
2. Set an hourly wage.
3. Post flyers around your neighborhood and at local stores to advertise your business.

For More Information: *www.freewindowcleaningtips.com*

101. YARD-SALE ASSISTANT

WHAT IS IT? You help a person to set up a yard sale by pricing items, laying them out, and posting flyers around the neighborhood directing people to the sale.

WHAT YOU NEED TO START:
- Nothing

Cost to Start: $0
Time to Get Started: Three hours
Skills Needed: Organizational and sales skills
Potential Customers: Family and neighbors

HOW TO GET STARTED:
1. Practice helping your parents put on a yard sale. Help by cleaning out the garage and house, pricing items, setting up tables, and posting signs around the neighborhood. You should also help sell items.
2. Set an hourly wage for the time that you help a person. Or you could request a percentage of all the profits that the yard sale makes. With the percentage way, people only have to pay out of the money that you help them to make.

3. Post flyers around your neighborhood to advertise your service. Tell all of your friends, as well as your parents' friends, to get the word out.

For More Information: *www.yardsalequeen.com; www.grandslamgaragesales.com*

RESOURCES

As you know, to start a business you'll need several forms and worksheets. If you've read this far, you've already come across some of these items, like the income statement and ledger. This Resources section contains all the other paperwork you'll need to start running your business. It even contains an entire business plan that you can use as a guide when you write your plan! Visit the book's Web sites, *quickcashforteens.com* to find other useful business forms and information.

Sample Press Release

FOR IMMEDIATE RELEASE [1]
Today's date
Contact:
Peter Bielagus
Phone XXX-XXX-XXXX

**America's top expert on young people and their money
offers $1,000 in venture capital to Young Entrepreneurs** [2]

Bedford, N.H., February 3, 2009, Financial author and speaker Peter Bielagus is offering $1,000 in venture capital to the young entrepreneur with the most interesting tale to tell. [3]

In preparation for his upcoming book *Quick Cash for Teens*, which is an entrepreneurship guide for students ages 12 to 21, Bielagus is collecting stories from young entrepreneurs all over the country. In return for their efforts, he is offering 100 free books to people who write the 100 top stories and a $1,000 grand prize to the entrepreneur with the best tale to tell.

That lucky grand prize winner will also receive a full day of entrepreneurship coaching from Bielagus.

"In writing this book, I really wanted to hear from the front lines," says Bielagus. "What are the actual problems that actual young entrepreneurs face? What was the smartest thing they did? What was the dumbest?" Bielagus's publisher, Sterling Publishing Co., Inc., expects the book to be out in 2009. [4]

To enter, participants must be between the ages of 12 and 21. Simply send a 250-word essay describing your business (either one that is up and running or one that is still in the planning stages) to *peter@peterbspeaks.com* with the word *Contest* in the subject line. [5]

Please include a description of how you came up with your business idea, how you got started (or plan to get started), what obstacles you faced, and what you would do with the $1,000.

Entries are due no later than April 28, 2009. Entries can also be mailed to Peter Bielagus, 123 Happy Street, Anywhere, NH USA 00000

Bielagus is available for interviews as an expert on young people and their money. To arrange an interview with Bielagus, please call him at 603-555-1234; he welcomes calls during weekends and holidays. For more information, visit www.peterbspeaks.com. [6]

[7]

Key to Press Release

Now, let's take a closer look at the press release. The numbers below correspond to the numbers at the end of entries in the press release:

1. This section states that this is an urgent press release. It's not about a story happening four months from now. It also shows the reporter how to get in touch with me.
2. This is the headline. The headline has one purpose: to get people to read on. It should be short, catchy, and in bold, large print.
3. The body of the press release should always begin with a place and time. Newspapers pay very close attention to local stories, so be sure to remind them that yours is a local story.
4. Be sure to include some live quotes in your press release. Remember, your job is to make it easy for reporters to write a story, and reporters love quotes.
5. Include an action item in your press release. Do you want people to show up to a certain place at a certain time? Do you want people to e-mail you or to send you their story via regular mail? Whatever it is you want, ask for it!

6. Most press releases are about a specific event. For example, your hat-making company is giving away 1,000 free hats to charity. However, feel free to include a little bit of information about your business in general in the press release. I have sent out well over 100 press releases. Often, reporters will call me not because they are interested in what the release said, but because they are doing a story on young people and money management.

7. What are those three number symbols for? They are just a journalistic code to signal that the press release is done! Don't forget them.

Sample Loan Agreement

CREDITOR: BORROWER:

_____   _____

_____   _____

_____   _____

_____   _____

Loan Amount: _____

Interest Rate: _____

Repayment Period: _____

Repayment Terms:

Borrower agrees to pay back Creditor the Loan Amount at the above

Interest Rate, over the above stated Repayment Period. Borrower will

make payments on a _____ basis (monthly, yearly, etc.).

If any loan payment is more than _____ days late, Borrower shall be

assessed a late fee of _____.

In the event Borrower cannot make the payments, Borrower agrees to

perform household chores for Creditor at a pre-agreed rate of $_____

per hour until the loan is paid off in full.

Agreed upon this _____ day of _____ in the year _____

Creditor's Signature _____

Borrower's Signature_____

Sample Invoice

Invoice # _____*
Date of invoice:_____

[Your business name, address, and contact information here:]
_____
_____
_____

TO [insert client's name and address here]:
_____
_____
_____

COST: **DESCRIPTION OF PRODUCTS OR SERVICES**
                   [include dates of purchase or service]:

_____   _____
_____   _____

TOTAL _____   **DUE TO**: [your business name here] _____

                   _____

Please make checks payable to "_____" and send to
the address above.
Payment is requested within _____ days.**
Thank you for your business!

_____

* *Always number your invoices to make them easy to track.*
** *Include information about how soon you expect to be paid.*

Sample Business Plan

The following is a fictional sample business plan written by a young entrepreneur named Ted Smith. As you can see, Ted just answered the questions on the Quick and Dirty Business Plan Worksheet on Page 93.

General Information:

The name of my business is Young American Editing, whose name is registered in the State of New Hampshire. The location of my business is 123 Happy Street, Anywhere, New Hampshire USA 01234.

The contact phone number is 603-555-1234.
The e-mail address is *xxx@yxxxxx.com.*
The Web site is *www.xxxxxxxxxx.com.*

Executive Summary

Young American Editing (YAE) is an editing service for companies who seek to connect with young Americans. While most editing companies offer merely a grammatical edit, YAE also offers, at no additional charge, a marketing review describing what young Americans think about a particular book, brochure, or commercial. YAE will target companies with professional editing needs that are trying to market to young Americans. We will ensure that all marketing materials are not only grammatically correct, but also are written in the casual, hip style that young Americans enjoy.

First Part: Identify Business

We sell an editing service and marketing copy review service. Companies submit their brochures, print advertising, catalogs, books, magazine issues, and even scripts for radio and TV ads to us. YAE first conducts a grammatical edit. Then, we review the material and ask these questions: Is this something a young American would connect with? Is this something that a young American would purchase, based on this content? Does it speak their language? We include a report with every editing job that gives suggestions on how our clients could make their materials hipper to young Americans. For the price of a grammatical edit, the clients also receive a marketing review from the same young Americans they are trying to reach.

Our prices for this all-inclusive service are at or below what most of our competitors charge for a grammatical edit alone. We're the "two for one" editing company.

Our market niche is unique as we have a group of young American editors who are not only skilled at the art of grammatical editing, but are also a good representation of the young American market. Because we use college students on an independent-contractor basis, we are also able to keep our costs down.

Second Part: Identify Management

I, Ted Smith, am the person running the business. I am a senior in high school and am currently taking two advanced placement English courses. My uncle owns a small company that publishes New England guidebooks, and I have worked for him as an editor since I was sixteen. What's more, as a high school student, I hear the concerns, complaints, and challenges of my generation every day. I run all of the day-to-day operations of the YAE. I will manage all of the financials. I will manage all of the marketing. I will make all of the executive decisions, and I will even do everything down to cleaning the office. Below is a brief schedule as to when I will perform each of the necessary business tasks:

Mondays:	Manage staff of editors
Tuesdays:	Marketing day
Wednesdays:	Executive planning and operations planning day
Thursdays:	Marketing day
Fridays:	Update financial statements and work on office paperwork

All of the editors are college English majors or graduate students majoring in marketing or English. They work on an independent-contractor basis, so there are no fixed costs to have these editors work for us. Our company pays about $5 per hour more than our top three competitors, so we are able to have our pick of the best college-age editors.

Third Part: Identify Market

The condition of the industry that I am in is terrific. As the baby boomers start to retire, companies are looking for their next giant batch of customers. Their research has led them to the 18- to 24-year-old demographic. Our target market is small companies who are trying to reach the 18- to 24-year-old age group. We are targeting small companies, because our low-price service will be most attractive to small companies that are seeking to keep their costs down.

We'll reach our customers primarily by word of mouth and through an aggressive outsourcing program. Because our operating costs are so low, we can provide our service cheaper than many marketing/editing companies can get with their own in-house staff. This price difference provides an ideal opportunity for them to outsource to us. We have also signed a deal with a marketing magazine to write one article a month on how to write copy that appeals to young Americans. This will give us exposure to more than 2 million readers per month, without costing a dime. We are going to conduct an initial mailing to the top 100 companies that we feel are most likely to use our service.

We charge $50 an hour in order to edit, with a minimum charge of one hour. We will offer a money-back guarantee; we just ask that dissatisfied clients fill out a short survey as to why they were unhappy with our service.

Our research tells us that most editing companies charge around $45 to

$65 an hour to perform an edit. However, these fees include only a grammatical edit. Were a company in need of a marketing edit, they would most likely have to pay another $45–$65 per hour for that service. For our $50 per hour, they receive both. This "two for the price of one" approach will be our self-seller. Our potential customers will think, *Why not go with YAE?* We will gain customers that our competitors cannot get, simply by offering a sensational product at a price below our competitors'.

We're preparing to put 10% of our profits into an account that we will use to cushion ourselves for emergencies, so as the business grows, it will get stronger and stronger because it will have a larger and larger cash reserve.

Fourth Part: Outline Operations

It won't cost that much to start the business. I already have most of the equipment and supplies necessary to start a service business. I am estimating a $1,000 start-up cost, but most of this money is going toward marketing and cash reserves. I'm using a computer that I already own; I'm using a special ring on my parent's landline; and I'm using my cell phone, which will cost $30 a month. Because I am using my parent's Internet connection, there is no charge.

All of our employees are independent contractors so there are no fixed costs associated with them. We charge our clients $50 an hour for an edit, and we pay our editors 50% of that, or $25 an hour. We hire mostly college students who are used to making between $8 and $15 per hour. Our high pay scale allows us to attract America's best and brightest.

The business requires no insurance and no licenses, which again allows us to keep our fixed costs down. We also do not need to put down any deposit money with any suppliers because all of the supplies necessary for my business can be bought at a local office supply superstore.

My father has promised to introduce me to his accountant and his lawyer. The accountant has agreed, as a favor to my father, to do the tax return for my business the first year for free. This lawyer and accountant, as well as my English teacher and my uncle, who owns the publishing company, have all agreed to serve on my board of advisors.

Fifth Part: Identify Risks

YAE is a low-risk business because we have very few fixed costs. Our biggest risk is that our business is rather easy to copy. However, while the idea is easy to copy, it will be extremely difficult for an existing company with large operating expenses to compete with our prices. My office is my bedroom and many of my fixed costs (such as electricity and Internet) are picked up by my parents. If we find companies trying to pitch our business model to their clients, we will simply begin pitching those very clients, mentioning that we are far less expensive. What's more, our business makes the perfect outsourcing opportunity for marketing and editing companies that have existing relationships with businesses that want to reach young

America. Rather than compete with our competitors, we will look to partner with them.

To further protect myself, I've established a separate business savings account in which I will put 10% of my after-tax business profits. This will serve as my emergency cushion for times when business might be slow.

Sixth Part: Schedule

FIRST 30 DAYS:

- Register domain name.
- Design Web site in MS Word and e-mail to Web designer.
- Choose business colors and logo.
- Print 500 business cards and stationery.
- Open five bank accounts.
- Draft press release.
- Make a list of family, friends, and target businesses to call.
- Call five names a week on target list.
- Follow up with e-mail.
- Get four filing boxes for accounting.
- Buy business ledger.
- Ask family and friends to preview Web site.
- Launch Web site.
- Have grand opening; send press release and e-mail to family and friends.

31 TO 60 DAYS FROM START:

- Create flyer.
- Print 100 flyers.
- Mail flyers to 100 target businesses.
- Write article on "writing in the language of young America."
- Send article to newspapers.
- Spend two hours researching online advertising.

- Prepare first month's cash-flow statement.
- Prepare first month's income statement.
- Prepare first month's balance sheet.
- Review financial statements: Where can I improve?

61 TO 90 DAYS FROM START:

- Change at least two lightbulbs in my parents' house to compact fluorescents.
- Ask all vendors if I can pay my bills later; shoot for 60 days after receipt of bill.
- Inquire from vendors if I am entitled to any discounts. (Buying in bulk? Agreeing to buy so much every month?)
- Arrange in-person meeting with accountant.
- Send "thank you" card to all current customers. Enclose a 10% off coupon and flyer to remind them of my $25 referral fee policy.
- Test online marketing, using two Google AdWords and spending no more than $200.
- Contact five businesses that would make good partners for my service (advertising agencies, publishers).

Seventh Part: Financial Analysis

START-UP COSTS:

Initial mailing:

Envelopes	$ 20
Paper	$ 20
Stamps	$ 40

Office supplies and set-up:

Book about grammar	$ 20
File cabinet	$ 100
Business cards/letterhead	$ 150
Web-site development	$ 150

Total Start-up Costs: **$ 500**

OPERATING EXPENSES:

Fixed costs:

Web-site hosting (1 year)	$ 100
One year office supplies (pens, etc.)	$ 20
Cell phone	$ 300
Internet	$ 0*
Landline	$ 0*

Total Fixed Costs: **$ 420**

Variable costs:

Annual mailing for outsourcing business:	$ 80

Total Variable Costs: **$ 80**

COST OF GOODS SOLD (COGS):

Paper printout of report:	$ 2
Cost of postage to mail report to client:	$ 2
Follow-up thank-you letter to client:	$ 1
Payment to independent contracting editor:	$ 25

Total COGS for one unit (one hour of work): **$ 30**

Free from parents.

My goal for YAE is to start the business for $1,000. All $1,000 of this money will come from my own savings. Of that $1,000, one-half, or $500, will be used for actual start-up costs, while the remaining $500 will be kept in a business savings account as an emergency cash reserve, should I not get any clients. This cash reserve can keep the business running for an

Beginning Balance Sheet			
ASSETS:		**LIABILITIES:**	
Cash:	$ 1,000	Owed to owners:	$1,000
Total Assets:	**$ 1,000**	**Total Liabilities:**	**$ 1,000**

Balance Sheet after Purchase of Supplies			
ASSETS:		**LIABILITIES:**	
Cash:	$ 500	Owed to owner:	$1,000*
Inventory:	$ 500		
Subtotal Assets:	**$ 1,000**	**Total Liabilities:**	**$1,000**
$500 in cash, $500 office supplies.			

entire year, without having one single client. My annual fixed costs, including an annual variable-cost mailing, are $500 per year.

A unit is defined as one hour, which is the minimum charge to our customers. YAE charges $50 per hour. Half of this money is given to the independent contracting editor. The report, postage, and follow-up thank-you letter cost a total of $5, which leaves me with a per unit profit of $20 for one hour. Keep in mind, this $5 cost is incurred only during the first hour. My per-unit profit for all hours after the first hour is $25 per hour.

To keep my estimates safe, let's assume that all of my clients hire YAE only for one hour (even though my research tells me the average length of an editing job is three hours). This means my break-even point is 25 units per year. (Again, this break-even point would be smaller if and when clients hire YAE for multiple hours.)

If I can sell 50 units in the first year, I will have covered all of my operating expenses for that year, plus earned back all of the start-up costs. My single biggest cost is the cell phone. I thoroughly investigated whether that was the cheapest plan, and so far, this appears to be the case. After six months into the business, I will begin experimenting with operating the business without the cell phone by not giving certain clients the number, to see if this creates any decrease in customer satisfaction. I am also considering making my minimum order two hours.

My initial research tells me that it is reasonable for a company like mine to sell 100 units per year in the first year. I arrived at this number by interviewing my editors, who will be working as independent contractors and discovering how often they work for other companies. I also called ten of

Yearly Income Statement (Estimated)

REVENUES:

Bank account interest:	$ 15
Sales (100 units):	$ 5,000
Total Revenues:	**$ 5,015**

COST OF GOODS SOLD (COGS):

Paper printout of report:	$ 200
Cost of postage to mail report to client:	$ 200
Follow-up thank-you letter to client:	$ 100
Payment to independent contracting editor:	$ 2.500
Total COGS:	**$ 3,000**
Gross Profit (Revenues – Total COGS):	**$ 2,015**

OPERATING EXPENSES

FIXED COSTS:

Web-site hosting (1 year):	$ 100
One year office supplies (pens, etc.):	$ 20
Cell phone:	$ 300
Internet:	$ 0 (free from parents)
Landline:	$ 0 (free from parents)
Total Fixed Costs:	**$ 420**

VARIABLE COSTS

Annual mailing:	$ 80
Total Variable Costs:	**$ 80**
Total Operating Costs:	**$ 500**
Profit before Taxes:	**$ 1,515**
Estimated Taxes:	**$ 455***
Net Profit:	**$ 1,060**

*$ 1,515 × 30%.

my target clients and asked them how often they hire editing and marketing services such as mine.

Based on this assumption, above and left are the income statement and balance sheet, and, on the next page, the cash-flow statement for my business. (Please remember that I assumed all sales would be first-hour sales, which are the least profitable for my company.)

Monthly Cash-Flow Statement March (Estimated)

TRANSACTION:	CASH IN:	CASH OUT:
Starting cash:	$ 500	
Sales (8 hours):	$ 400	
Interest:	$ 1.25	
Paper printout of report:		$ 16
Cost of postage to mail report to client:		$ 16
Follow-up thank-you letter to client:		$ 8
Payment to independent contracting editor:		$ 200
Web-site hosting (1 month):		$ 8
One month office supplies (pens, etc.):		$ 1.60
Cell phone:		$ 30
Subtotals:	$ 401.25 (revenue)	$ 121.65 (expenses)
Taxes: $401.25 – $121.65 × 30% =		$ 36.49
Total:	$ 585.16	

Monthly Cash-Flow Statement April (Estimated)

TRANSACTION:	CASH IN:	CASH OUT:
Starting cash:	$ 585.16	
Sales (12 hours):	$ 600	
Interest:	$ 1.25	
Paper printout of report:		$ 24
Cost of postage to mail report to client:		$ 24
Follow-up thank-you letter to client:		$ 12
Payment to independent contracting editor:		$ 300
Web-site hosting (1 month)		$ 8
One month office supplies (pens, etc.)		$ 1.60
Cell phone		$ 30
Subtotals:	$ 601.25 (revenue)	$ 375.60 (expenses)
Taxes: $601.25 – $375.60 × 30% =		$ 67.70
Total:	$1,118.72	

Conclusion

YAE is entering a hot market as companies are trying to connect with young Americans. My fixed costs are about as low as they can be, making it easy for me to compete and making it easy for my competitors to consider outsourcing much of their business to me.

GLOSSARY

accounting system: A system to handle the money that goes in and out of your business

accounts payable: Bills that you need to pay but haven't yet

accounts receivable: Bills you have sent to your customers that are waiting to be paid

AdWords: Trigger words that allow your Web site to come up first in a Google Internet search

assets: The stuff your business owns, including cash

ATM: A computerized electronic machine that performs basic banking functions, handling check deposits and withdrawals

balance sheet: A financial document that lists a company's net worth

bandwidth: Capacity for data transfer of an electronic communications system. The bandwidth determines the amount of transfer (traffic) that a website can handle

bookkeeper: A person who organizes and prepares your financial statements

bookkeeping system: A process used for preparing and monitoring the financial statements of your business

borrower: The person borrowing the money (duh!)

bounced: The term used to describe what happens to a check written on a checking account that has insufficient funds

break-even number: The number of units of your product or service that you need to sell to cover all operating costs

business: A group or an individual that charges to solve a problem

business hours: The hours when you actually are open to customers

business ledger: A notebook with preprinted columns to help you keep track of revenues and expenses

business plan: A road map describing how you will start and grow your business

byline: A one- or two-sentence description of a business, used in advertising

cancel: The process by which one terminates a check

capitalism: An economic system in which individuals, not governments, own their own businesses, banks, and homes and are responsible for solving the majority of society's problems

CEO: Chief executive officer of a company

CFO: Chief financial officer of a company

check: A legal contract to exchange money

check-clearing policy: A policy, written by the bank, which doesn't allow checks to be converted into cash immediately

checking account: A bank account that allows you to write checks against the account to transfer money

CMO: Chief marketing officer of a company

competitive advantage: An advantage over competitors gained by offering customers greater value, through lower prices or by providing more goods or services

compound interest: Interest that is paid on both principal and interest already earned

controller: Someone who works under the CFO in a company

COO: Chief operations officer of a company

cost of goods sold (COGS): Costs directly related to the product itself, which are not incurred until the product is actually made and sold. The total of all these costs is the **total cost of goods sold.** The cost per unit is the **unit cost of goods sold.**

credit cards: Plastic cards that let you pay for products and services by borrowing from a company

creditor: The person loaning the money

credits: On an income statement, this is money coming in

C Suite: The top officers in a company, such as the CFO and CEO

customers: The people who give you money for your products and services

debit: On an income statement, this is money being paid out

debit card: A plastic card that allows you to instantly remove money from your checking account without using checks

debt: Money that you owe

debt financing: The act of paying for the start-up costs of a company by borrowing money

demand: A measure of how aggressively people want to buy something

depreciation: The act of subtracting a portion of an asset's value from your income statement to account for that asset's loss in value over time

diversification: The act of spreading your money out over several different investments to protect yourself from risk

domain registration: The annual charge to register your Web site address or "domain"

earnings: A company's profits

economics: The study of how we produce, distribute, and consume goods and services in our society

economic system: A procedure for solving society's problems, specifically dealing with the management of scarce resources

endorse: To sign the back of a check so it can be cashed

entrepreneur: Someone who starts and operates his or her own business

equity: Money that you own

equity financing: The act of paying for a company's start-up costs by selling part of the business to someone else

estimated taxes: Taxes paid by business owners four times a year, based on estimates of their earnings

executive assistant: A person who assists the C Suite with everyday tasks

expenses: Things your business spends money on

finance: To pay for something

financial plan: A plan that a business makes about how to spend its money

financing strategy: A plan made to pay business costs

Five S Formula: Formula for evaluating a potential business. It should be Simple, Safe, use your Skills, be Satisfying, and be a Self-seller

fixed costs: Costs that don't change from month to month

funds-availability policy: Another name for check-clearing policy

goodwill: A company's regard in the eyes of the public

gross profit: Your profit before subtracting operating costs and taxes

hyperlinks: Virtual doorways that connect Web pages and Web sites

income tax: Fees charged to individuals or businesses by the federal, state, and (sometimes) local government, calculated as a percentage of income

independent contractor: A person hired to perform only a specific job. Not an employee

index mutual fund: A mutual fund that does not have a manager, but buys every stock on the market, using a computer program

Individual Retirement Arrangement (IRA): A savings account in which income taxes on certain deposits and all gains are deferred until withdrawals are made, typically at or near retirement age

initial public offering (IPO): The name of the event where shares of a company are sold to the public for the first time

interest: The fee you are charged when you rent or borrow money.

interest rate: The percentage of a loan that is charged as the fee for borrowing the money

Internal Revenue Service (IRS): The agency of the United States government that collects federal taxes

inventory: Saleable product you have on hand

investing: The practice of risking your money in hopes that it will grow to be a larger sum

investment bank: A bank that helps companies raise money by selling shares of the company to the public

invoices: Bills for products or services

landing page: The first page that a visitor to a Web site sees

law of supply and demand: A concept of capitalist economics that describes effects on price and quantity and how they relate

liabilities: The monies your business owes

logo: A small, simple symbol or picture that helps people recognize your business

maker: The person who writes the check

marketing plan: An outline of how you will get more customers

market price: The halfway point between the highest price the buyer is willing to pay and the lowest price the seller is willing to sell for

merchant account: A bank account established with a credit-card processor that is linked to your bank account. It allows your business to accept credit cards

micro-testing: A miniature advertising campaign that allows a business to quickly determine if its products or services are desirable to customers, for very little money. Typically micro-testing is done entirely online

multimedia advertising: Targeting your customers in several areas at once

mutual fund: A money pool formed by a group of investors and headed by one manager

negotiation: The art of establishing a difficult relationship

net profit: Profit left after deducting all expenses and paying taxes

net worth: The amount you get when you subtract a company's liabilities from its assets. This is value of the business to the owner

niche: Marketing term used to describe how your business is unique and different from all the others that it competes with

noncash expense: An expense that doesn't require you to give away actual cash

office hours: Times when your business is closed to customers, but you the owner are still working

operating costs: Basic expenses that a business must continue to pay in order to stay open

opportunity: A situation in which someone is willing to pay to have a problem solved

organizational chart: A tree diagram that a company uses to determine who works under whom

organizational plan: A plan that spells out the specific tasks that each person in the company will be doing and justifies why these people were chosen for the tasks

organizational structure: Who does what work in a company

outsourcing: The practice of hiring another business to do part of your company's work

owner's equity: Another term for net worth

payee: The person to whom a check is written

per-use tax: A tax that you pay for services only when you use them

Pop3 e-mail account: An e-mail account that uses your domain name as your e-mail address

principal: The original amount you borrowed on a loan

products: Items produced and sold

profit: The money a business owner keeps after paying all expenses

profit before taxes: The money a business has earned after subtracting all expenses *except* taxes owed to state and local governments

public: Term used to describe a company whose shares are available for sale to everyone (the public)

repayment period: The amount of time you have to pay back a loan

repayment terms: The specific details of a loan agreement that outline how and when the money will be paid back

retail: A business that sells directly to consumers

return on investment (ROI): A calculation to determine how much money you made on your initial investment

revenue: The money collected from selling products and services to customers

reward: A measure of the return you get for taking a risk on a investment

risk: A measure of the probability that you will lose your money when making an investment

Roth IRA (Individual Retirement Arrangement): An investment account, designed to encourage people to save for retirement, that protects you from taxes

routing number: Number on a check used to identify which bank the checking account is located at

sales call: An in-person visit or phone call in which you approach someone in your target market to get him or her to buy your product or service

sales tax: A fee charged by a government when something is bought and sold

savings account: A bank account with a higher interest rate than a checking account, typically used for storing money long-term

search engine: Computer software used to search data for specified information; or a site on the World Wide Web that uses search software to locate key words at other sites

server: A hard drive that stores all your Web site's information. This is usually a computer in a network that is used to provide services to other computers in the network

services: Useful labor that does not produce a product

shares: Pieces of a company sold to the public in order to raise money

shopping cart: The virtual equivalent of a grocery store shopping cart, used for shopping online

simple interest: Setup in which an investment pays interest only on the principal

socialism: An economic system in which the government or community owns and administers the means of production and distribution of goods

societies: Groups of people who have banded together to help solve the problems of the group

sole proprietorship: Business setup in which one person owns a business and the assets within it

solutions: The answers to problems. In the business world, solutions come in the form of products and services

start-up costs: One-time expenses needed to start a business

stock market: A place (either real or in cyberspace) where shares of companies are bought and sold

sub-ledgers: These are specific business ledgers that support the main ledger (accounting books)

supply: In economics, a measure of how aggressively a business wants to sell a product or service. The higher the price, the more a producer will try to supply that product or service

synergy: Situation in which the whole group of businesses or people working together is greater than the sum of the parts

targeting: The act of focusing on only those customers most likely to buy your product

target market: The group of people who are your ideal customers

taxes: Fees we pay to local, state, and national governments to solve the societal problems that businesses either cannot or should not solve

tax ID number: A number that allows the government to easily monitor a business and collect sales and income tax

tax refund: Money you receive when you have sent in too much tax money to the government

tax return: A document summarizing how much an individual or business has earned and spent and how much it owes in taxes

tax time: Late January to April 15 every year in the United States, when people are preparing their tax returns for the prior year

testing: In marketing, a term used to describe trying different variations of an advertisement or of a product's price

testimonial: A positive statement from one of your satisfied customers about your product or service

track: A system fused to measure marketing effectiveness. Tracking determines exactly how the customer found out about your business

transaction fees: Costs that occur when a customer buys something from your Web site

transfer: The processing space it takes to load a Web page

tweaking: The act of making slight changes to a business idea so it meets the criteria of the Five S Formula

variable costs: Operating costs that can increase or decrease

venture capital: Money available for investing a new business

withholding: The process by which the employer of a salaried worker takes income taxes out of his or her paycheck and sends the appropriate amounts to the federal and state governments

wholesaler: A business that sells to retail businesses

Acknowledgments

To say a book is "by" a particular author is a bit of a lie. It is truly a group effort. Therefore, I need to thank the following group for their efforts in this book. (Please note two things: One, these folks are listed in no particular order, and two, I was too lazy to alphabetize.)

Ken Atchity, my literary manager, and his whole AEI team, most notably Mike Kuciak and Brenna Lui. Ken and AEI have maintained an unwavering belief in me, regardless of career highs and lows.

My editor at Sterling, Meredith Hale, for her patience and great feedback.

Carly Bornstein, for her indispensable research and editing abilities, and Melissa Bratter, for giving some hope to a hopelessly disorganized man.

Of course, my parents, Barbara and Justin Bielagus, my brother Ryan and his wife, Diane. You are my unpaid, overworked team of consultants and advisors, and I can't thank you enough for your help.

Also thank you to all the young entrepreneurs who helped contribute their stories. Best of luck to all of you.

While there are many others who contributed, the following names float to the top: Todd Norwood, Sean Stephenson, Michael Simmons, Sheena Lindahl, Kathy Parker, Keith Rousseau, Jim Tyson, Lori Beath, Ernesto Anguilla, Jayme and Laura Simoes of Louis Karno and Co., Dan Hebert of New Hampshire Jumpstart, Jennifer Howard of Answersmart, and Steve Alten of Adopt an Author.

And finally, Susan Leahy and Jared Patrick of *www.freewayguides.com*. These two invited me to a party at Book Expo, where I met my editor, Meredith, and soon after signed a deal to publish this book.

INDEX

Attention, Teachers!

Quick Cash for Teens is part of *Adopt-An-Author,* an innovative nationwide nonprofit program gaining attention among educators for its success in motivating tens of thousands of reluctant secondary school students to read. The program combines informational guides and fast-paced thrillers with an interactive Web site AND direct contact with the author. All teachers receive curriculum materials and posters for their classrooms. The program is FREE to all secondary school teachers and librarians.

For more information and to register for Adopt-An-Author, go to *www.AdoptAnAuthor.com*

Quick Cash for Teens and all Sterling titles are available at a discount when purchasing in quantity (10 copy minimum) for sales promotions or corporate use. Special editions, including personalized covers, excerpts, and corporate imprints can be created when purchasing in large quantities. For more information, please call Premium Sales at 212-532-7160 or email *specialsales@sterlingpublishing.com.*

Peter Bielagus speaks to parents, teachers, nonprofits, and corporations on how they can get young Americans excited about personal finance and entrepreneurship. To learn more about speaking and availability, please visit *www.peterbspeaks.com.*